Financial Control Blueprint: Building a Path to Growth and Success

DG. Junior

Published by DG Junior, 2023.

FINANCIAL CONTROL BLUEPRINT: BUILDING A PATH TO GROWTH AND SUCCESS

First edition. June 6, 2023.

ISBN: 979-8223019343

Written by DG. Junior.

Also by DG. Junior

Essential Coputer Skills

Basics of Programming: A Comprehensive Guide for Beginners

Get Your Finances In Order

Where Can I Invest? Unlocking a World of Opportunities

FROM IDEA TO PROFIT: A Guide for New Entrepreneurs on Building a Successful Business

Standalone

Financial Control Blueprint: Building a Path to Growth and Success

Table of Contents

To my mother who was my first fiancial advisor
(That I can write this book is testimony to her success)

Financial Control Blueprint: Building a Path to Growth and Success

By DG Junior

A Comprehensive Guide to Mastering Your Finances and Achieving Financial Freedom

June 2023

Contents

Preface

In this book, we will dive deep into the realm of financial control, guiding you step by step towards building a path to growth and success. By understanding the importance of financial control and implementing the strategies outlined in this book, you will be able to take charge of your personal or business finances, make informed decisions, and achieve your financial goals.

Through a series of practical exercises and insightful advice, you will learn how to assess your current financial situation, create a budget, manage cash flow effectively, build an emergency fund, control and reduce debt, invest for growth, manage risks through insurance, optimize tax planning, monitor progress, and ultimately create long-term wealth.

Financial control is a continuous process, and this book emphasizes the importance of regularly monitoring and adjusting your strategies as needed. With the right knowledge, tools, and discipline, you can gain control over your financial destiny and create a solid foundation for future success.

Embark on this transformative journey towards financial control today, and unlock the doors to a brighter, more prosperous future.

Chapter 1: Introduction

1.1 Understanding Financial Control

Financial control constitutes the bedrock of effective financial management, encompassing a series of processes aimed at meticulous oversight of financial activities. This vigilance ensures optimal resource utilization, goal adherence, and risk mitigation. Central to this is the maintenance of precise financial records, meticulous analysis of financial data, and consequent informed decision-making.

1.1.1 The Essence of Financial Vigilance

At its core, financial control involves maintaining a delicate equilibrium between income and expenses, managing debts, optimizing taxes, and prudently investing surplus funds. It's akin to piloting a ship – steady navigation is required to reach your intended financial destination.

Navigating the Financial Waters

Imagine your financial journey as a vast ocean, and you are at the helm of your financial ship. Financial control becomes your navigational compass, helping you chart a course amidst the changing tides of income and expenses. Just as a skilled sailor adjusts the sails to catch the wind, you fine-tune your financial decisions to harness the currents of opportunity.

Balancing Income and Expenses

One of the cardinal aspects of financial control is striking a harmonious balance between your income and expenses. This balance acts as the keel of your financial vessel, ensuring stability even in the face of turbulent economic waters. By conscientiously monitoring your income sources and managing your expenditures, you prevent capsizing and remain afloat.

The Art of Debt Management

Effective financial control extends its vigilant gaze to the realm of debts. Much like trimming excess weight to keep a ship buoyant, managing debts helps you maintain financial buoyancy. Smart debt management involves distinguishing between good debts that fuel growth and bad debts that weigh you down. By strategically paying off debts and leveraging them judiciously, you steer clear of potential financial storms.

Optimizing the Tax Compass

In the labyrinth of financial waters, taxes stand as formidable obstacles. Financial control empowers you to navigate through this maze by optimizing your tax strategies. Just as a skilled navigator chooses the most efficient route, you explore legal avenues to minimize your tax burden. This prudent approach ensures your hard-earned resources remain available for the voyage ahead.

Sailing Towards Investment Proficiency

No financial voyage is complete without investments – they are the wind that fills your sails, propelling you forward. Financial control equips you with the knowledge to assess investment opportunities critically. You analyze risk and potential returns, diversify your investment portfolio, and select investments aligned with your financial goals. Like a skilled navigator who studies the stars to guide the ship, you navigate the investment universe with insight and precision.

Reaching Your Financial Destination

Just as a ship's captain aims for a specific harbor, your financial journey has a destination – your long-term financial goals. Financial control serves as your compass, guiding you steadily toward these aspirations. With each careful maneuver, you inch closer to the shores of financial security, independence, and ultimately, success.

In the subsequent chapters, we will delve even deeper into the intricate components of financial control. We will explore strategies for assessing your financial health, crafting effective budgets, managing cash flow, reducing debts, making strategic investments, mitigating risks, optimizing taxes, and setting long-term goals. As we embark on this comprehensive exploration, you'll gather the tools, insights, and understanding needed to become the captain of your financial ship – confidently charting a course toward growth, stability, and the realization of your dreams.

Remember, just as a captain navigates through storms and calms, your commitment to financial vigilance will guide you through both challenging and prosperous times. The journey ahead is one of empowerment and transformation, and I invite you to embrace it wholeheartedly.

So, let's unfurl the sails of financial understanding, set our course toward knowledge, and embark on a voyage that promises to reshape your financial destiny.

1.1.2 Fostering Financial Insight

Beyond the mechanics of financial control lies a profound truth – the empowerment to make informed financial decisions. This empowerment, akin to a beacon piercing through the financial fog, illuminates a path toward stability, growth, and the eventual triumph of your financial journey.

The Power of Informed Decision-Making

Imagine standing at a crossroads, armed with a map that reveals the terrains ahead. Such is the power of informed financial decision-making. By exercising astute financial control, individuals and businesses alike are bestowed with this transformative ability. It's the compass that enables you to distinguish between financial routes, assess risks, and plot the most favorable course to your goals.

A Virtuous Cycle of Stability

At the heart of fostering financial insight is the creation of a virtuous cycle. This cycle begins with meticulous financial control, which generates accurate data and insights. These insights, in turn, pave the way for even more refined financial control. Like the gears of a well-oiled machine, this cycle propels you toward a stable and secure financial foundation.

Nurturing Growth Amidst Uncertainty

Life is rife with uncertainties, and the financial realm is no exception. However, armed with financial insight, you possess the tools to weather these storms and even flourish amidst uncertainty. Just as a seasoned sailor navigates turbulent waters with expertise, your financial insight equips you to make agile decisions, seize opportunities, and adapt to changing circumstances.

Building Bridges to Financial Triumph

Consider your financial insight as the bricks with which you construct the bridge to prosperity. Each decision, each step guided by your financial acumen, adds another layer to this bridge. As it spans the chasm between financial struggle and triumph, you'll find yourself walking confidently toward a future characterized by achievement and contentment.

A Resilient Foundation for Prosperity

The environment cultivated by financial insight is not one of chance, but rather of calculated intention. This proactive approach to financial management acts as a resilient foundation upon which prosperity can be built. It's a vantage point from which you can view your financial landscape with clarity, identify potential obstacles, and strategize ways to surmount them.

The Journey Ahead

As we embark on this journey through the Financial Control Blueprint, remember that every piece of knowledge gained, every strategy honed, contributes to the cultivation of your financial insight. Each chapter we explore, each concept we delve into, adds a layer to the robust edifice of your financial acumen.

In the upcoming chapters, we will dive into the depths of assessing your current financial situation, crafting effective budgets, mastering cash flow management, taming debts, leveraging investment opportunities, mitigating risks, optimizing taxes, and setting your sights on long-term goals. Along this voyage, your financial insight will not only guide you but also empower you to navigate the complexities of personal and business finances with finesse.

So, let's hoist the sails of financial insight, catch the winds of knowledge, and steer our course toward a horizon of financial stability, growth, and triumph. As we navigate these waters together, remember that the journey is as rewarding as the destination – an evolution toward mastery and a transformative shift in your financial future.

1.2 Significance of Financial Control for Businesses

Within the realm of businesses, the significance of financial control is unparalleled, transcending size and industry. This strategic practice forms the cornerstone for the effective management of financial resources, maximization of profits, and mitigation of financial risks.

1.2.1 Navigating Financial Horizons

In the vast expanse of financial landscapes, businesses chart their courses through turbulent waters every day. In this unpredictable realm, financial control emerges as the guiding lighthouse, casting its steady beam to illuminate the path forward. Its resolute presence ensures that the limited and valuable resource of finances is judiciously allocated to support the grand tapestry of operational objectives.

The Guiding Light of Financial Control

Picture a stormy night at sea, with waves crashing and currents swirling. Amidst this chaos, a lighthouse stands tall, its beacon piercing through the darkness, offering a guiding light to ships seeking safe harbors. Similarly, financial control assumes the role of this guiding light for businesses, dispelling uncertainties and guiding decisions that steer the course of financial success.

Optimal Allocation of Resources

A core facet of financial control is the meticulous allocation of financial resources. Just as a seasoned captain assesses wind and tide to navigate efficiently, financial control enables businesses to evaluate their financial health, analyze data, and strategically allocate funds. This allocation isn't haphazard; it's a strategic choreography that ensures every financial move is aligned with overarching operational goals.

Sailing Through Operational Objectives

Operational objectives are the destinations toward which a business sails. Financial control acts as the map that plots the most efficient routes, avoiding treacherous currents and hidden reefs. By ensuring that financial resources are channeled into the right avenues, financial control facilitates the achievement of operational milestones and the realization of broader business aspirations.

Unveiling Opportunities Amidst Challenges

Business waters can be tempestuous, marked by unexpected storms and unforeseen obstacles. Yet, financial control empowers businesses to not merely weather these challenges but to uncover opportunities amidst them. Like a skilled navigator who spots a potential shortcut, financial control identifies financial inefficiencies and suggests course corrections to navigate challenges successfully.

A Symphony of Financial Governance

Consider financial control as the conductor of an intricate symphony, harmonizing the various financial instruments to create a melodious composition. It ensures that financial decisions align with business goals, orchestrating an interplay between income, expenses, investments, and debts. This symphony, when conducted skillfully, results in financial equilibrium and operational harmony.

Upholding Stability in Volatile Seas

Just as a lighthouse provides stability in tumultuous weather, financial control offers steadiness amidst economic volatility. Businesses equipped with sound financial control mechanisms are better poised to weather economic storms, ensuring continued operations, employee well-being, and sustained growth even when external forces create waves.

The Voyage Ahead

As we navigate through the chapters of this guide, envision yourself as the captain of your business vessel, steering through the complexities of financial waters. The principles and practices of financial control, which we will delve into further, will serve as your guiding compass, your strategic map, and your unyielding lighthouse. Together, we will explore strategies for assessing financial health, optimizing cash flows, taming debts, seizing investment opportunities, managing risks, and optimizing taxes.

The journey may have its challenges, but armed with financial control, you are equipped to conquer the seas of uncertainty and navigate toward the shores of business success. As we delve deeper into the Financial Control Blueprint, embrace the empowerment that comes with mastering the art of financial navigation, and set sail on a voyage that promises growth, resilience, and the realization of your business's fullest potential.

1.2.2 Safeguarding Profitability

Amid the intricate dance of financial management, safeguarding profitability emerges as a fundamental pillar. This vigilant sentry stands guard, ensuring that your business's financial fortress remains strong and resilient. Through meticulous analysis of revenue streams, expenditure patterns, and overall profitability, businesses gain the power to not only protect their earnings but also enhance them.

The Fortification of Financial Health

Imagine profitability as the lifeblood of your business, coursing through its veins and sustaining its vitality. Just as a vigilant guardian watches over a castle, financial control diligently monitors this lifeblood. By meticulously scrutinizing revenue sources, assessing expenditure trends, and evaluating the big picture of profitability, financial control safeguards the very essence of your business's health.

Unveiling Inefficiencies

Think of profitability safeguarding as a detective on a relentless quest for clues. It unveils inefficiencies and irregularities that might otherwise go unnoticed. Through detailed analysis, it shines a light on areas where resources are squandered or underutilized. Like a skilled investigator, financial control identifies the "leaks" in the financial ship, allowing you to plug them promptly.

Implementing Cost-Saving Measures

The vigilant guardian of profitability doesn't merely uncover inefficiencies; it takes proactive measures to address them. Just as a skilled doctor prescribes the right treatment, financial control suggests prudent cost-saving measures. These measures could range from optimizing supply chains to streamlining operational processes, all aimed at bolstering profitability.

Optimizing Revenue-Generation

Profitability is a delicate equilibrium between inflows and outflows. Financial control understands this balance intimately and, like a conductor fine-tuning an orchestra, optimizes revenue-generation processes. It identifies opportunities to amplify revenue streams, whether through strategic pricing, innovative product offerings, or exploring untapped markets.

The Art of Profitability Enhancement

Consider the process of profitability safeguarding as a canvas, and financial control as the artist wielding the brush. With each calculated stroke, financial control adds layers of insight, allowing you to paint a more vivid picture of your business's financial landscape. As you blend revenue analysis, expenditure evaluation, and strategic foresight, you create a masterpiece of enhanced profitability.

A Continuous Pursuit of Excellence

Much like a seasoned athlete relentlessly hones their skills, financial control ensures the continuous pursuit of excellence in profitability. It isn't a one-time endeavor but a perpetual cycle of assessment, adjustment, and advancement. With financial control as your coach, you refine your profitability strategies, fine-tuning them as your business evolves.

Charting the Course Ahead

As we delve into the chapters ahead, envision profitability safeguarding as your vigilant guardian, accompanying you on your financial journey. With each insight gained, each strategy honed, you empower your business to not only weather financial challenges but to thrive amidst them. The practices we'll uncover – assessing financial health, optimizing cash flows, strategic debt management, investment prowess, risk mitigation, and tax optimization – all contribute to the symphony of profitability enhancement.

So, let's journey forward, guided by the principles of financial control, and navigate through the intricacies of safeguarding and enhancing profitability. Armed with this knowledge and empowered by these strategies, you're poised to steer your business toward greater financial strength, resilience, and a horizon of prosperity.

1.2.3 Mastering the Cash Flow Symphony

In the grand orchestration of financial management, mastering the cash flow symphony emerges as a pivotal movement. Just as a skilled conductor harmonizes various instruments to create a melodic masterpiece, financial control orchestrates the intricate movement of cash within a business. By deftly tracking inflows and outflows, businesses not only optimize the management of working capital but also lay the foundation for sustained growth and expansion.

Conducting the Financial Orchestra

Imagine your business as a symphony, with different financial components acting as instruments. The role of financial control is akin to that of a conductor, skillfully guiding each instrument to play in harmony. In this symphony, cash flow takes center stage, its rhythm dictating the cadence of your business's financial performance.

Balancing the Notes of Inflows and Outflows

Cash flow, much like musical notes, comes in different forms – revenue, payments, investments, and expenditures. Financial control ensures these notes are balanced, creating a harmonious melody that sustains the business's operational rhythm. It scrutinizes the timing of cash inflows against outflows, ensuring that the business meets its financial obligations while maintaining a healthy surplus.

Optimizing Working Capital Management

Think of working capital as the orchestra's instruments, each playing a unique role in the overall performance. Financial control ensures that each instrument is finely tuned, optimizing working capital management. This orchestration involves managing inventory levels, extending payables, and accelerating receivables – all aimed at striking the right balance between liquidity and operational efficiency.

Meeting Financial Obligations

Much like a conductor keeps time during a performance, financial control ensures that financial obligations are met punctually. By monitoring cash flow, it anticipates upcoming expenses and prepares the necessary resources to fulfill them. This proactive approach prevents last-minute scrambles and maintains the business's reputation for reliability.

Paving the Way for Growth and Expansion

A harmonious cash flow symphony sets the stage for growth and expansion, much like a well-orchestrated performance captures the audience's attention. Financial control secures a robust cash flow that fuels future endeavors – be it venturing into new markets, launching innovative products, or investing in technological upgrades. This financial stability becomes the launchpad for ambitious undertakings.

The Ongoing Symphony of Financial Control

Consider the cash flow symphony as a perpetual performance, with financial control serving as the unwavering conductor. Its role doesn't end after a single performance; rather, it continues to refine, adjust, and enhance the symphony over time. With each refined note, financial control strengthens your business's ability to navigate financial fluctuations and capitalize on opportunities.

Charting Harmonious Progress

As we progress through the chapters ahead, envision financial control as your steadfast conductor, guiding you through the complexities of cash flow management. Together, we'll explore strategies for assessing financial health, creating effective budgets, optimizing cash flows, reducing debt, navigating investments, mitigating risks, and optimizing taxes. These components, like the sections of an intricate symphony, contribute to the harmonious financial performance of your business.

So, let's embrace the role of the conductor, skillfully guiding the cash flow symphony, and navigate through the melodies of financial control. Armed with these insights and strategies, you're poised to orchestrate a business performance that resonates with stability, growth, and the promise of a resounding financial future.

1.3 The Blueprint Approach: Your Roadmap to Financial Mastery

Embedded within this comprehensive guide is the Financial Control Blueprint, a roadmap that systematically unravels the intricacies of financial control, leading you towards mastery over your financial landscape.

1.3.1 Embarking on the Journey

In the grand orchestration of financial management, mastering the cash flow symphony emerges as a pivotal movement. Just as a skilled conductor harmonizes various instruments to create a melodic masterpiece, financial control orchestrates the intricate movement of cash within a business. By deftly tracking inflows and outflows, businesses not only optimize the management of working capital but also lay the foundation for sustained growth and expansion.

Conducting the Financial Orchestra

Imagine your business as a symphony, with different financial components acting as instruments. The role of financial control is akin to that of a conductor, skillfully guiding each instrument to play in harmony. In this symphony, cash flow takes center stage, its rhythm dictating the cadence of your business's financial performance.

Balancing the Notes of Inflows and Outflows

Cash flow, much like musical notes, comes in different forms – revenue, payments, investments, and expenditures. Financial control ensures these notes are balanced, creating a harmonious melody that sustains the business's operational rhythm. It scrutinizes the timing of cash inflows against outflows, ensuring that the business meets its financial obligations while maintaining a healthy surplus.

Optimizing Working Capital Management

Think of working capital as the orchestra's instruments, each playing a unique role in the overall performance. Financial control ensures that each instrument is finely tuned, optimizing working capital management. This orchestration involves managing inventory levels, extending payables, and accelerating receivables – all aimed at striking the right balance between liquidity and operational efficiency.

Meeting Financial Obligations

Much like a conductor keeps time during a performance, financial control ensures that financial obligations are met punctually. By monitoring cash flow, it anticipates upcoming expenses and prepares the necessary resources to fulfill them. This proactive approach prevents last-minute scrambles and maintains the business's reputation for reliability.

Paving the Way for Growth and Expansion

A harmonious cash flow symphony sets the stage for growth and expansion, much like a well-orchestrated performance captures the audience's attention. Financial control secures a robust cash flow that fuels future endeavors – be it venturing into new markets, launching innovative products, or investing in technological upgrades. This financial stability becomes the launchpad for ambitious undertakings.

The Ongoing Symphony of Financial Control

Consider the cash flow symphony as a perpetual performance, with financial control serving as the unwavering conductor. Its role doesn't end after a single performance; rather, it continues to refine, adjust, and enhance the symphony over time. With each refined note, financial control strengthens your business's ability to navigate financial fluctuations and capitalize on opportunities.

Charting Harmonious Progress

As we progress through the chapters ahead, envision financial control as your steadfast conductor, guiding you through the complexities of cash flow management. Together, we'll explore strategies for assessing financial health, creating effective budgets, optimizing cash flows, reducing debt, navigating investments, mitigating risks, and optimizing taxes. These components, like the sections of an intricate symphony, contribute to the harmonious financial performance of your business.

So, let's embrace the role of the conductor, skillfully guiding the cash flow symphony, and navigate through the melodies of financial control. Armed with these insights and strategies, you're poised to orchestrate a business performance that resonates with stability, growth, and the promise of a resounding financial future.

Unveiling the Treasure Trove of Knowledge

Just as a seasoned explorer sets out with a map and compass, you're armed with the Financial Control Blueprint.

This blueprint is your guiding map, leading you through the intricate terrain of financial management. Within its pages lie a treasure trove of knowledge, waiting to be uncovered and applied to your unique financial landscape.

Navigating the Path to Empowerment

Embarking on this journey is a deliberate step towards empowerment. The Financial Control Blueprint is more than a set of guidelines – it's a roadmap to financial sovereignty. With each chapter you traverse, you'll gain insights that demystify financial complexities, empowering you to make informed decisions and navigate challenges with confidence.

A Toolbox of Strategies and Techniques

As you delve into the blueprint's content, you'll discover a toolbox overflowing with strategies and techniques. These tools aren't mere abstractions; they are practical instruments that you can wield to shape your financial destiny. From budgeting tactics to debt reduction strategies, from investment insights to tax optimization techniques – each tool is designed to enhance your financial dexterity.

From Understanding to Action

The blueprint bridges the gap between understanding and action. It's not just about acquiring knowledge; it's about putting that knowledge into practice. Much like a craftsman hones their skills through practice, you'll refine your financial acumen by implementing the principles and strategies laid out in the blueprint.

Your Personal Financial Odyssey

Consider this journey as your personal financial odyssey. With each chapter, you set sail to new horizons, uncovering insights that empower you to navigate the intricacies of financial control. The challenges you encounter become opportunities for growth, and the victories you achieve form the milestones of your progress.

Charting the Transformation

As we navigate through the chapters ahead, envision this journey as a transformational process. Just as a caterpillar metamorphoses into a butterfly, you too will undergo a financial metamorphosis. You'll shed misconceptions, embrace new perspectives, and emerge with the wings of financial mastery.

The First Step Awaits

The blueprint's call is clear – the journey awaits your initiative. By turning the pages and absorbing the knowledge within, you're setting sail on a path that promises to reshape your financial landscape. Each concept you internalize, each strategy you deploy, brings you closer to a future defined by financial stability, growth, and triumph.

So, let's take that first step together, opening the door to transformation and embracing the wisdom of the Financial Control Blueprint. With each step you take, you're not just traversing chapters; you're advancing towards a future where financial control is not just a concept, but a way of life.

1.3.2 The Power of Structure

Imagine building a magnificent skyscraper without a blueprint – the result would be chaos, devoid of coherence and stability. In much the same way, the Financial Control Blueprint serves as the architectural design for your financial future. At its core, this blueprint embodies a structured approach, meticulously guiding you through a sequence of steps that collectively elevate your financial acumen. This systematic framework isn't just a roadmap; it's a potent tool that empowers you to translate knowledge into tangible and sustainable results.

Laying the Foundation of Understanding

Just as a solid foundation is vital for any architectural marvel, understanding the fundamentals of financial control is crucial. The blueprint commences with this bedrock, providing you with a comprehensive understanding of financial principles. As you delve into each chapter, you're not merely acquiring isolated knowledge; you're constructing a robust base upon which financial mastery can be erected.

Progressive Steps Toward Mastery

Consider the blueprint as a staircase leading to financial proficiency. Each step you ascend builds upon the previous one, gradually enhancing your financial expertise. This progression isn't arbitrary; it's meticulously designed to equip you with the skills needed to conquer intricate financial challenges.

A Toolbox of Strategies

Embedded within this structured approach is a toolbox brimming with strategies. These strategies aren't disjointed pieces of advice; they're carefully curated techniques that seamlessly integrate into your financial journey. From budgeting methods to investment tactics, from risk management practices to tax optimization principles – each strategy serves as a building block, contributing to the solid edifice of financial control you're constructing.

Empowering You to Take Action

A blueprint is useless if it remains on paper. Similarly, the Financial Control Blueprint is a call to action. It's designed to be wielded, applied, and translated into real-world financial decisions. By following its systematic guidance, you're not just accumulating knowledge; you're catalyzing transformation.

The Beauty of Tangible Results

Think of the blueprint as an alchemical formula that turns knowledge into gold – tangible and valuable outcomes. It's not a mere theoretical exercise; it's a dynamic process that propels you toward financial stability, growth, and success. The systematic nature of the blueprint ensures that your efforts yield measurable results.

A Symphony of Achievement

Envision your journey through the blueprint as a symphony, with each chapter playing a distinct yet harmonious note. As you progress, these notes blend together to create a melodious composition – your financial success story. The power of structure ensures that each note contributes to the overall masterpiece.

Charting a Future of Mastery

As you traverse the blueprint's structured path, visualize yourself as a craftsman honing their skills. Each step, each concept, each strategy is a chisel that refines your financial acumen. Your efforts culminate in a masterpiece that is not just your financial control, but your financial mastery.

So, let's embrace the power of structure, and with each turn of the page, let's construct a future defined by financial proficiency. The blueprint is not merely a guide; it's a catalyst that transforms aspirations into achievements. As we navigate this structured journey, remember that the transformation you seek is not distant – it's a series of deliberate and empowered steps away.

1.3.3 Versatility and Adaptability

In the realm of finance, as in nature, no two paths are identical. Recognizing the uniqueness inherent in every financial journey, the Financial Control Blueprint stands as a beacon of adaptability. Just as a chameleon seamlessly blends into its surroundings, the blueprint flexes and adjusts to accommodate a spectrum of scenarios, ensuring its relevance and effectiveness across diverse financial landscapes.

Tailoring Solutions to Your Reality

Consider the blueprint as a skilled tailor, meticulously crafting solutions to fit your financial contours. It doesn't impose a one-size-fits-all approach; rather, it embraces the nuances of your circumstances. Whether you're an individual managing personal finances or a business navigating complex markets, the blueprint bends and weaves, ensuring that its principles align with your reality.

A Spectrum of Financial Landscapes

Imagine the financial world as a sprawling landscape, replete with peaks and valleys, meadows and rivers. The blueprint isn't confined to a single trail; it's a versatile guide that traverses this diverse terrain. Its principles apply to businesses of various sizes, to individuals with varying financial goals, and to a multitude of economic contexts.

A Tool for All Seasons

Just as a versatile tool has applications beyond a single task, the blueprint transcends specific financial challenges. It equips you with strategies that are as applicable in times of abundance as they are during economic downturns. This adaptability ensures that you're not left stranded when circumstances change; rather, you possess the tools to navigate through uncertainty.

Fostering Resilience Through Adaptation

Adaptability is the cornerstone of resilience. The blueprint's ability to bend and flex strengthens your financial resilience. By embracing diverse scenarios and tailoring its strategies, it empowers you to pivot, adjust, and navigate through uncharted waters with confidence.

A Blueprint for Your Financial Story

Envision the blueprint as a dynamic narrative, with its adaptable nature allowing it to seamlessly integrate into your unique financial story. Each chapter becomes a plot point, each strategy a twist, and the entire blueprint a roadmap that guides your journey. The adaptability it offers ensures that you're the protagonist, steering your narrative toward financial success.

Charting a Flexible Path Forward

As we embark on this blueprint-guided journey, remember that adaptability is your ally. Each strategy you learn, each concept you absorb, is a tool that can be modified to suit your circumstances. Embrace this flexibility as you navigate through financial challenges and seize opportunities with dexterity.

Your Blueprint, Your Way

The blueprint is not a rigid doctrine; it's a malleable framework that respects the individuality of your financial expedition. It acknowledges that your journey is yours alone, and it offers its guidance in a way that's as unique as your financial fingerprint.

So, let's celebrate the versatility and adaptability of the blueprint, and as we venture forth, let's weave its principles into the fabric of your financial reality. Whether you're treading a well-worn path or blazing a new trail, the blueprint is your steadfast companion – adjusting, molding, and ultimately, empowering you to craft a financial story that's truly your own.

1.3.4 Bridging Theory and Action

In the realm of financial management, theory without action is like a ship without a rudder – directionless and unproductive. Recognizing this, the Financial Control Blueprint serves as a bridge that spans the gap between theory and action. It's more than a collection of theoretical concepts; it's a pragmatic toolkit meticulously designed to empower you with actionable strategies. With its guidance, knowledge transforms into the currency of impactful financial decisions.

Empowering Through Practicality

Imagine the blueprint as a craftsman's workshop, where theoretical ideas are transformed into tangible creations. It takes financial theories off the shelf and places them in your hands as powerful tools. These tools are not mere abstractions; they are actionable strategies that can be implemented in the real world, yielding measurable outcomes.

From Concepts to Calculated Decisions

Consider the blueprint as a translator, converting complex financial concepts into a language of calculated decisions. It distills intricate theories into actionable steps, enabling you to make informed choices. By following its guidance, you're not just amassing knowledge; you're converting that knowledge into a currency that drives financial progress.

Applied Wisdom for Real-World Challenges

The blueprint acknowledges that the real world is fraught with challenges and complexities. It doesn't shy away from these realities; instead, it equips you to confront them head-on. With its actionable strategies, you're armed to navigate financial storms, capitalize on opportunities, and overcome obstacles with confidence.

A Toolkit of Transformation

Envision the blueprint as a toolkit, and each strategy it offers as a finely honed instrument. Just as a skilled craftsman selects the right tool for a specific task, you'll find the blueprint's strategies fitting seamlessly into your financial endeavors. From budget creation to investment evaluation, from debt reduction to risk mitigation – each tool contributes to your toolkit of financial mastery.

Catalyzing Change Through Application

The true power of the blueprint lies not in its theoretical elegance, but in its application. It's a catalyst that drives change, enabling you to actively shape your financial destiny. By integrating its strategies into your financial routine, you're cultivating a culture of action and propelling yourself toward success.

Creating Your Financial Tapestry

Imagine the blueprint as a loom, and each actionable strategy as a thread. As you weave these threads together, a rich and intricate tapestry emerges – your financial story. Each decision you make, each strategy you implement, adds another layer of depth and complexity to this tapestry.

Charting the Path Forward

As we navigate the chapters ahead, remember that the blueprint is not just a theoretical discourse; it's a call to action. Each concept we explore, each strategy we unveil, is a stepping stone toward meaningful financial decisions. By embracing the actionable nature of the blueprint, you're embarking on a transformative journey – one where knowledge isn't just acquired, but actively applied to sculpt a future of financial stability and triumph.

1.3.5 Paving the Way for Success

Envision the Financial Control Blueprint as a masterful architect laying the foundation for your financial success. It's not a mere collection of ideas; it's a roadmap to crafting a triumphant financial future. This blueprint is the culmination of principles and strategies meticulously designed to empower you – not just with knowledge, but with actionable tools. These tools enable you to navigate through financial challenges, seize opportunities, and march confidently toward a horizon of unparalleled triumph.

A Blueprint for Actionable Success

Think of the blueprint as a treasure map, guiding you through the labyrinth of financial intricacies. It's not a map to be gazed upon from a distance; it's a map to be followed, step by step, as you unearth the riches of financial control. The blueprint isn't just about learning; it's about doing – about actively sculpting your financial reality.

A Holistic Financial Landscape

Imagine the blueprint as an artist's palette, each strategy a stroke of color that contributes to a vivid and holistic financial landscape. It doesn't focus on isolated areas; it addresses the entirety of your financial canvas. From budgeting to investment, from risk management to tax optimization, the blueprint ensures that no facet of your financial journey remains untouched.

Empowerment in Action

The true empowerment lies not in knowledge alone, but in its application. The blueprint empowers you to transform knowledge into action, turning concepts into results. It's like a captain who not only knows the navigational charts but expertly steers the ship to its intended destination. Through actionable steps, you'll navigate financial waters with prowess.

The Triumph Over Challenges

Picture the blueprint as a shield, protecting you against financial storms. It equips you to face challenges head-on, transforming them from insurmountable obstacles into stepping stones toward growth. Debt becomes a conquerable adversary, risks evolve into manageable variables, and taxes metamorphose into opportunities for optimization.

The Symphony of Financial Triumph

Envision your financial journey as a symphony, with the blueprint as the conductor guiding the harmonious notes. Each strategy you implement, each decision you make, contributes to this symphony of financial triumph. It's not just about a single performance; it's about a lifelong composition of stability, growth, and enduring success.

The Road Ahead

As we venture into the depths of the blueprint's insights, remember that your journey doesn't end with knowledge. It's a journey of action, of transformation, of triumph. By weaving the blueprint's principles into your financial fabric, you're paving the way for a future defined by financial stability, growth, and the unwavering confidence that comes with mastery.

So, let's embark on this journey together – a journey where knowledge becomes empowerment, where principles become action, and where action becomes a symphony of financial success. As we traverse through the blueprint's chapters, let's seize the tools it offers and carve a path that leads not just to financial control, but to an expanse of triumph that knows no bounds.

In the upcoming chapters, we will delve deeper into each facet of the Financial Control Blueprint, unraveling the layers of financial control and providing you with the insights and skills necessary to construct a robust financial foundation. Together, let's embark on this transformative journey toward financial mastery and success.

Chapter 2: Assessing Your Current Financial Situation

2.1 Evaluating Your Financial Health

At the outset of your journey toward enhanced financial control, it's imperative to gauge the health of your current financial landscape. This assessment provides a clear snapshot of your overall financial standing and lays the groundwork for crafting effective strategies. As you embark on this evaluation, consider the following pivotal factors:

2.1.1 Calculating Your Net Worth

In the realm of financial navigation, your net worth stands as a reliable compass, directing you toward your fiscal destination. This fundamental metric transcends mere numbers – it is a beacon that illuminates your current financial path and guides your future course. Calculating your net worth is akin to unfurling a treasure map; by subtracting your liabilities from your assets, you unearth a pivotal figure that encapsulates your financial standing at this juncture. This numerical revelation serves as more than a snapshot; it becomes your starting point, a reference against which you can chart your progress, and a foundation upon which your financial aspirations will be built.

The Math Behind the Magic

At its essence, calculating your net worth is a straightforward arithmetic endeavor. It entails deducting your liabilities, or debts, from your assets. The resulting figure unveils the true extent of your financial holdings, offering a panoramic view of your fiscal worth.

Assets: The Building Blocks

Assets encompass the tangible and intangible elements that contribute to your financial arsenal. From savings accounts to investments, real estate properties to valuable possessions, assets embody your financial resources. They are the bricks that lay the foundation of your net worth calculation.

Liabilities: The Debts to Settle

On the flip side, liabilities embody your financial obligations – the debts you owe to creditors and financial institutions. These may include credit card balances, mortgages, student loans, or any other financial commitments. By subtracting liabilities from your assets, you gain insight into the net result of your financial endeavors.

A Compass for Progress

The calculated net worth serves as more than a mere numerical outcome. It's a dynamic tool that facilitates a multitude of insights. As you embark on your financial journey, this figure becomes your guiding star, allowing you to monitor your progress over time. Just as a sailor relies on the compass to navigate uncharted waters, your net worth offers direction amidst the ever-shifting tides of your financial landscape.

Anchoring Your Financial Goals

Your net worth provides an anchor point for your financial goals. It delineates where you currently stand and, in turn, informs the trajectory you aspire to achieve. As you set your sights on short-term triumphs and long-term accomplishments, your net worth acts as a reference, allowing you to gauge the impact of your financial decisions on your overall fiscal picture.

The Journey of Progress

Picture your financial journey as a scenic road trip, with your net worth as the mile marker. Just as each milestone signifies progress toward your destination, each recalculated net worth measurement offers a tangible representation of your advancement. The incremental increase becomes a testament to your financial acumen and prudent decision-making.

A Legacy of Progression

As you calculate your net worth today, recognize that it's not merely a numerical exercise. It's a step toward a future of empowerment, stability, and growth. Your net worth isn't static; it's a living testament to your financial journey. As you make strategic choices and implement sound financial practices, this compass will guide you through changing landscapes, ultimately leading to a legacy of financial progression.

In traversing the financial terrains ahead, remember that your net worth isn't just a calculation – it's a reflection of your commitment, an embodiment of your financial prowess, and a harbinger of the prosperous horizons that await.

2.1.2 Gauging Income Stability

Imagine your income sources as the pillars upon which your financial edifice stands. Just as a solid foundation is imperative for a sturdy structure, the stability and reliability of your income sources lay the groundwork for your entire financial journey. As you embark on this critical assessment, envision your income streams as the symphony that orchestrates your fiscal harmony.

The Crucial Pulse of Stability

Income stability is the heartbeat of your financial health. Just as a steady rhythm sustains life, a stable income ensures the vitality of your financial existence. Begin your evaluation by scrutinizing the dependability of each income source. Is it consistent, or does it ebb and flow unpredictably? Stability is the bridge between financial uncertainty and unwavering confidence.

Covering the Spectrum: Expenses and Aspirations

Delve deeper by examining the pivotal question: Does your income provide a secure umbrella that shelters both your essential expenses and your loftier financial aspirations? Is it substantial enough to not only meet your day-to-day needs but also propel you toward your goals? A thorough evaluation ensures that your income is not just a fleeting rain but a sustained downpour of financial fulfillment.

Mapping the Journey: A Strong Foundation

Think of income stability as the bedrock upon which your financial expedition is charted. Just as a seasoned sailor prefers calm waters, a stable income allows you to navigate your financial voyage with confidence. It underpins your ability to weather storms, seize opportunities, and chart a course toward lasting financial success.

Harmonizing Aspirations: The Income-Expense Synchrony

As you assess income stability, consider the symphony between your income and expenses. Do they harmonize in a melodious balance, or do dissonances arise? A stable income allows you to orchestrate this symphony effectively, ensuring that your expenses are not a discordant note that throws your financial melody off-key.

The Stronger Together Paradigm

A stable income doesn't merely cover your financial needs – it propels you forward. It empowers you to not only maintain financial equilibrium but also to embrace growth. Your stable income becomes a partner in your financial dance, offering the surefootedness required to take confident steps toward your goals.

Foundation for Financial Fortitude

In essence, the stability of your income isn't just a facet of your financial health; it's the bedrock upon which your financial fortitude is built. Just as a skyscraper relies on its foundation for height and stability, your financial journey hinges on the steadfast nature of your income. A strong foundation ensures that your financial aspirations have a solid platform from which to ascend.

A Symphony of Confidence

As you gauge your income stability, envision a symphony where each note represents a source of income, each instrument symbolizes a revenue stream. When these instruments play in harmony, your financial symphony resonates with confidence, resilience, and the promise of a harmonious financial future.

As you navigate the chapters ahead, remember that income stability isn't merely a numerical consideration; it's the orchestrator of your financial harmony. Through its stable rhythm, you can craft a melody of financial fulfillment, where expenses are met, aspirations are embraced, and the cadence of your financial journey is nothing short of a harmonious symphony of success.

2.1.3 Peering into Savings and Emergency Fund

Imagine your savings and emergency fund as a resilient fortress, standing guard against the unpredictable tempests of life. Just as a fortress shields its inhabitants from external threats, your savings and emergency fund shield you from financial vulnerabilities. As you embark on this exploration, visualize these reserves as a haven of security, ready to weather unforeseen storms.

The Sanctum of Savings

Your savings are more than just numbers; they represent your aspirations, dreams, and a safety net for the future. Begin your journey by delving into the depths of your savings reserves. Take stock of their magnitude and significance. Are they substantial enough to provide you with a sense of financial security and empowerment?

The Guardian of Emergencies

An emergency fund is your financial guardian, standing sentinel against unexpected twists of fate. As you examine this fund, consider its robustness. Can it withstand the impact of sudden income disruptions or unanticipated expenses? Just as a lighthouse guides ships through tumultuous waters, your emergency fund guides you through the turbulent seas of financial uncertainty.

The Power of Preparedness

Analyze the readiness of your emergency fund. Is it poised to swiftly intervene when life throws unexpected challenges your way? Just as a firefighter stands ready to douse flames, your emergency fund should be primed to extinguish financial fires. By ensuring its adequacy, you assure yourself the ability to face crises head-on, without undue financial strain.

The Resilience Test

Consider your emergency fund as a resilience test for your financial health. Can it absorb the impact of a medical emergency, an unforeseen job loss, or a sudden vehicle repair? Much like a bridge tested against the weight of passing vehicles, your emergency fund's strength is evaluated against the pressure of life's unforeseen demands.

The Shelter Against Uncertainty

In a world of uncertainties, your savings and emergency fund offer the solace of certainty. They serve as your shelter against the storms of life, providing a safe harbor when the seas become rough. As you peer into these financial reservoirs, reflect on their role as more than just funds – they are your shield, your protector, and your instrument for maintaining financial equilibrium.

The Unseen Peace of Mind

The true value of a well-stocked emergency fund transcends mere numbers. It bestows upon you a priceless peace of mind – an assurance that you are equipped to handle whatever life throws your way. Just as a sentinel watches over a citadel, your emergency fund watches over your financial well-being.

Building Financial Fortitude

The process of peering into your savings and emergency fund is not merely an exercise in numbers; it's a quest to build financial fortitude. It's about fortifying your financial castle, reinforcing its walls, and ensuring that it remains impervious to unexpected breaches. It's a testament to your commitment to your own financial security and well-being.

A Beacon of Stability

As you journey through the chapters ahead, remember that your savings and emergency fund are more than just resources – they are beacons of stability. They light your way through the darkness of financial uncertainty, providing a guiding light toward a future where unexpected challenges are met with resilience, and where the unpredictability of life is met with the unwavering strength of your financial sanctuary.

2.1.4 Unveiling Credit Score Clarity

Picture your credit score as a window into your financial soul, offering insights into your creditworthiness and financial health. Much like a report card, your credit score showcases your financial behavior, influencing not only your borrowing power but also your access to a realm of opportunities. As you unveil the clarity of your credit score, you're embarking on a journey of self-discovery, where numbers become narratives of your fiscal journey.

The Financial Report Card

Your credit score is more than just a digit; it's a testament to your financial character. Just as a report card encapsulates your academic journey, your credit score encapsulates your financial behavior. Begin by understanding its significance –

it's not a mere metric; it's a gauge of how lenders perceive your reliability as a borrower.

The Influencer of Loan Terms

Your credit score holds the keys to favorable loan terms and interest rates. It's akin to a backstage pass, granting you access to a world of financial opportunities. A robust credit score can unlock doors to mortgages, car loans, and personal loans with lower interest rates, saving you substantial amounts of money over time.

The Opportunity Enabler

Beyond loans, your credit score opens doors to a myriad of opportunities. It can influence your ability to secure an apartment lease, attain favorable insurance premiums, and even impact your job prospects in certain industries. A healthy credit score isn't just about financial prowess; it's about expanding the horizons of your financial journey.

The Comprehensive Evaluation

Conducting a comprehensive review of your credit score is more than a casual glance; it's a deep dive into your financial narrative. Scrutinize the factors that contribute to your score – from payment history and credit utilization to types of credit and new credit inquiries. Is your credit score a mirror reflecting disciplined financial behavior?

A Reflection of Creditworthiness

Ask yourself: Does your credit score mirror your creditworthiness? A high credit score reflects a history of responsible credit management, punctual payments, and prudent credit utilization. On the other hand, a lackluster score may point to missed payments, high credit card balances, or limited credit history.

The Catalyst for Progress

Consider your credit score as a catalyst for your financial progress. Just as a catalyst accelerates a chemical reaction, your credit score can accelerate your access to financial goals. A strong score can shorten the path to homeownership, expedite your dream of owning a car, and catalyze your ability to secure credit when you need it most.

The Hurdles of a Lackluster Score

A lackluster credit score isn't a roadblock; it's a hurdle that can be overcome. Just as an athlete trains to leap over obstacles, you can undertake steps to improve your credit score. Timely payments, judicious credit card usage, and strategic credit management can transform your credit score from a hindrance to a stepping stone.

Charting Your Credit Odyssey

As you peer into the world of credit score clarity, envision it as a treasure map guiding your credit odyssey. It reveals the hidden pathways to financial opportunities, helping you navigate the labyrinth of borrowing and lending. Armed with credit score clarity, you wield a tool that not only empowers your present financial decisions but also shapes the trajectory of your financial future.

A Tapestry of Financial Identity

Remember, your credit score isn't just a number; it's a tapestry woven from your financial behaviors. It reflects your commitment to financial responsibility, your ability to manage credit, and your readiness to seize opportunities. As you weave the threads of financial prudence, your credit score becomes a masterpiece that influences not only your financial options but also the very fabric of your financial life.

2.1.5 Safeguarding Through Insurance Coverage

Imagine insurance coverage as a shield that fortifies your financial castle. In the kingdom of financial control, safeguarding your assets and well-being is paramount. Just as a knight's armor offers protection in times of battle, insurance coverage shields you against the unforeseen adversities that life may unleash. As you peer into the realm of insurance, you're casting a watchful eye over your financial fortress, ensuring its robustness.

The Armor of Protection

Your insurance coverage is more than just a policy; it's a potent form of protection. Begin your exploration by scrutinizing your coverage across various domains. From health and life insurance to property and liability coverage, each policy weaves a strand of security that strengthens your financial resilience.

The Sentinel of Health

Health insurance stands as a sentinel, guarding your well-being against the perils of illness and injury. Assess your health coverage – does it encompass your medical needs and provide a safety net for unexpected medical expenses? A comprehensive health policy ensures that your health remains a priority, even in the face of medical challenges.

The Guardian of Life

Life insurance is a guardian angel that watches over your loved ones. Evaluate your life coverage – is it sufficient to secure your family's future in the event of your absence? A robust life policy ensures that your legacy endures, providing financial support and stability to those you hold dear.

The Fortress of Property

Property insurance acts as a fortress, shielding your assets against the ravages of unforeseen events. Scrutinize your property coverage – does it safeguard your home, belongings, and investments? Comprehensive property insurance guarantees that your hard-earned assets remain protected, even amidst the tumult of accidents or disasters.

The Shield of Liability

Liability coverage is the shield that guards you against legal and financial repercussions. Examine your liability policies – do they shield you from potential legal liabilities and financial obligations? A well-structured liability coverage ensures that you're fortified against unforeseen circumstances that may arise.

The Tapestry of Resilience

As you assess your insurance coverage, envision it as a tapestry woven from threads of resilience. Each policy is a thread that contributes to the overall fabric of your financial security. Just as a tapestry strengthens a garment, insurance coverage fortifies your financial well-being.

The Legacy of Preparedness

Consider insurance as a legacy of preparedness that you bestow upon yourself and your loved ones. It's a testament to your foresight, a gift of security that transcends time. As you scrutinize your coverage, recognize that it's not just about policies – it's about creating a legacy of protection and stability.

The Pillars of Financial Control

In the grand architecture of financial control, insurance coverage forms the sturdy pillars that uphold your financial structure. It's the assurance that even in the face of uncertainty, you stand unshaken. Your insurance coverage isn't just a set of policies; it's a testament to your commitment to shielding your assets, preserving your well-being, and ensuring that your financial fortress remains unassailable.

A Shield of Empowerment

As you journey through the chapters ahead, remember that insurance coverage isn't a mere transaction; it's an act of empowerment. It's about equipping yourself with the tools to brave the storms, navigate the challenges, and emerge stronger on the other side. With insurance as your shield, you're not merely a spectator of your financial destiny – you're the valiant protagonist of your own financial epic, steadfastly steering toward a future of resilience and security.

2.2 Reviewing Your Financial Goals

The cornerstone of effective financial control rests upon the clarity of your goals. As you embark on assessing your financial landscape, take a moment to revisit and refine your financial aspirations. This review process sets the stage for informed decision-making and strategic planning.

2.2.1 Short-Term Goals in Focus

Visualize your financial journey as a garden of aspirations, where short-term goals are the vibrant blooms that grace your path. These goals, much like delicate petals, hold the power to transform your financial landscape. As you delve into the realm of short-term objectives, you're embarking on a journey of nurturing and growth, where every goal achieved paves the way for even greater accomplishments.

The Stepping Stones of Progress

Short-term goals serve as the stepping stones that bridge your present with your future. Just as a well-placed stone allows you to cross a river, accomplishing short-term goals propels you forward on your financial odyssey. Begin by focusing your attention on these goals – they are the practical, tangible manifestations of your aspirations.

The Tapestry of Dreams

Delve into the rich tapestry of short-term objectives. Do you dream of a much-needed vacation? Is credit card debt casting a shadow over your financial horizon? Are you nurturing an emergency fund, ready to shield yourself from the unexpected? Each goal represents a thread woven into the fabric of your financial aspirations.

The Power of Scrutiny

As you scrutinize your short-term goals, envision them as seeds waiting to flourish. What care and attention do they require? Just as a gardener tends to each plant's unique needs, you must nurture your goals with strategic planning, dedicated effort, and timely actions.

The Catalyst for Momentum

Accomplishing short-term goals isn't a mere checkbox exercise; it's a catalyst for momentum. Just as the first step of a journey sets the pace, achieving short-term objectives propels you forward, infusing your financial journey with a surge of energy. These achievements embolden you to tackle more ambitious undertakings.

The Ripple Effect

Consider short-term goals as ripples in a pond. When you achieve one goal, the impact extends far beyond the initial accomplishment. The discipline, determination, and knowledge gained create a ripple effect that influences subsequent financial decisions and actions.

The Nexus of Practicality and Aspiration

Short-term goals embody the nexus of practicality and aspiration. They are the tangible outcomes of your financial dreams, translating abstract desires into concrete actions. By focusing on short-term goals, you align your aspirations with actionable steps, creating a harmonious blend of vision and reality.

The Lighthouse of Achievement

As you navigate the seas of financial growth, let your short-term goals be the lighthouse that guides your way. Each accomplished goal emits a beam of achievement, illuminating the path toward your broader objectives. Just as a lighthouse helps sailors avoid rocky shores, your achieved short-term goals help you steer clear of financial pitfalls.

The Art of Celebration

Celebrate each short-term victory as a brushstroke on the canvas of your financial masterpiece. The joy of achievement is not just a momentary elation; it's a testament to your dedication, discipline, and determination. These celebratory moments fuel your financial journey with positivity and enthusiasm.

The Prelude to Grandeur

Remember, short-term goals aren't the destination; they are the prelude to grandeur. Each accomplished goal sets the stage for more ambitious endeavors. By nurturing and achieving your short-term aspirations, you're sowing the seeds of success that will eventually yield a bountiful harvest of financial triumphs.

2.2.2 Medium-Term Dreams Unveiled

Envision your financial journey as a canvas, where medium-term goals are the vivid strokes that shape your masterpiece. These goals, with their time horizon spanning 3 to 10 years, are the bridges between your short-term accomplishments and your long-term aspirations. As you unveil the tapestry of medium-term dreams, you're embarking on a journey of envisioning, planning, and manifesting your aspirations.

The Horizon of Possibilities

Medium-term goals stretch before you like a horizon of possibilities. They encompass a diverse spectrum of ambitions, from planting the seeds of homeownership to nurturing the garden of entrepreneurial endeavors or securing a foundation for your child's education. Each goal is a brushstroke that adds depth and dimension to your financial landscape.

The Refinement of Direction

Delve into the heart of your medium-term goals to refine your financial direction. In a world of ever-evolving desires, a closer look at these goals ensures that your financial trajectory remains aligned with your changing aspirations. It's the compass that keeps you on course, ensuring that you're charting a path that resonates with your evolving desires.

The Bridge Between Timeframes

Medium-term goals act as bridges connecting your present with your future. They provide a structured conduit for your ambitions to materialize over a span of years. Like a gardener tending to a sapling, nurturing your medium-term goals requires deliberate planning, consistent effort, and a vision of the flourishing outcome.

The Canvas of Entrepreneurship

If entrepreneurial pursuits beckon, your medium-term goals might involve the birth and growth of a business venture. Delve into the intricacies of this dream – from market research and business plans to funding strategies and scalability. Every stroke of planning and execution contributes to the canvas of your entrepreneurial vision.

The Foundation of Education

Perhaps your medium-term aspirations revolve around funding your child's education. Consider the financial canvas required – tuition fees, educational resources, extracurricular activities. By meticulously planning and executing, you lay a sturdy foundation for your child's academic journey.

The Dream of Homeownership

For some, medium-term goals involve the realization of homeownership. This dream involves envisioning the ideal abode, saving for a down payment, and navigating the intricacies of real estate. As you unveil this dream, you're sculpting the very space where memories will be crafted and cherished.

The Symphony of Savings

Medium-term goals often dance to the rhythm of savings. Just as a conductor guides an orchestra, you orchestrate your finances to accommodate these aspirations. The tempo might involve increasing your savings rate, exploring investment opportunities, and aligning your financial instruments with the symphony of your goals.

The Evolution of Desires

As you peer into the realm of medium-term dreams, recognize that desires are dynamic. What you yearn for today may evolve over time. By closely examining and revisiting your medium-term goals, you ensure that your financial journey is a reflection of your ever-changing aspirations.

The Legacy of Vision

Remember, medium-term goals aren't merely destinations; they are the legacy of your vision. Each goal accomplished signifies not only a milestone but a testament to your ability to manifest your aspirations. As you nurture and unveil your medium-term dreams, you're painting a canvas that encapsulates your determination, foresight, and commitment to creating a future that aligns with your heart's desires.

2.2.3 The Grandeur of Long-Term Goals

Imagine your financial journey as a tapestry woven with threads of time, and long-term goals as the majestic patterns that emerge over a decade or more. These goals hold the promise of profound transformation, embodying the pinnacle of your aspirations. As you explore the grandeur of long-term objectives, you embark on a journey of vision, dedication, and legacy-building.

The Tapestry of Transformation

Long-term goals are the master strokes that shape the tapestry of your financial future. Spanning a decade or more, they encompass ambitions of retirement tranquility, wealth accumulation, or the creation of a lasting financial legacy. Each goal represents a chapter in the story of your life, written with meticulous consideration and unwavering intent.

The Symphony of Retirement

Retirement planning is a symphony that plays softly in the background of your financial journey. As you approach this long-term goal, consider the notes of financial security, leisure pursuits, and quality of life. Craft a retirement vision that harmonizes with your desires, ensuring that your golden years are a symphony of fulfillment.

The Canvas of Wealth Accumulation

Wealth accumulation is a canvas awaiting your strokes of strategic brilliance. Delve into the hues of investment portfolios, diversified assets, and compounding growth. With each stroke of financial wisdom, you're painting a future that boasts not only prosperity but the freedom to pursue life's passions.

The Legacy of Financial Footprints

Crafting a financial legacy is akin to leaving footprints on the sands of time. It involves considering the impact you wish to have on future generations or charitable causes. As you etch your legacy, ponder the values and principles you want to impart, ensuring that your financial journey is a testament to purpose and impact.

The Essence of Specificity

Long-term goals demand a touch of specificity. Much like a sculptor chiseling intricate details, your long-term goals should be etched with clarity, precision, and depth. Define not only the goal itself but also the milestones, strategies, and timeline that will guide your journey.

The Yardstick of Measurability

Measurability becomes your yardstick of progress. Break down your long-term goals into quantifiable metrics – be it a target retirement corpus, a certain net worth, or an annual income in retirement. Measurability empowers you to track your progress and make informed adjustments along the way.

The Thread of Life Alignment

Long-term goals are interwoven with the fabric of your life's overarching narrative. Consider how each goal aligns with your values, passions, and aspirations. Just as a skilled weaver selects threads that harmonize to create a masterpiece, you align your long-term goals to contribute to the symphony of your life's story.

The Legacy You Craft

As you stand at the threshold of long-term aspirations, recognize that you're crafting a legacy – a legacy of foresight, determination, and impact. Each decision, each step, becomes a brushstroke that adds depth to the canvas of your financial journey. The grandeur of long-term goals is not just in their accomplishment, but in the story they tell about your commitment to crafting a life of significance and fulfillment.

2.2.4 SMART Goals: Your North Star

In the vast expanse of goal setting, the North Star of SMART criteria shines brightly, illuminating your path with clarity and purpose. Each letter in SMART – Specific, Measurable, Attainable, Relevant, and Time-bound – acts as a guiding light, ensuring that your goals are not merely wishes, but well-defined roadmaps to success. As you embrace the essence of SMART goals, you embark on a journey of precision, focus, and accomplishment.

The Specific Blueprint

A goal without specificity is like a ship without a compass. Specificity is the compass that directs your efforts with unwavering precision. By defining your goal in explicit terms, you create a blueprint that outlines the destination, the journey, and the landmarks along the way.

The Measurable Milestones

Milestones are the markers that measure your progress. Measurability injects your goals with substance and tangibility. It transforms vague notions into concrete targets that you can track, celebrate, and adjust. With measurable milestones, you gain a clear understanding of how far you've come and how much further you have to go.

The Attainable Horizon

An unattainable goal is a mirage that fades as you approach. Attainability ensures that your goals are rooted in reality and feasibility. While ambition is encouraged, setting goals that are within your reach empowers you to channel your efforts effectively, ensuring that every step brings you closer to the summit.

The Relevant Connection

Relevance is the thread that connects your goals to your broader vision. A relevant goal resonates with your aspirations, aligns with your values, and contributes to your overall objectives. It's the heartbeat that infuses your goals with purpose and significance, making every endeavor a meaningful step on your journey.

The Time-Bound Commitment

Time is the essence that fuels action. A goal without a timeline is a dream deferred. By setting a time-bound aspect to your goals, you create a sense of urgency and accountability. A timeline serves as a reminder that your goals are not distant fantasies, but commitments that demand your attention and effort.

The Compass for Your Expedition

SMART goals become the compass for your goal-setting expedition. They guide your decisions, illuminate your path, and steer you toward your desired destination. Regularly revisiting and refining your SMART goals ensures that they remain the constant North Star, keeping you on track even as the landscape of life evolves.

The Journey of Mastery

As you embrace SMART goals, recognize that it's not just about achieving individual objectives; it's a journey of mastery. Each SMART goal you set and achieve hones your ability to envision, plan, and execute with precision. It's a testament to your commitment to continuous growth and progress.

The Symphony of Achievement

Envision your financial journey as a symphony, where SMART goals compose the melodic notes that create harmonious progress. Just as a symphony requires each instrument to play its part, your SMART goals work in concert to orchestrate your financial success. With each note of specificity, measure, attainability, relevance, and timeliness, you compose a symphony of achievement that resonates with fulfillment and triumph.

2.3 Analyzing Income and Expenses

Financial control hinges on the mastery of your income and expenses. By meticulously dissecting these aspects, you unravel valuable insights into your financial behaviors and pave the way for strategic optimization.

2.3.1 Symphony of Income Analysis

Picture your financial journey as a grand symphony, and at its opening notes is the melodic performance of income analysis. This harmonious examination dissects the various instruments of your revenue streams – the steady hum of salary, the dynamic crescendo of business earnings, the harmonic resonance of investments, and the gentle undertones of rentals. As you discern the stability and composition of your income, you are orchestrating the rhythm that will guide your financial performance.

Conducting the Financial Orchestra

Much like a conductor meticulously directs every instrument in an orchestra, income analysis allows you to conduct the financial symphony of your life. By understanding the diverse sources of your income, you're not only aware of their individual melodies but also their collective harmony. This awareness empowers you to make informed decisions and fine-tune your financial composition.

The Cadence of Stability

Stability is the heartbeat of your financial symphony. Just as a steady rhythm provides a foundation for musical expression, a stable income ensures a strong financial base. Analyze the predictability and consistency of your income sources – is your salary a reliable refrain, or do business earnings introduce fluctuations? This assessment sets the tone for your financial composition.

The Crescendo of Business Earnings

For entrepreneurs and business owners, business earnings add a dynamic crescendo to your financial symphony. Dive into the intricacies of your business revenue – are you achieving consistent growth, or are there seasonal variations? As you examine this melody, you're not only assessing financial performance but also identifying opportunities for expansion and optimization.

The Harmonic Resonance of Investments

Investments introduce a harmonic resonance to your financial composition. Delve into the world of stocks, bonds, real estate, and other investment vehicles. How do they contribute to your overall income? Are they creating a balanced and diversified melody, or is there room for adjustments to achieve optimal performance?

The Melody of Rentals

If you're a landlord, rentals introduce their unique melody to the symphony. Explore the stability of rental income, evaluate occupancy rates, and consider the impact of maintenance costs. This melody, if well-tuned, can create a steady undercurrent that enriches your financial performance.

Setting the Rhythm for Financial Performance

Just as a conductor sets the rhythm for a musical performance, income analysis establishes the tempo of your financial journey. It dictates the pace at which you can move toward your goals, make investments, and allocate resources. By understanding the nuances of your income sources, you're not only orchestrating your financial symphony but also preparing for the harmonious melodies of expenses, savings, and investments that will follow.

Fine-Tuning and Refining

Remember, income analysis isn't a one-time performance; it's an ongoing symphony that requires fine-tuning and refining. Regularly revisit your income sources, track their performance, and adjust your financial composition as needed. Just as a skilled conductor ensures that every note is played with precision, you, too, have the power to orchestrate a symphony of financial success through insightful income analysis.

2.3.2 Choreographing Expense Analysis

In the grand production of your financial journey, expense analysis takes center stage as a meticulously choreographed performance. Just as a skilled choreographer arranges every move with precision, you're tasked with delineating your expenses into a harmonious routine. This dance between fixed and variable categories – encompassing essentials like rent or mortgage, utilities, groceries, entertainment, and transportation – creates a symphony of insight. Through this granular exploration, you unveil areas primed for prudent cost reduction.

The Dance of Fixed and Variable Expenses

Expenses, much like dancers, take various forms – some adhering to a predetermined routine, while others exhibit fluidity. Fixed expenses, akin to the lead dancers, include the unchanging essentials such as rent or mortgage and utilities. Variable expenses, like the ensemble, introduce spontaneity and variety, encompassing groceries, entertainment, dining out, transportation, and more.

The Essence of Essentials

Fixed expenses are the backbone of your choreography – the foundation upon which your financial routine rests. Just as a dance routine revolves around key movements, your financial routine centers on essentials that sustain your lifestyle. These unchanging costs demand careful consideration and alignment with your overall financial goals.

The Flourish of Variable Spending

Variable expenses add the flourish and flair to your financial choreography. These flexible elements introduce color and vibrancy to your routine. While they allow for spontaneity and enjoyment, they also present opportunities for mindful decision-making. Delve into these expenses – from leisure activities to dining experiences – and evaluate their alignment with your financial priorities.

The Art of Prudent Cost Reduction

Expense analysis unveils opportunities for prudent cost reduction – the art of optimizing your spending without sacrificing value. As a choreographer seeks seamless transitions between movements, you seek seamless ways to trim unnecessary expenses. Can you find more cost-effective alternatives without compromising quality? Can you identify areas where moderation can lead to substantial savings?

The Rhythmic Review

Just as a choreographer reviews each step for precision, embark on a rhythmic review of your expenses. Regularly revisit your spending patterns, analyze fluctuations, and identify any deviations from your financial choreography. This practice ensures that your financial routine remains aligned with your goals and aspirations.

The Choreography of Progress

Expense analysis isn't solely about restriction; it's a choreography of progress. It's a deliberate and thoughtful arrangement of your financial resources to support your objectives. By refining your financial routine, you're not only optimizing your current performance but also laying the groundwork for a graceful and harmonious financial future.

The Ongoing Performance

Remember, the choreography of expense analysis is an ongoing performance. Just as a dance evolves with each practice, your spending habits may shift with changing circumstances. Stay attuned to your financial choreography, make adjustments as needed, and ensure that every step is a deliberate and purposeful move toward your financial aspirations. As you master the art of choreographing your expenses, you're orchestrating a symphony of financial control and success.

2.3.3 The Dance of Cash Flow

In the grand ballroom of financial management, the dance of cash flow takes center stage. With grace and precision, you step onto the dance floor of your financial reality, comparing the elegant movements of your total income to the rhythmic steps of your total expenses. As you sway to this financial waltz, a harmonious melody emerges – one where your income gracefully surpasses your expenses. This analysis illuminates the cadence of your financial well-being, revealing insights that guide your journey to prosperity.

The Choreography of Income and Expenses

Much like a choreographer orchestrates the movements of dancers, you orchestrate the flow of your financial resources. Your income, the lead dancer, takes center stage, supported by the ensemble of your expenses. Each step of this choreography affects the overall performance – ensuring that your income leads, your expenses follow, and the dance remains harmonious.

The Graceful Melody of Positive Cash Flow

Positive cash flow is the graceful melody that emanates from this dance. It signifies a financial rhythm where your income elegantly outpaces your expenses. This melody, akin to a soothing symphony, is a testament to your ability to manage your resources effectively and make informed financial decisions.

The Reflection of Financial Well-Being

As you engage in the dance of cash flow, you're presented with a reflection of your financial well-being. Are the movements fluid and synchronized, or do they stumble and falter? By comparing income and expenses, you gain insight into your financial cadence – is it harmonious and sustainable, or is there a need for adjustment?

The Insights Beneath the Surface

Beneath the surface of this financial dance lie valuable insights. A positive cash flow suggests that you have a surplus – funds that can be directed toward savings, investments, and debt reduction. On the other hand, a negative cash flow indicates a deficit – a signal to review your spending patterns and make necessary adjustments.

The Dance of Decisions

The dance of cash flow is also a dance of decisions. It prompts you to evaluate your financial choreography – Are there areas where expenses can be trimmed without sacrificing essentials? Can you allocate surplus funds strategically to accelerate your progress toward financial goals? Each decision you make impacts the flow of this dance and influences the melody it produces.

The Ongoing Choreography

Like any performance, the dance of cash flow is ongoing. It requires continuous monitoring, adjustment, and refinement. Just as a dancer practices tirelessly to perfect their routine, you, too, must practice mindful financial management to ensure that the dance of cash flow remains a harmonious and prosperous symphony.

The Symphony of Financial Harmony

As you master the art of the cash flow dance, you contribute to the symphony of financial harmony. Your graceful steps of income and expenses create a composition that resonates with stability and progress. This symphony not only reflects your current financial state but also serves as a guiding rhythm toward your future financial goals. So, step onto the dance floor of cash flow with confidence, for each movement you make brings you closer to the crescendo of financial success.

2.4 Assessing Debt and Liabilities

A comprehensive understanding of your debt and liabilities is pivotal in your journey toward financial control. By confronting these financial obligations head-on, you fortify your foundation and empower strategic decision-making.

2.4.1 The Tapestry of Debt Inventory

Imagine crafting a tapestry of your financial landscape – a vivid portrayal of your commitments and obligations. This intricate artwork, known as a debt inventory, weaves together the threads of your financial responsibilities. Each thread represents a debt – from credit card balances to student loans, mortgages to car loans. With each thread meticulously woven, you paint a comprehensive portrait of your financial tapestry, noting outstanding balances, interest rates, and monthly payments.

The Weaver of Financial Commitments

As the weaver of this tapestry, you take on the role of an artist, carefully selecting each thread to create a harmonious composition. Each debt thread is a brushstroke, contributing to the overall picture of your financial landscape. By laying out your debts in this organized manner, you gain clarity and insight into your financial obligations.

The Threads of Debt Variety

Just as a tapestry boasts threads of different colors and textures, your debt inventory encompasses a variety of financial obligations. Some threads may be light and manageable, while others may be heavier and more burdensome. Lay them all out, from the smallest personal loan to the largest mortgage, creating a mosaic of debts that form the backdrop of your financial journey.

The Depth of Outstanding Balances

Each thread of your debt tapestry carries a numeric weight – the outstanding balance. These balances are the foundation of your tapestry, dictating the size and shape of each thread. By documenting these balances, you unveil the financial load you're carrying and set the stage for strategies to manage and reduce them.

The Intricacies of Interest Rates

Interest rates add nuances to your tapestry, much like shading and gradients in a painting. Some threads may bear high interest rates, casting a darker hue of financial strain. Others may be graced with lower rates, contributing to a lighter and more optimistic tone. As you map out these rates, you identify areas where strategic action can lead to interest savings.

The Melody of Monthly Payments

In the symphony of your financial tapestry, monthly payments are the recurring notes that create a rhythm. Each debt thread contributes to this melody, with varying monthly payments that echo across your financial landscape. By documenting these payments, you gain a sense of the financial commitments that must be honored regularly.

The Portrait of Financial Responsibility

When your debt inventory is complete, you unveil a portrait of your financial responsibility. This portrait goes beyond numbers; it tells a story of your financial past and present. It serves as a foundation for debt management strategies, repayment plans, and informed financial decision-making.

The Journey Ahead

Just as an artist revisits their canvas, you, too, will revisit and update your debt inventory as your financial journey evolves. It becomes a living tapestry, reflecting your progress in managing and reducing debt. With this portrait in hand, you're equipped to navigate the path of debt reduction, financial freedom, and ultimately, the creation of a brighter and more prosperous financial tapestry.

2.4.2 Balancing the Debt-to-Income Ratio

In the intricate dance of financial equilibrium, one crucial partner is the debt-to-income ratio. This mathematical relationship is the pivot upon which your financial balance rests. It quantifies the interplay between your monthly debt payments and your monthly income. By deciphering this ratio, you unveil valuable insights into your debt burden and your capacity to manage additional financial commitments.

The Mathematical Choreography

Imagine the debt-to-income ratio as a carefully choreographed dance. On one side of the stage stands your monthly debt payments, each representing a financial commitment you must honor. On the other side stands your monthly income, the lifeline of your financial well-being. The dance they perform together reveals the delicate balance between your financial obligations and your earning capacity.

The Numerical Harmony

As these two partners dance, they create a numerical harmony known as the debt-to-income ratio. This ratio is a reflection of your financial health – a numeric representation of your ability to juggle existing debts while considering the feasibility of taking on more. The lower the ratio, the more balanced your financial equilibrium; the higher the ratio, the more it tilts toward potential financial strain.

The Insightful Interpretation

Interpreting the debt-to-income ratio requires a discerning eye. Is your dance floor dominated by debt payments, or is income taking center stage? A higher ratio suggests that a significant portion of your income is allocated to debt, potentially limiting your financial flexibility. Conversely, a lower ratio indicates a healthier balance, freeing up more of your income for savings, investments, and pursuing your financial goals.

The Capacity for New Commitments

Beyond its role as a financial mirror, the debt-to-income ratio also serves as a litmus test for managing new commitments. As you contemplate additional financial responsibilities – whether it's a new loan or an investment opportunity – your debt-to-income ratio provides a gauge. It signals whether you have the capacity to take on new financial obligations without compromising your existing financial stability.

The Quest for Balance

Just as dancers strive for perfect balance and synchronization, you, too, aim to achieve equilibrium in your financial dance. A balanced debt-to-income ratio indicates that your financial partners – debt payments and income – are performing in harmonious coordination. If the dance seems uneven, it's an invitation to reassess your financial choreography, explore debt reduction strategies, and fine-tune your income streams.

The Ongoing Performance

Remember, the dance of the debt-to-income ratio is an ongoing performance. As your financial circumstances evolve, so does this ratio. Regularly revisiting this metric allows you to monitor your financial rhythm, make informed decisions, and adjust your choreography accordingly.

The Path to Financial Symphony

As you master the dance of the debt-to-income ratio, you're sculpting the path to a financial symphony. Your steps toward achieving a balanced ratio echo the movements of responsible financial management. Just as dancers practice diligently to perfect their routine, you, too, refine your financial routine to create a balanced and melodious financial future.

2.4.3 Strategies for Debt Repayment

Debt repayment is a strategic art form, a choreography of financial liberation. Within this dance, two prominent methods emerge – the debt snowball and the debt avalanche. Each method is a sequence of graceful movements that guide you toward the grand finale of debt freedom. As you engage with these strategies, you orchestrate a symphony of financial empowerment, taking charge of your journey toward debt liberation.

The Debt Snowball: A Sequence of Triumphs

Imagine the debt snowball as a series of triumphant steps on your path to debt freedom. In this method, you start by addressing your smallest debts first. Picture these smaller debts as snowflakes that you gather and roll into a snowball. With each small victory, your snowball grows, gaining momentum and size.

The Momentum of Small Wins

The brilliance of the debt snowball lies in its focus on psychology. By conquering smaller debts early, you experience a series of victories. This psychological boost propels you forward, building momentum and enthusiasm for the journey ahead. As the snowball gains mass, it eventually gathers enough force to tackle larger debts with renewed confidence.

The Debt Avalanche: Scaling Heights of Savings

Contrastingly, envision the debt avalanche as a climb toward financial peaks. In this method, you ascend by targeting debts with the highest interest rates. Like a skilled mountaineer, you conquer the most challenging obstacles first, inching your way toward the summit of debt freedom.

The Strategy of Interest Optimization

The debt avalanche is grounded in a strategic principle – minimizing interest payments. By prioritizing high-interest debts, you minimize the long-term cost of your debts. This method is akin to chipping away at the steepest part of a mountain, progressively easing your ascent as you move toward debts with lower interest rates.

The Choreography of Your Debt Dance

Both the debt snowball and the debt avalanche are choreographies of financial discipline. They guide your steps toward debt liberation, each with its unique rhythm and tempo. The choice between them hinges on your personal style and financial priorities. Whether you seek the momentum of small victories or the optimization of interest savings, both methods lead you to the same triumphant destination.

The Grand Finale of Debt Freedom

As you engage in the dance of debt repayment, envision the grand finale – a stage bathed in the radiant glow of debt freedom. The snowball rolls larger, the avalanche surges higher, and with each debt conquered, you inch closer to the spotlight of financial liberation. These strategies empower you to orchestrate your journey, to curate each movement toward a debt-free crescendo.

The Ongoing Performance

Remember, debt repayment is an ongoing performance. Just as a dancer refines their routine with each practice, you refine your approach to debt repayment as your financial circumstances evolve. Whether you're rolling the snowball or conquering the avalanche, every step is a testament to your commitment and resolve.

The Symphony of Financial Triumph

Ultimately, debt repayment is a symphony of financial triumph. The choreography of the snowball or the avalanche, guided by your choices and determination, shapes a melodic journey toward debt freedom. With each debt settled, you compose a harmonious narrative of financial empowerment, leading to a standing ovation of debt liberation and a brighter, debt-free future.

2.4.4 Embracing Financial Obligations

Imagine a symphony where debt and liabilities join in harmonious accord, creating the melody of financial obligations. Within this orchestration, obligations extend beyond debts, encompassing a wide spectrum of responsibilities that demand your timely attention and fulfillment. From mortgage payments to insurance premiums, these notes in your financial composition form a symphony of commitment, revealing the depth and breadth of your financial responsibilities.

The Versatility of Financial Obligations

Much like a symphony's diverse instrumentation, your financial obligations encompass a variety of notes. Some notes may be soft and gentle, representing routine bills and payments. Others may be more pronounced, like the bold crescendo of mortgage installments or loan repayments. Collectively, they create a symphony of financial commitments that resonate through your financial landscape.

The Spectrum of Responsibility

Every obligation in this symphony carries its own significance. Your mortgage payment, for instance, represents your commitment to homeownership and a place of sanctuary. Insurance premiums are the safeguarding chords, protecting your assets and well-being. These financial notes are a reflection of your responsible stewardship, ensuring that promises are honored and obligations are met.

The Choreography of Fulfillment

Just as a conductor guides each instrument in a symphony, you orchestrate the fulfillment of these financial obligations. Each payment, each commitment met on time, contributes to the rhythm and harmony of your financial composition. Your choreography of fulfillment ensures that the symphony plays on smoothly, free from dissonance or disruption.

The Balance of Financial Symphony

Maintaining the balance within this symphony is essential. As you fulfill your obligations, you strike a chord of financial stability. However, just as a symphony requires attention to detail and continuous practice, your financial obligations demand ongoing vigilance. By embracing these responsibilities and ensuring their timely fulfillment, you maintain the balance that underpins your financial well-being.

The Reward of Responsible Stewardship

Embracing financial obligations isn't merely a duty; it's an act of responsible stewardship. Each payment, each commitment met, is a testament to your dedication to financial health. By fulfilling these obligations, you create a melody of financial integrity, one that echoes through your life and resonates with the rewards of disciplined financial management.

The Ongoing Symphony

Remember, the symphony of financial obligations is ongoing. Just as a symphony has multiple movements, your financial journey consists of various obligations that evolve over time. Regularly reviewing and adjusting your choreography ensures that your symphony remains in tune, playing a harmonious melody that supports your broader financial goals.

The Symphony of Fulfillment

As you embrace your financial obligations, you contribute to a symphony of fulfillment. Each note, each commitment met, adds to the resonance of your financial well-being. With each obligation honored, you enrich the harmonious composition of your financial life, creating a symphony that celebrates your dedication, responsibility, and commitment to a prosperous future.

With these sections, you've set the stage for a comprehensive exploration of assessing one's current financial situation. The subsequent layers of this chapter will delve deeper into each facet, empowering you to unravel the intricacies of your financial landscape and establish the cornerstone for an empowered financial future.

Chapter 3: Creating a Budget

3.1 Setting Financial Goals

In the symphony of financial management, setting clear and harmonious goals acts as the conductor's baton, guiding each note of your budget. These goals, like musical motifs, infuse purpose and direction into your budgeting endeavors. To create a harmonious budget, consider the following when setting your financial goals:

3.1.1 Prioritize Goals

Envisioning your financial journey as a symphony, where each note contributes to a harmonious composition, you step into the role of a skilled conductor. Just as a composer carefully arranges musical themes, you embark on the task of determining the hierarchy of your financial goals. This act of classification lends structure and purpose to your aspirations, creating a roadmap that guides your allocation of resources.

Short-Term Crescendos

In this musical analogy, short-term goals play the role of vibrant crescendos. These are the immediate, attention-commanding notes that demand swift action. They encompass endeavors such as establishing an emergency fund, paying off high-interest debts, or affording a well-deserved vacation. As you prioritize these short-term crescendos, you infuse your financial symphony with a sense of urgency and accomplishment.

Medium-Term Melodies

Transitioning to a more measured tempo, medium-term goals resonate as enduring melodies within your financial composition. With a horizon spanning three to ten years, these melodies include acquiring a home, nurturing a business venture, or investing in education. Crafting these medium-term melodies adds depth and richness to your financial symphony, contributing to a harmonious progression.

Long-Term Harmonies

The enduring harmonies of long-term goals echo through the years, shaping the very essence of your financial symphony. These are the profound compositions that encompass retirement planning, wealth accumulation, and the establishment of a lasting legacy. As you meticulously integrate these long-term harmonies, you forge the grand narrative of your financial journey, ensuring that each note resonates with purpose.

A Symphony of Priorities

In your role as conductor, you adeptly weave these goals together, creating a symphony of priorities. The short-term crescendos, medium-term melodies, and long-term harmonies harmoniously interplay, forming a coherent and purposeful financial composition. Through this symphonic arrangement, you establish a framework for allocating resources effectively, ensuring that each note contributes melodically to the overarching opus of your financial success. As you set the stage for your financial symphony, remember that the prioritization of goals is the conductor's baton that guides your journey toward harmony and triumph.

3.1.2 Specificity and Measurability

In the intricate symphony of financial goal-setting, the beauty lies in the precision of each note – much like the creation of a beautiful melody. Your financial goals, akin to musical notes, gain resonance and significance when crafted with specificity and measurability. Instead of vague notions that linger like distant echoes, embrace the clarity of well-defined objectives.

Crafting Distinct Notes

Imagine your financial goals as individual musical notes, each contributing to the composition of your financial symphony. To make these notes truly resonate, infuse them with distinctness. Replace the vague refrain of "save money" with a clear and resonant goal, such as "save $5,000 for a down payment on a house within one year." By assigning a numerical value and a specific purpose, you bring each note to life, giving it a defined place within the grand musical arrangement.

Harmonizing with Measurability

Just as a melody gains depth and harmony through measured progression, your financial goals flourish when accompanied by measurable milestones. Attach tangible metrics to your aspirations. Consider the example of "pay off debt" – transform this into a harmonious goal by specifying "pay off $10,000 credit card debt in 18 months." This not only defines the direction but also provides a clear gauge of progress as you traverse your financial composition.

The Focal Points of Your Budget

As you craft these finely tuned and resonant goals, they evolve into the focal points of your financial budget. Each goal becomes a guiding theme, steering your allocation of resources and setting the tempo for your financial journey. Just as a melody thrives on distinct and well-defined notes, your budget gains structure and purpose through the presence of these specific and measurable financial objectives.

Enhancing the Symphony of Your Finances

In the grand symphony of your financial life, the precision of specificity and measurability serves as the conductor's baton. It directs the rhythm, ensures alignment, and guides your financial performance. These meticulously crafted goals transform your financial composition into a masterpiece, where each note resonates with clarity, purpose, and achievement. As you continue to compose your financial symphony, remember that every well-defined goal is a resonant note that harmonizes with the broader opus of your financial success.

3.1.3 Realistic and Attainable

In the symphony of financial goal-setting, achieving harmony requires a delicate balance – much like an orchestra playing within its abilities. As you compose your financial aspirations, the principles of realism and attainability become the guiding notes that ensure a harmonious alignment between your goals and your budget's capacity.

Crafting Goals with Precision

Just as a skilled conductor tailors the composition to the capabilities of the orchestra, your financial goals should harmonize with your current financial situation. The crafting of goals that are realistic and attainable is akin to selecting musical pieces that complement the skills of the musicians. It prevents dissonance between your aspirations and your budget's potential, allowing for a seamless integration of both.

Averting Dissonance

While ambition serves as a driving force, setting goals that surpass the boundaries of your budget's capacity may introduce dissonance into your financial symphony. Much like a cacophony of out-of-tune instruments, overly ambitious goals can strain your resources and lead to frustration. The pursuit of financial success is a journey, not a sprint – and just as a well-paced symphony unfolds, your goals should progress in harmony with your financial reality.

Striving for Balanced Crescendos

As you set your sights on financial horizons, remember that each goal should inspire without overwhelming. Strive for a balanced crescendo, where your aspirations uplift and energize you, yet remain well within the realm of the achievable. This balance ensures that your financial symphony flows smoothly, allowing for consistent progress without disruptive strains.

A Symphony of Balance

In the grand composition of your financial journey, the notes of realism and attainability play a crucial role. They provide the necessary cadence that allows your financial aspirations to harmonize with your budget's capabilities. Just as an orchestra creates a harmonious masterpiece by playing within its abilities, your financial goals become a resonant melody when crafted with precision, ensuring that each note contributes to the symphony of your success.

3.1.4 Time-Bound

In the symphony of financial goal-setting, time is the conductor that shapes the rhythm of your aspirations. Just as timing is crucial in music, it is equally pivotal in defining and achieving your financial objectives. Infusing each goal with a specific timeline is akin to setting a rhythmic beat, propelling you forward in your financial journey.

The Musical Metronome of Time

Consider time as the metronome that dictates the pace of your financial composition. Much like the tempo in music, a specific timeline adds structure and urgency to your goals. It transforms a vague objective into a harmonious melody, with each note aligning to the rhythmic beat of progress.

Creating a Sense of Urgency

A time-bound goal is not merely a point on the calendar; it's a powerful motivator. Just as a crescendo builds anticipation in music, a time-bound goal creates a sense of urgency that fuels your determination. This urgency urges you to take consistent action, propelling you closer to the final chord of achievement.

Setting the Tempo of Progress

Just as a composer sets the tempo of a musical piece, you set the tempo of your financial journey through time-bound goals. This tempo ensures that you're moving steadily toward your desired financial crescendo. It prevents complacency, encourages consistent effort, and ensures that each note of progress is played at the right moment.

Harmonizing Your Financial Symphony

As you craft your financial goals, remember that each goal gains depth and purpose when set within a specific timeframe. This temporal element transforms your aspirations into a symphony of achievement, where every note resonates with progress. With time-bound goals, you're not just envisioning a future – you're orchestrating the rhythm of your financial success, ensuring that each step brings you closer to the harmonious finale.

3.2 Developing a Realistic Budget

Your budget, akin to a musical composition, harmonizes your income and expenses into a balanced melody. As a conductor orchestrates each section, follow these steps to compose a realistic budget that resonates with your financial goals:

3.2.1 Track Income

In the grand symphony of financial management, your income takes center stage as the conductor of resources. As you embark on the composition of your budget, gather the diverse instruments of your income to create a harmonious financial overture.

Assembling the Financial Ensemble

Imagine yourself as the composer, assembling the musicians of your financial orchestra. Collect the various instruments of your income – the resonant notes that contribute to your financial melody. These instruments include your salary, business revenue, investments, rental income, and any other financial harmonies that contribute to your financial score.

Crafting the Baseline Rhythm

Your total monthly earnings, like the foundational beat of a composition, set the baseline rhythm for your budget. This sum of income serves as the rhythmic pulse that drives your financial composition forward. It establishes the tempo for your budget's creation, dictating the pace at which you allocate resources and fulfill your financial obligations.

The Tempo of Financial Progress

Just as a conductor guides musicians to create a coherent and harmonious piece, you orchestrate your financial journey by tracking your income. This financial ensemble, composed of various sources, plays a vital role in setting the tone for your budget's symphony. By meticulously tracking your income, you lay the groundwork for a well-structured budget that aligns with your financial goals.

The Conductor of Resources

Your income, like a skilled conductor, directs the allocation of resources in your financial composition. It determines the balance between spending, saving, and investing – each note harmonizing to create a melody of financial stability and progress. As you track and orchestrate your income, you guide your budget toward a harmonious and prosperous financial performance.

3.2.2 Identify Fixed Expenses

In the symphony of budgeting, fixed expenses form the recurring themes that provide structure and continuity to your financial composition. Just as a musical composition features recurring melodies, your budget incorporates fixed expenses that play a consistent role in your financial symphony.

The Repetitive Refrain of Fixed Expenses

Picture your budget as a musical score, with each category representing a distinct musical motif. Fixed expenses are the refrain that repeats throughout your financial melody. These unwavering notes include essentials like rent or mortgage payments, utility bills, loan repayments, and insurance premiums. They create a rhythmic cadence, ensuring that your budget's melody remains steady and predictable.

Crafting Stability and Predictability

Much like a refrain anchors a song, fixed expenses anchor your budget. Their predictability adds a layer of stability to your financial composition. Just as a well-executed refrain elicits familiarity and comfort, identifying fixed expenses brings a sense of order and predictability to your budgeting efforts.

Maintaining Harmonious Budgeting

As you identify fixed expenses, you establish the framework for your budget's composition. These recurring notes are the building blocks of financial stability, ensuring that your budget's melody flows smoothly. By acknowledging and accounting for these fixed expenses, you create a harmonious balance between consistent obligations and your financial aspirations.

The Rhythmic Cadence of Financial Success

In the symphony of your budget, fixed expenses serve as the rhythmic cadence that guides your financial performance. Their repetition adds a sense of structure, allowing you to allocate resources with precision and purpose. By identifying and harmonizing these fixed notes within your budget, you lay the foundation for a symphony of financial success that resonates with stability and progress.

3.2.3 Consider Variable Expenses

Just as a musical composition features dynamic and evolving melodies, your budget embraces the nuanced rhythms of variable expenses. These melodies, like musical phrases that shift and adapt, encompass a range of spending – from everyday essentials to leisure activities – and add depth to the harmonious composition of your financial plan.

Creating Intricate Melodies of Spending

Imagine your budget as a symphony of spending, with each category representing a unique musical motif. Variable expenses create intricate melodies within this symphony. These melodies encompass a spectrum of spending habits, including groceries, dining out, entertainment, transportation, and personal care. They introduce diversity and texture, enriching your budget's overall composition.

The Ebb and Flow of Financial Melodies

Variable expenses introduce an element of fluidity and adaptability to your budget. Like a skilled musician improvising within a musical piece, these expenses shift and evolve from month to month. While they may vary in tempo and intensity, they contribute to the overall rhythm and harmony of your financial composition.

Balancing Dynamics and Harmony

Just as a musical composition requires a delicate balance between dynamics and harmony, your budget thrives on managing variable expenses. While these expenses may fluctuate, their inclusion ensures that your budget captures the multifaceted nature of your financial life. They add color and vibrancy to your budget's symphony, reflecting the diversity of your spending patterns.

Weaving a Complete Financial Score

Incorporating variable expenses into your budget is akin to weaving intricate melodies into a larger musical score. They infuse vitality and depth, contributing to the richness of your financial plan. By considering and accommodating variable expenses, you create a budget that harmoniously captures the rhythms of both predictable obligations and spontaneous indulgences, resulting in a well-rounded financial symphony.

3.2.4 Account for Irregular Expenses

In the grand orchestration of your budget, just as a symphony might introduce unexpected musical twists, life presents irregular expenses that add unique dynamics to your financial composition. These occasional crescendos emerge in the form of annual subscriptions, vehicle maintenance, medical costs, and other non-recurring items. By accounting for these sporadic notes, you fortify your budget's resilience, allowing it to gracefully adapt to unforeseen financial variations without missing a harmonious beat.

Unveiling the Unpredictable Notes

Think of your budget as a symphony with its ebb and flow, featuring both anticipated rhythms and unexpected surprises. Irregular expenses are akin to the unexpected musical elements that arise in a symphony, adding layers of complexity and intrigue to the overall performance. These irregular notes, such as an annual membership renewal or a sudden car repair, punctuate your financial journey with moments of financial variation.

Creating a Resilient Financial Melody

Just as a skilled conductor prepares the orchestra for unexpected musical shifts, accounting for irregular expenses equips your budget to handle financial surprises. These occasional crescendos require specific attention and allocation within your budget composition. By incorporating these irregular notes into your financial symphony, you ensure that your budget remains adaptable, ready to navigate unexpected variations without disrupting its melodic flow.

Adapting without Missing a Beat

In the symphony of budgeting, the ability to adapt without missing a beat is paramount. By accounting for irregular expenses, you embrace the unpredictable nature of financial life while maintaining the rhythm of your budget's composition. These sporadic notes serve as a reminder that even in the most harmonious of financial plans, there is room for the unexpected, allowing you to navigate the ever-changing financial landscape with grace and poise.

3.2.5 Set Savings Targets

In the intricate composition of your budget, akin to a composer weaving themes into a symphony, the section dedicated to savings takes center stage. Just as a powerful melody resonates within a musical masterpiece, the savings component of your budget is a potent tune that echoes your financial aspirations. This section invites you to define specific categories for your savings endeavors – an emergency fund, retirement savings, future investments – and allocate funds harmoniously. This financial melody not only enriches your budget's harmony but also contributes to the grand opus of your long-term financial journey.

Crafting a Symphony of Savings

Imagine your budget as a symphony where each category represents a distinctive musical motif. The savings section, with its carefully crafted categories, is a symphony of its own. Just as a composer carefully arranges themes and motifs to create a harmonious piece, you allocate funds to different savings categories with purpose and intent. Each category represents a unique note, contributing to the overall melody of financial progress.

The Resonance of Financial Aspirations

Savings targets within your budget resonate with your deepest financial aspirations. Much like a resonant musical note, these savings categories create a powerful and enduring sound within your financial composition. Whether it's the security of an emergency fund, the promise of a comfortable retirement, or the potential of future investments, each category adds depth and resonance to your budget's symphony.

A Melodic Journey to Financial Opulence

As a symphony's melody carries listeners on a journey, the savings targets in your budget guide you on a melodic path toward financial opulence. Each allocation, each contribution to a savings category, becomes a step forward in your financial voyage. Just as a composer's careful arrangement of notes creates a compelling musical narrative, your deliberate savings plan weaves a narrative of financial security, growth, and eventual triumph.

Contribution to the Grand Opus

Ultimately, the savings targets you set within your budget contribute to the grand opus of your long-term financial symphony. Each note, each category, harmonizes with the others to create a masterpiece of financial stability and success. Your budget becomes a score that guides you through life's financial crescendos and diminuendos, ensuring that your financial journey is accompanied by a harmonious melody of savings and progress.

3.2.6 Factor in Debt Repayment

Within the symphony of financial responsibility, debt repayment emerges as a crucial movement, akin to a recurring refrain that adds depth and purpose to the composition. Just as a skilled composer carefully weaves recurring motifs throughout a musical masterpiece, your budget allocates a dedicated portion to honor your debt obligations. This harmonious integration of debt repayment aligns with your chosen strategy, guiding your financial symphony toward a triumphant, debt-free finale.

Harmonizing Responsibility and Progress

Imagine your budget as a musical score, and debt repayment as a melodic motif that runs through its heart. Just as a recurring musical theme creates a sense of cohesion and direction within a composition, your dedicated allocation for debt repayment ensures that financial responsibility is harmonized with progress. This harmonious interplay guides your budget's symphony towards a resolution where debt burdens are lightened and financial freedom takes center stage.

Conducting Your Debt Repayment Symphony

In the grand orchestra of your budget, debt repayment holds a conductor's baton, guiding the rhythm and tempo of your financial movement. Much like a conductor shapes the dynamics of a musical piece, you shape the trajectory of your debt repayment strategy. Every payment becomes a note, every milestone a crescendo, as you move steadily closer to the harmonious resolution of a debt-free existence.

A Crescendo of Financial Liberation

Debt repayment within your budget mirrors the ebb and flow of musical dynamics. The allocation toward debt reduction is a crescendo of financial liberation, building in intensity as you make consistent payments and witness your debt balances decrease. This crescendo adds texture and depth to your financial symphony, creating a sense of accomplishment and propelling you toward the ultimate climax of debt freedom.

A Triumphant Finale

As a symphony reaches its final notes, your budget's dedication to debt repayment sets the stage for a triumphant finale. The disciplined allocation, the focused strategy, and the persistent effort all culminate in a resolution where debt is conquered. Your financial symphony concludes on a high note, paving the way for future movements of growth, investment, and prosperity.

3.2.7 Adjust as Needed

Within the ever-changing musical landscape of life, the art of adjustment takes center stage. Just as a conductor fine-tunes a performance to resonate with the acoustics of a venue, you too must regularly review and adjust your budget to harmonize with shifts in your financial circumstances. Flexibility becomes your baton, guiding your financial symphony towards optimal resonance and harmony.

The Maestro of Flexibility

Imagine yourself as the maestro of your financial orchestra, guiding each note and instrument with precision. Just as a seasoned conductor adapts to the unique nuances of a performance space, you too must adapt your budget to the nuances of your financial journey. Your role as conductor involves monitoring the tempo of your income, the rhythm of your expenses, and the melody of your savings, making subtle adjustments as needed to ensure a seamless and harmonious composition.

Fine-Tuning the Financial Melody

In the symphony of your budget, fine-tuning is your secret weapon. Much like a musician adjusts their instrument to achieve perfect pitch, you must adjust your budget to maintain financial harmony. Life's changing cadences – unexpected expenses, income fluctuations, or new financial goals – require nimble adjustments to your budget's melody. This ongoing process of fine-tuning ensures that your financial symphony remains on track and melodious.

Harmonizing with Life's Variations

Just as a composer embraces variations in melody and tempo, you too must embrace the variations that life presents. Your budget is not static but a living, breathing composition that evolves alongside your circumstances. By staying attuned to these variations, you can make proactive adjustments to your budget's harmony, ensuring it remains aligned with your goals even as life's tempo changes.

Achieving Symphony through Flexibility

In the grand theater of financial management, flexibility is your virtuoso performance. It allows you to adapt your budget to the ever-changing rhythm of life, creating a symphony of financial stability and success. Just as a conductor orchestrates the perfect performance through adjustments, you too orchestrate your financial future by fine-tuning your budget. With each adjustment, you play a key role in shaping your financial masterpiece, ensuring that your symphony of financial control remains captivating and harmonious.

3.3 Categorizing Expenses

Your budget, like a musical composition, gains structure through categorization. Each category forms a distinct musical motif, contributing to the overall harmony of your financial symphony. Common expense categories include:

3.3.1 Essential Expenses

In the grand symphony of your budget, essential expenses serve as the foundational notes that lay the groundwork for your financial composition. These notes are the fundamental tones that create the harmonious melody of your financial life. Just as a composer carefully selects the base chords of a piece to establish its tonality, you must meticulously consider these essential expenses to establish the tonality of your budget.

Building the Musical Foundation

Imagine your budget as a musical score, and essential expenses as the building blocks of its structure. These expenses encompass the necessities that sustain your daily life – housing costs, utilities, groceries, transportation, and healthcare. Much like the sturdy pillars that support a grand concert hall, these essential expenses provide the structural integrity that your budget relies upon.

The Rhythmic Heartbeat

Just as a strong rhythm sets the heartbeat of a musical composition, essential expenses set the financial heartbeat of your budget. They provide the consistent and predictable pulse that underlies your financial melody. By recognizing and allocating resources to these essential elements, you ensure a steady and reliable rhythm in your budget, creating a solid foundation upon which your financial goals can flourish.

Stability in Uncertain Times

In times of change and uncertainty, essential expenses act as the steady rhythm that anchors your financial composition. Like the unwavering beat of a metronome, these expenses remain constant, providing stability amidst the ebb and flow of life's challenges. By accounting for these necessities in your budget, you create a sense of security and assurance, allowing you to navigate the ever-changing symphony of your financial journey.

Harmonizing the Essentials

Just as the low tones of a cello complement the bright tones of a flute, essential expenses harmonize with other components of your budget. They provide a counterpoint to discretionary spending and savings goals, creating a balanced and harmonious composition. By acknowledging the importance of these fundamental notes, you ensure that your financial melody remains rich and resonant, creating a symphony of financial well-being.

3.3.2 Discretionary Expenses

Just as a skilled conductor adds embellishments to a musical piece, discretionary expenses add a touch of artistry and flair to your budget composition. These expenses are the brushstrokes of color that enhance the canvas of your financial life. Imagine your budget as a work of art, with discretionary expenses serving as the vibrant hues that bring it to life.

Painting with Financial Creativity

In the grand tableau of your budget, discretionary expenses represent your creative expression. These are the choices you make to infuse your financial journey with enjoyment, pleasure, and experiences. Like an artist selecting the perfect brushstroke, you curate discretionary expenses that align with your values and aspirations. Dining out, entertainment, travel, hobbies, and shopping are all strokes of financial creativity that contribute to the overall masterpiece.

Adding Nuance and Texture

Just as a skilled musician adds delicate embellishments to a melody, discretionary expenses add nuance and texture to your financial composition. These non-essential expenses introduce a layer of complexity and depth, elevating your budget from a mere list of transactions to a symphony of experiences. They allow you to indulge in life's pleasures and create cherished memories, adding a dynamic and multi-dimensional aspect to your financial landscape.

Balancing the Palette

Just as an artist balances warm and cool tones to create visual harmony, you must balance discretionary expenses with other budget categories. These expenses provide a touch of vibrancy and excitement, but they must be harmoniously integrated into your overall financial picture. By thoughtfully allocating resources to discretionary expenses, you ensure that they enhance rather than overshadow the essential components of your budget.

Enriching the Symphony

In the grand symphony of your financial life, discretionary expenses serve as the embellishments that enrich the overall composition. They bring a sense of joy, spontaneity, and delight to your budget, creating a harmonious blend of responsible financial planning and joyful living. By carefully selecting and managing these discretionary expenses, you create a symphony that resonates with both fiscal prudence and the art of living fully.

3.3.3 Debt Payments

Within the intricate symphony of your budget, the debt payments category emerges as a distinctive and purposeful movement. This is the segment where you address your financial obligations head-on, orchestrating a journey toward debt elimination. Just as a musical composition seamlessly transitions between different movements, your budget strategically allocates funds to honor your debts, creating a harmonious progression toward financial liberation.

Crafting Financial Melody

Think of your debt payments as the carefully composed notes that contribute to the rhythm and melody of your financial composition. Each payment, whether it's towards credit card debt, student loans, or other obligations, plays a crucial role in the overall harmony of your budget. Just as a skilled musician strikes the right chords to create a pleasing tune, your debt payments contribute to the cadence of your financial well-being.

The Momentum of Progress

As the conductor of your financial orchestra, you set the tempo for debt repayment. With each payment, you build momentum and advance toward your goal of becoming debt-free. This movement within your budget creates a sense of purpose and achievement, much like a musical passage that propels the composition forward. The consistency and dedication you bring to this movement amplify the sense of progress in your financial journey.

Resonating with Financial Freedom

The debt payments movement is more than a financial obligation; it's a declaration of your commitment to financial freedom. Just as a well-executed musical movement evokes emotions, your debt repayment efforts resonate with determination and empowerment. This section of your budget transforms your financial symphony from a composition burdened by debt to a harmonious expression of control and liberation.

Harmony in Balance

While the debt payments movement is vital, it's essential to strike a balance between debt repayment and other budget categories. Just as a symphony requires a delicate equilibrium between different instruments, your budget needs a thoughtful allocation of resources to ensure all financial aspects work together in harmony. By integrating debt payments into your budget's composition, you create a symphony that embodies both financial responsibility and the pursuit of a brighter, debt-free future.

3.3.4 Savings and Investments

Amidst the symphony of your budget's composition, the savings and investments category emerges as a majestic crescendo, signaling your unwavering commitment to future financial growth. This segment represents the harmonious fusion of foresight and discipline, encompassing a symphony of melodies – from the steadfast rhythm of an emergency fund to the anticipatory cadence of retirement savings and investment accounts. Together, these harmonies contribute to the grand symphony of your long-term financial success.

The Overture of Financial Security

Imagine your savings and investments as the overture that sets the stage for your financial security. Just as a musical overture captures the essence of an entire composition, this category encapsulates your determination to safeguard your financial well-being and create a prosperous future. Each note within this segment resonates with the anticipation of a strong financial foundation.

The Melodic Echoes of Preparedness

The emergency fund takes center stage within this category, its melody echoing preparedness and resilience. Just as a recurring motif weaves through a musical piece, your emergency fund serves as a constant refrain, providing a safety net for unexpected financial challenges. This melody ensures that your financial composition remains resilient and adaptable, regardless of the unexpected twists that life may bring.

Harmonizing with Retirement Ambitions

As the symphony progresses, the retirement savings melody joins the ensemble. This harmonious movement embodies your aspirations for a secure and fulfilling retirement. Similar to the way a melody evolves and develops in a musical piece, your retirement savings steadily grows, weaving a harmonious tapestry of financial comfort for your golden years.

Investment Accounts: An Optimistic Prelude

The investment accounts segment adds an optimistic prelude to your financial symphony. Just as a prelude captures the audience's attention and sets the tone for the rest of the performance, your investments signal a belief in your future financial potential. This melody resonates with the hope of growth and prosperity, creating a forward-looking and dynamic element within your budget's composition.

A Unified Symphony of Growth

As the conductor of your financial orchestra, you orchestrate the various melodies within the savings and investments category to create a unified symphony of growth. Each note, each contribution, and each decision harmoniously blend to produce a composition that embodies your dedication to securing your financial future. Through this category, your budget becomes a dynamic and evolving piece, adapting to your changing circumstances while maintaining a consistent theme of long-term prosperity. By categorizing your expenses, you compose a budget that harmonizes various financial notes into a coherent and purposeful composition. Each category contributes to the overall rhythm and melody, ensuring that your financial symphony is both structured and harmonious.

3.4 Implementing Budgeting Tools

Creating a budget is like orchestrating a symphony – precision and coordination are essential. To conduct this financial symphony effectively, consider utilizing various budgeting tools:

3.4.1 Spreadsheets

Envision a masterful musical score, meticulously notated to orchestrate a flawless performance. In the realm of financial management, spreadsheets emerge as the virtuoso conductors of your budgeting symphony. Much like a composer tailors notes to create a harmonious melody, spreadsheets like Microsoft Excel or Google Sheets enable you to compose your budget's intricate rhythm. Through customization and careful data input, these digital orchestrators bring to life a visual representation of your financial composition.

A Prelude to Precision

Consider spreadsheets as the prelude to your financial precision. Just as a prelude captures the essence of a musical piece, spreadsheets encapsulate the intricacies of your financial landscape. Each cell, each formula, and each tab corresponds to a distinct financial note, contributing to the symphony of your budget's creation. Through spreadsheets, you embark on a journey of meticulous planning and informed decision-making.

Customization: The Composer's Canvas

Spreadsheets offer a canvas for your financial artistry. Like a composer carefully selecting instruments and arranging notes, you tailor your spreadsheet template to match your unique financial landscape. Income streams become harmonious chords, expenses transform into melodic phrases, and categories form the thematic motifs that shape your budget's composition. With every cell you fill, you create a visual representation of your financial aspirations.

Building Blocks of Clarity

Imagine each cell in your spreadsheet as a building block of financial clarity. Just as musical notation clarifies the performer's intentions, spreadsheet cells clarify your financial transactions. Income figures, expense breakdowns, and savings allocations harmonize to reveal a comprehensive overview of your financial journey. This clarity empowers you to make informed decisions and orchestrate your budget with finesse.

Symphony of Calculation

Within each cell, formulas and functions interweave to create a symphony of calculation. Much like the intricate interplay of musical notes, these calculations harmonize to depict the intricate relationship between your income and expenses. From summing up monthly totals to calculating savings rates, spreadsheets ensure the accuracy and coherence of your financial score.

Visual Symphony, Tangible Progress

As you populate cells and manipulate formulas, your spreadsheet becomes a visual symphony of your financial reality. The rows and columns dance in a rhythm that mirrors your income, expenses, and aspirations. Just as a musical score captures the ebb and flow of a composition, your spreadsheet captures the evolving dynamics of your budget. Tangible progress emerges as cells light up with figures, revealing the notes of your financial success.

In the grand orchestra of financial management, spreadsheets take center stage, guiding you through the creation of a harmonious budget. Each cell, formula, and calculation contributes to the intricate melody of your financial composition, offering a visual representation of your aspirations and a roadmap to your financial crescendo. Through the symphonic precision of spreadsheets, you conduct a masterpiece of financial control and orchestrate the harmonies of your future prosperity.

3.4.2 Budgeting Apps

Envision a seasoned conductor on the podium, deftly guiding the orchestra's tempo and dynamics. In the symphony of financial management, budgeting apps step into this role with finesse and precision. Apps such as Mint, YNAB (You Need a Budget), and PocketGuard become your digital maestros, orchestrating a harmonious financial composition. Through automation, insights, and real-time guidance, these apps ensure that you stay in tune with your budget, creating a symphony of financial control.

Conducting Financial Harmony

Much like a conductor ensures each instrument harmonizes seamlessly, budgeting apps help you achieve financial harmony. These digital maestros choreograph the intricate dance between income and expenses, tracking each transaction and categorizing it with precision. Your financial overture unfolds under their watchful eye, ensuring that every note contributes to the overall symphony of your budget.

Automated Symphonies

Imagine an orchestra that plays itself – budgeting apps transform this fantasy into reality. These apps automate the process of expense tracking, capturing financial transactions with the elegance of a virtuoso. With each swipe of your card or online purchase, the app records the transaction, categorizes it, and adds it to your financial score. This automation eliminates the manual effort, allowing you to focus on the creative nuances of your budget.

Insights: The Conductor's Baton

Just as a conductor wields a baton to shape the orchestra's performance, budgeting apps offer insights that shape your financial decisions. These digital conductors analyze your spending patterns, revealing trends and tendencies. They highlight areas where you can fine-tune your budget's composition, guiding you toward financial optimization. Through graphical representations and data-driven analyses, these insights become your financial conductor's baton, directing your budget's performance.

Real-Time Guidance: Musical Mastery

In the midst of a live performance, a conductor offers real-time guidance to ensure flawless execution. Similarly, budgeting apps provide immediate feedback and guidance. They send alerts and reminders, notifying you of upcoming bills, expenses, or budget targets. This real-time interaction keeps you attuned to your financial goals, allowing you to make adjustments on the fly and maintain the rhythm of your budget.

The Symphony of Progress

As you navigate the financial landscape with the assistance of budgeting apps, you embark on a symphony of progress. The app's algorithms and functionalities become the instrumental sections of your budget's performance, each playing a crucial role in maintaining balance and harmony. Through their guidance, automation, insights, and alerts, these digital maestros guide your financial composition toward a resounding finale of success.

In the grand symphony of financial management, budgeting apps stand as your dedicated conductors, orchestrating a melodious blend of income, expenses, and aspirations. Through their automated precision, insightful direction, and real-time guidance, these apps elevate your budget to a virtuoso performance, ensuring that every financial note strikes the perfect chord.

3.4.3 Envelope System

Close your eyes and imagine a symphony orchestra – the woodwinds, strings, brass, and percussion sections each contributing their unique sound. In the realm of financial management, the envelope system takes on a similar role, assigning specific monetary "instruments" to various expense categories. Just as a conductor directs each section of the orchestra, you allocate predetermined amounts of cash to labeled envelopes, ensuring a harmonious and controlled financial performance.

The Ensemble of Envelopes

Visualize a collection of envelopes, each adorned with a label denoting a different aspect of your financial composition. Like sections of a symphony orchestra, these envelopes represent distinct expense categories – groceries, entertainment, transportation, and more. Each envelope holds a designated amount of cash, acting as a musical score that guides your spending.

The Conductor's Role

As a conductor shapes the orchestra's performance, you wield the baton of financial allocation. At the beginning of each budget cycle, you allocate a specific sum of money to each envelope. This allocation mirrors the conductor assigning instruments to various sections of the orchestra. Just as each section contributes to the symphony's overall sound, each envelope contributes to your financial melody.

A Tangible Experience

Imagine reaching into an envelope labeled "Groceries" and withdrawing cash as you head to the supermarket. This tangible interaction provides a visceral connection to your budget – a real-time awareness of your spending. The physical act of removing cash from the envelope mimics a musician playing their instrument, contributing to the larger musical arrangement.

Balancing the Score

Much like a conductor ensures that no section of the orchestra overpowers the others, you maintain equilibrium within your budget's composition. When an envelope runs low, it's a signal to exercise restraint in that particular spending category. This dynamic mirrors a conductor's role in maintaining harmony and balance among various musical elements.

Limitations and Creativity

While the envelope system instills discipline and control, it may also require creative adjustments. Just as a composer may adapt a musical piece to suit the orchestra's capabilities, you might need to modify your spending if an envelope is depleted before the budget cycle ends. This flexibility encourages inventive financial solutions and resourceful money management.

The Grand Finale

In the final crescendo of your budget's performance, the envelope system ensures that you stay in tune with your financial goals. As you allocate, spend, and replenish each envelope, you actively engage with your budget's composition. This tangible and visual approach transforms your financial management into an orchestrated experience, where every transaction becomes a note in the symphony of your financial success.

The envelope system, like a symphony conductor, directs the flow and allocation of financial resources. Each envelope represents a musical section, contributing its unique sound to the overall composition. Through tactile interaction and strategic allocation, this system creates a tangible connection to your budget, empowering you to conduct your financial affairs with harmony and precision.

3.4.4 Online Banking Tools

Imagine a conductor skillfully wielding a baton, guiding an orchestra through a mesmerizing symphony. In the realm of financial management, online banking tools assume a comparable role – that of a conductor – orchestrating and harmonizing the intricate notes of your monetary affairs. Just as a conductor ensures each instrument plays its part, these digital tools categorize expenses, set limits, and provide insights to maintain the harmonious composition of your financial journey.

The Baton of Automation

Much like a conductor's baton directs the tempo and dynamics of a musical piece, online banking tools automate and streamline various financial processes. These digital conductors categorize your transactions, seamlessly separating essentials from discretionary expenses. Just as a conductor ensures that each instrument's timing is impeccable, online banking tools ensure accurate and timely tracking of your spending.

Categorizing the Instruments of Expense

Imagine the various sections of an orchestra – strings, woodwinds, brass – each contributing its unique sound. Online banking tools categorize your expenses in a similar manner. They identify and classify transactions into distinct groups such as housing costs, entertainment, groceries, and more. This meticulous categorization allows you to visualize the composition of your spending symphony.

Setting Limits for Harmonious Spending

A conductor ensures that no section of an orchestra overpowers the others. Similarly, online banking tools help you set spending limits for different categories. Just as a conductor adjusts the volume of instruments to maintain balance, these tools notify you when you approach or exceed your spending limits. This ensures that your financial symphony remains melodious and aligned with your budget.

Insights for a Finely-Tuned Composition

A conductor's keen insight shapes the orchestra's performance. Online banking tools offer you valuable insights into your financial habits. They provide visual representations of your spending patterns, enabling you to identify areas where adjustments are needed. Like a conductor guiding the interpretation of a musical piece, these insights guide your financial decisions, fine-tuning your budget's composition.

Adapting to Change

Life's tempo can change unexpectedly, much like a musical piece taking an unexpected turn. Online banking tools remain vigilant, adjusting to shifts in your financial landscape. Whether it's a new expense category or an irregular spending pattern, these tools adapt and ensure that your financial symphony continues to play harmoniously.

Maintaining Rhythm Amidst Change

As a conductor maintains rhythm and harmony throughout a performance, online banking tools uphold the rhythm of your financial symphony. They ensure that your budget stays on track, even as life's tempo fluctuates. Just as a conductor guides an orchestra through intricate passages, these tools guide you through the complexities of financial management, keeping your composition melodious and aligned with your goals.

Online banking tools, much like a skilled conductor, play a pivotal role in guiding and harmonizing your financial journey. With their automated categorization, spending limits, and insights, they ensure that your financial symphony remains balanced, cohesive, and attuned to your aspirations.

By selecting the right budgeting tools, you conduct your financial symphony with precision and finesse. Just as a conductor shapes the performance, these tools shape your budget, ensuring its rhythm and melody harmonize seamlessly.

In the next chapter, we will delve into the intricacies of managing cash flow effectively, a crucial movement in your financial symphony. Join us as we explore the importance of cash flow management and techniques to enhance its harmonious flow.

Chapter 4: Managing Cash Flow Effectively

4.1 Importance of Cash Flow Management

Cash flow management forms the backbone of financial stability, akin to conducting a symphony to perfection. This section elaborates on the significance of cash flow management and its role in maintaining liquidity, stability, growth opportunities, and informed decision-making.

4.1.1 Liquidity: The Essence of Financial Harmony

Imagine your financial symphony as a grand orchestral performance. Just as a conductor ensures that each instrument is ready to play its note, liquidity ensures that your financial instruments are prepared for every financial note you encounter.

Visualizing Liquidity: The Conductor's Baton

In the world of music, a conductor wields a baton that guides the orchestra, setting the rhythm, tempo, and intensity of the performance. Liquidity plays a similar role in your financial journey. It is the guiding force that orchestrates the flow of cash, ensuring that your financial instruments are in tune and ready to play their part.

Think of liquidity as the conductor's baton, gracefully directing the movement of financial resources. Just as the conductor's baton brings together various instruments to create a harmonious composition, liquidity brings together your income, expenses, and financial obligations to create a symphony of stability.

Covering Daily Expenses: The Melody of Stability

In a musical piece, a melody serves as the central theme that carries the composition forward, creating a sense of coherence and continuity. Similarly, proper cash flow management acts as the underlying melody that supports your day-to-day financial activities.

Liquidity ensures that you have the necessary funds to cover routine expenses, pay bills, and meet your financial obligations seamlessly. Just as a melody provides structure and stability to a musical piece, liquidity provides the essential foundation for your financial stability. It eliminates the dissonance of worrying about whether you can meet your financial commitments, allowing you to focus on the harmonious progression of your financial goals.

Handling Emergencies: The Safety Net of Sound

In the realm of music, unexpected disruptions can occur during a performance – a missed note, a technical glitch, or an unforeseen challenge. Similarly, financial challenges can arise unexpectedly, threatening to disrupt the rhythm of your financial journey. This is where liquidity steps in as the safety net of sound.

Liquidity cushions you against unexpected financial hurdles, much like a protective sound that catches you when you stumble. An emergency fund, fueled by proper cash flow management, provides the resilience needed to address unforeseen expenses, medical emergencies, or sudden income disruptions. Just as a well-prepared musician can seamlessly recover from a minor mistake, a well-managed liquidity ensures you can navigate financial challenges without missing a beat.

Harmony and Beyond: The Symphony of Financial Success

A successful orchestra delivers a performance that resonates with harmony and leaves a lasting impact on the audience. Similarly, a well-managed liquidity ensures that your financial performance remains harmonious and stress-free. Whether you're playing the daily notes of routine expenses, conducting the complex melodies of investments, or addressing unexpected financial crescendos, liquidity stands as the conductor's baton, guiding you through the symphony of your financial life.

In the grand composition of your financial journey, liquidity serves as the unifying force that allows you to create, innovate, and pursue your aspirations. It harmonizes your income and expenses, ensures stability, and provides the safety net needed to handle life's unexpected variations. With liquidity as your guiding baton, your financial symphony will resonate with success, confidence, and a melody of prosperity.

4.1.2 Stability: The Melodic Assurance

In the orchestra of your financial life, where each financial decision and action plays a role like musical notes in a symphony, stability takes center stage as the melodic assurance that creates a harmonious and confident composition. Just as a well-orchestrated musical piece relies on stable notes and rhythms, your financial journey thrives on the stability of cash flow and financial well-being.

Stabilizing Finances: The Resonance of Harmony

Imagine a musical ensemble performing a captivating piece – each instrument contributes to the overall harmony, and the stability of each note ensures a captivating performance. Similarly, in your financial world, stability is the resonating force that ensures each financial note plays its part.

Financial stability mirrors the harmony found in music. It's the alignment of your income, expenses, and financial goals, creating a synchronized melody that rings true. Just as a well-tuned instrument produces a clear and resonant sound, stable finances produce a reassuring and confident financial environment.

Stress Reduction: The Soothing Chord

Think about a soothing melody that calms your mind and eases your worries. Stable cash flow operates in a similar fashion, playing the soothing chord of stress reduction in your financial life. When your income and expenses are in harmony, you reduce the dissonance of financial uncertainty.

Stable cash flow minimizes stress by ensuring that you have the necessary funds to meet your obligations. It reduces the need to rely on excessive debt or credit, freeing you from the anxiety of juggling financial burdens. Just as a harmonious musical performance captivates the audience and takes away their worries, stable cash flow creates a serene financial atmosphere that allows you to focus on what truly matters.

Navigating with Confidence: The Guiding Melody

A skilled navigator knows how to steer a ship through tumultuous waters. In your financial journey, stability serves as the guiding melody that helps you navigate through the unpredictable currents of life. When your cash flow is stable, you can face financial challenges with confidence and poise.

Stability empowers you to handle unexpected expenses, economic fluctuations, or personal setbacks without losing your financial footing. It's like having a well-rehearsed musical piece to fall back on during an impromptu performance. Stable finances allow you to make decisions from a place of strength and assurance, ensuring that you stay on course toward your financial goals.

The Symphony of Assurance

In the grand symphony of life, stability is the assurance that each note will be played with precision and confidence. It's the undercurrent that supports your financial performance, allowing you to create beautiful melodies without the distraction of discordant notes. Just as a symphony conductor ensures that each section of the orchestra is in sync, your stable financial foundation orchestrates your financial instruments to create a harmonious and balanced financial composition.

In essence, stability in cash flow management is not merely a concept but a transformative force that shapes your financial narrative. It's the gentle hum that underscores your financial decisions, the rhythm that guides your fiscal steps, and the melody that resonates through every aspect of your financial life. By embracing stability as the melodic assurance in your financial symphony, you lay the groundwork for a future composed of confidence, security, and financial well-being.

4.1.3 Growth Opportunities: The Crescendo of Financial Progress

In the symphony of your financial journey, growth opportunities emerge as the crescendo – the exhilarating rise in intensity that captivates and propels the composition forward. Just as a musical piece builds anticipation through crescendos, effective cash flow management orchestrates your financial performance to embrace and amplify growth opportunities, fostering a future filled with financial advancement and prosperity.

Musical Growth Analogies: Building Crescendos

Think of a musical composition that gradually builds momentum, each note contributing to an ever-increasing intensity. Similarly, your financial growth mimics the crescendos in music. As you allocate resources wisely, balance your cash flow, and make strategic financial decisions, you're crafting a composition of financial growth.

Just as a well-timed crescendo elevates the emotional impact of a musical piece, seizing growth opportunities enhances your financial performance. Whether you're an individual or a business, effective cash flow management acts as the conductor, guiding the rhythm and timing of your financial crescendo.

Pursuing Ventures: Laying the Foundation

In music, crescendos signify pivotal moments – the building blocks that lead to a climactic point in the composition. Similarly, effective cash flow management lays the foundation for pursuing ventures that drive financial growth. It provides the necessary resources to invest in new projects, expand operations, or explore innovative avenues.

Imagine a business looking to launch a new product line. Proper cash flow management ensures that there are sufficient funds to cover research and development costs, production expenses, and marketing initiatives. This financial stability enables the business to pursue the venture confidently, knowing that the crescendo of growth is well-supported.

Seizing Favorable Conditions: Capitalizing on Stability

In music, a skilled performer seizes the moment when conditions are favorable – perhaps when the acoustics of the venue are ideal or the audience is most receptive. Likewise, financial stability enables individuals and businesses to capitalize on favorable market conditions.

When your cash flow is effectively managed, you're in a better position to recognize and seize opportunities presented by the market. This might involve investing in stocks when prices are low, expanding operations during periods of economic growth, or entering new markets when the timing is optimal.

Harmonizing Growth and Stability

The beauty of a musical composition lies in the delicate balance between different elements – melody, harmony, rhythm, and intensity. Similarly, the art of effective cash flow management harmonizes growth and stability. While pursuing growth opportunities is exhilarating, it must be supported by a stable financial foundation.

Growth without stability is like a crescendo without proper build-up – it lacks the depth and resonance that make it impactful. Through prudent cash flow management, you ensure that your pursuit of growth is rooted in financial stability, allowing you to create a symphony of financial progress that resonates for years to come.

The Orchestra of Financial Progress

Imagine your financial journey as a grand orchestral performance, where each decision and action contributes to the overall composition. Growth opportunities serve as the crescendos that elevate your financial symphony, adding layers of excitement and achievement. Just as a conductor guides the orchestra through dynamic changes in intensity, effective cash flow management guides you through the intricate interplay of growth and stability.

By recognizing the parallels between musical crescendos and financial growth, you embrace the power of effective cash flow management. With every well-executed note of financial discipline, you build towards a crescendo of progress, ensuring that your financial symphony resonates with accomplishment, prosperity, and the fulfillment of your aspirations.

4.1.4 Decision Making: The Harmonic Analysis

In the world of music, a skilled composer carefully analyzes musical notes, harmonies, and rhythms to create a masterpiece. Similarly, in the realm of finance, accurate cash flow analysis serves as the harmonious analysis that guides your decision-making process. Just as a composer's choices shape the direction of a musical composition, your financial decisions are influenced by the careful analysis of your cash flow.

Analyzing Finances: Composing Financial Strategies

Consider the process of composing a musical piece. A composer carefully analyzes each musical note, considering its contribution to the overall composition. Similarly, analyzing cash flow involves dissecting the inflows and outflows of your financial resources. This analysis provides insights into your financial "composition," revealing patterns, strengths, and areas that require adjustment.

By comparing the meticulous analysis that goes into crafting a musical composition with the scrutiny applied to cash flow, you understand the critical role of analysis in both realms. Just as a composer strives for coherence and beauty in their music, your cash flow analysis aims for coherence and success in your financial decisions.

Informed Choices: The Melody of Financial Decisions

Imagine a musician selecting the perfect note to complete a melodic phrase. Each note is carefully chosen to evoke the desired emotional response. Similarly, accurate cash flow analysis empowers you to make informed choices that shape your financial landscape.

For instance, when considering investments, a thorough cash flow analysis helps you assess whether you have the necessary funds to allocate without compromising your daily operations. This analysis also aids in evaluating the potential return on investment and the timeline for achieving financial goals.

Similarly, pricing strategies can be guided by cash flow analysis. Understanding your cash inflows and outflows helps you set prices that cover costs, ensure profitability, and align with market dynamics. Just as a musician adjusts tempo and dynamics to convey emotion, your pricing decisions are adjusted based on your financial analysis to convey value and financial sustainability.

Ensuring Harmonious Outcomes: Aligning with Objectives

In music, harmonies create a pleasing blend of different notes, resulting in a balanced and delightful sound. In the financial world, harmonious outcomes are achieved through proper analysis that aligns financial decisions with overarching objectives.

Accurate cash flow analysis ensures that your financial decisions harmonize with your broader goals. For instance, if your objective is to expand your business, cash flow analysis helps you determine the optimal timing and resources needed for expansion. It also ensures that expansion plans don't disrupt the harmony of your existing operations.

Just as a conductor balances the various sections of an orchestra to create a harmonious performance, cash flow analysis balances the different elements of your financial strategy. It ensures that your decisions resonate with your financial objectives and contribute to the overall symphony of your financial success.

The Symphony of Decision Making

As you navigate the complex landscape of financial decisions, envision yourself as a conductor guiding an intricate symphony. The notes you choose – based on accurate cash flow analysis – contribute to the harmonious composition of your financial journey. By drawing parallels between musical composition and financial decision-making, you appreciate the artistry and precision required to orchestrate a symphony of successful financial choices. Just as a conductor's masterful guidance leads to a captivating musical performance, your mastery of cash flow analysis leads to a compelling and harmonious financial path.

4.2 Analyzing Cash Flow Patterns

Understanding the rhythm and movement of cash flow is crucial for effective management. This section delves into analyzing cash flow patterns, including cash inflows, cash outflows, seasonal variations, and the cash flow cycle.

4.2.1 Cash Inflows: The Crescendo of Income Streams

Imagine your financial landscape as a grand symphony, with each note representing a source of cash flowing into your life. Similar to the rising crescendos that captivate audiences in a musical performance, cash inflows infuse your financial composition with energy and vitality. These inflows, much like the crescendos in music, mark moments of growth, abundance, and potential.

Musical Representation: The Dynamic Rise

In the realm of music, crescendos are passages where the volume and intensity of sound gradually increase, creating a sense of anticipation and excitement. Cash inflows play a similar role in your financial symphony. Each inflow represents a surge of financial resources, contributing to the crescendo of your overall financial well-being.

Visualize a musical piece building towards a powerful crescendo – the culmination of effort and artistry. Similarly, your cash inflows build momentum, reflecting your hard work, investments, and financial endeavors. These moments of financial crescendo propel you forward, allowing you to achieve your goals and aspirations.

Tracking Sources: Unveiling the Melodies

Just as a composer carefully selects musical instruments to create a rich tapestry of sound, you must identify and track the diverse sources of your cash inflows. These sources can include your salary, business revenue, investments, rental income, and any other financial harmonies that contribute to your financial composition.

Tracking these sources provides a comprehensive view of your financial landscape. It helps you understand the diverse melodies that contribute to your financial symphony. Moreover, by identifying and quantifying each source, you gain clarity on the specific role it plays in your overall financial performance.

Consistency and Frequency: The Rhythm of Inflows

In music, rhythm creates the heartbeat of a composition. Similarly, the rhythm of cash inflows is the heartbeat of your financial journey. Analyzing the consistency and frequency of these inflows offers valuable insights into your financial health.

Consider a musical piece with a steady and consistent rhythm – it exudes stability and coherence. Similarly, cash inflows that occur at regular intervals provide stability to your financial situation. A consistent paycheck, reliable business revenue, and recurring investments contribute to a harmonious financial rhythm.

Furthermore, understanding the frequency of cash inflows allows you to plan and allocate resources effectively. Just as a composer arranges notes in a pattern to create rhythm, you can arrange your financial activities to align with the rhythm of your inflows. This synchronization enhances your financial efficiency and ensures that you can meet your financial obligations without missing a beat.

Harmonizing Your Financial Composition

Envision your cash inflows as the rising crescendos that elevate your financial symphony. Each source of cash adds depth and dimension to your composition, allowing you to create intricate melodies of financial growth and stability. Just as a composer strategically places crescendos to create emotional impact, you can strategically manage and leverage your cash inflows to achieve your financial goals.

By drawing parallels between musical crescendos and cash inflows, you appreciate the dynamic and rhythmic nature of your financial journey. As you track sources, analyze consistency, and align your activities with the rhythm of your inflows, you orchestrate a symphony of financial success. Embrace the crescendos of income streams and let them harmonize with the other elements of your financial composition, creating a symphony that resonates with prosperity and fulfillment.

4.2.2 Cash Outflows: The Choreography of

Expenditures

Imagine your financial journey as an intricate dance performance, where each step represents a cash outflow from your financial stage. Similar to the choreography that guides dancers' movements, cash outflows choreograph the rhythm of your financial life. This elegant dance, like a well-rehearsed routine, involves careful coordination and precision.

Choreographing Cash Outflows: The Dance of Expenses

In the world of dance, choreography is the art of designing sequences of movements that convey emotions and tell a story. Similarly, cash outflows are the choreography of your financial narrative. Each expenditure, whether a necessity or a choice, contributes to the storyline of your financial journey.

Visualize the grace and coordination of a dance performance, where every movement is intentional and contributes to the overall composition. Similarly, your cash outflows should be intentional and aligned with your financial goals. Just as a choreographer ensures that each step serves a purpose, you must ensure that each expenditure supports your financial objectives.

Categorization and Tracking: The Steps of Financial Movement

Just as a dance routine comprises various steps and movements, your financial choreography consists of different types of expenses. Categorizing and tracking these expenses is akin to documenting each dance move. It provides clarity and insight into where your financial resources are allocated.

Expenses can be categorized into fixed and variable, essential and discretionary. Categorization allows you to see the patterns and themes in your financial dance. It highlights where your resources are flowing and helps you evaluate whether these movements align with your overall financial performance.

Timing and Regularity: The Rhythm of Financial Choreography

In dance, timing and rhythm are crucial for a seamless performance. Similarly, understanding the timing and regularity of your cash outflows is essential for financial planning. Some expenses, like rent and utility bills, have a fixed rhythm – they occur at regular intervals. Others, like discretionary spending, might have a more variable beat.

Consider a dance routine where each movement is in sync with the music's tempo. Similarly, aligning your cash outflows with their timing ensures that your financial choreography remains harmonious. By knowing when and how much to allocate for each expense, you create a rhythm that supports your financial goals.

Creating a Financial Masterpiece

Envision your cash outflows as the choreography that shapes your financial dance. Each expenditure is a deliberate step that contributes to the elegance and beauty of your financial routine. By choreographing your expenses, categorizing them, and understanding their timing, you create a financial masterpiece that reflects your values and aspirations.

Just as a dance captivates its audience with its movements, your financial choreography captivates your financial well-being. Every expenditure, whether essential or discretionary, contributes to the intricate pattern of your financial dance. Embrace the choreography of expenditures and ensure that each step aligns with your financial symphony, guiding you toward a harmonious and fulfilling financial future.

4.2.3 Seasonal Variations: Adapting to Financial Seasons

Just as music evolves with the changing seasons, your financial symphony experiences its own seasonal variations. These fluctuations in cash flow are like the shifting melodies of different musical seasons, each requiring a unique approach to maintain the harmony of your financial composition.

Musical Seasons: The Ebb and Flow of Cash Flow

In music, each season brings a distinct ambiance – the warmth of summer, the crispness of fall, the stillness of winter, and the renewal of spring. Similarly, your cash flow experiences different seasons influenced by factors like holidays, industry trends, or personal events.

Imagine your cash flow as a musical score that transitions through these seasons. Just as a composer adjusts the mood of a composition to match the changing seasons, you too must adapt your financial strategies to align with the rhythm of your financial year.

Adjusting Budgeting: Harmonizing with the Seasons

As the seasons influence the type of music played, seasonal variations influence your financial melody. Recognizing these variations allows you to adjust your budgeting and financial planning. For example, holiday seasons might bring increased expenses, while certain months could see fluctuations in income.

Consider how musicians alter their compositions to capture the essence of each season. Similarly, you can fine-tune your budget to accommodate higher spending during festive times or prepare for leaner months. By understanding the financial patterns of different seasons, you can allocate resources more effectively and ensure your financial symphony remains in tune.

Ensuring Continuous Harmony: The Adaptive Conductor

In a musical performance, the conductor adapts the tempo and dynamics to match the changing mood of the piece. Similarly, you must be the adaptive conductor of your financial symphony. By embracing seasonal variations, you maintain continuous financial harmony.

Just as a musician seamlessly transitions between musical seasons, you transition between financial phases with flexibility and foresight. Adaptability ensures that your financial journey remains harmonious, regardless of the season. It allows you to address challenges, seize opportunities, and maintain stability throughout the year.

A Harmonious Year-Round Symphony

Envision your financial journey as a year-round symphony, each season bringing its own notes and melodies. By acknowledging and embracing seasonal variations, you create a well-orchestrated financial composition. Like a skilled composer, you adjust your financial strategies to ensure that every season contributes to the overall harmony of your financial symphony.

As the conductor of your financial orchestra, you harmonize your budgeting and planning with the changing seasons, allowing your financial melody to resonate with the ebb and flow of cash flow. Just as music captures the essence of each season, your financial symphony captures the essence of your financial journey, creating a beautiful and harmonious masterpiece year after year.

4.2.4 Cash Flow Cycle: The Tempo of Financial Progression

In the grand orchestral performance of your financial journey, the cash flow cycle takes center stage as the conductor of your monetary movements, dictating the tempo and rhythm of your financial progress. Just as a well-conducted musical piece requires a steady and harmonious tempo, understanding and optimizing your cash flow cycle is essential for orchestrating a smooth and melodious financial symphony.

Musical Tempo Analogies: The Rhythmic Pulse of Cash Flow

Imagine your cash flow cycle as the tempo of your financial composition, setting the pace at which money flows in and out of your accounts. Similar to how a musical tempo guides the rhythm of a piece, your cash flow cycle guides the rhythm of your financial activities. The tempo can vary depending on the nature of your financial endeavors, but maintaining a consistent and controlled rhythm is crucial for financial stability and success.

Just as a skilled conductor adjusts the tempo to evoke specific emotions in a musical piece, you have the power to influence and adjust your cash flow cycle to align with your financial goals. Whether it's speeding up the tempo during periods of growth or slowing it down to weather economic downturns, understanding your cash flow cycle enables you to make strategic financial decisions.

Identifying Bottlenecks: Ensuring Smooth Crescendos

In music, a bottleneck can disrupt the flow of a composition, causing a momentary pause or imbalance in the melody. Similarly, bottlenecks in your cash flow cycle can lead to disruptions and challenges in your financial journey. These bottlenecks can manifest as delays in receiving payments, extended payment terms from clients, or fluctuations in customer demand.

By identifying and addressing these bottlenecks, you ensure the smooth progression of your financial symphony. Much like a composer tweaks the arrangement of musical notes to eliminate dissonance, you can optimize your cash flow cycle by negotiating better payment terms, streamlining invoicing processes, or diversifying your income streams to reduce the impact of potential bottlenecks.

Optimizing Progression: The Conductor of Cash Movement

Just as a conductor guides each section of an orchestra to play in harmony, you take on the role of the conductor in your financial symphony. You have the ability to optimize the progression of your cash flow cycle, ensuring that every financial note is played at the right time and in the right sequence.

Optimizing your cash flow progression involves strategically managing both inflows and outflows. For instance, you can accelerate the tempo by offering incentives for early payments from clients or implementing automated payment systems. On the other hand, you can adjust the tempo by extending payment terms with suppliers or using financial instruments like lines of credit to bridge temporary gaps.

Harmonizing Your Financial Tempo

Visualize your financial journey as a symphony in which the cash flow cycle sets the tempo. Just as a conductor's skill influences the emotional impact of a musical piece, your mastery of cash flow management influences the overall harmony of your financial symphony. By comparing the cash flow cycle to the tempo of music, you gain a deeper understanding of its significance in maintaining financial stability and propelling your financial goals.

Whether you're navigating through a soft and soothing Adagio or sprinting through an energetic Allegro, your ability to analyze, adapt, and optimize your cash flow cycle ensures that your financial symphony remains harmonious and well-orchestrated. As you conduct the tempo of your financial progress, remember that every note played contributes to the symphony of your financial success.

Chapter 5: Building and Maintaining an Emergency Fund

5.1 Understanding the Importance of an Emergency Fund

5.1.1 Financial Security: An Ensemble of Stability

In the grand symphony of your financial journey, the concept of financial security stands as a powerful ensemble of stability, akin to the harmonious arrangement of instruments in an orchestra. Just as a skilled conductor ensures that every instrument plays in harmony to create a captivating musical performance, your emergency fund orchestrates financial stability that resonates throughout your life.

Visualizing a Safety Net: Comparing an Emergency Fund to a Safety Net in a Musical Performance

Imagine attending a mesmerizing orchestral performance. The trapeze artist gracefully glides through the air, secured by a safety net below. Similarly, your emergency fund serves as a safety net, ready to catch you in times of unexpected financial acrobatics. In the world of music, as in finances, uncertainties are a constant presence. Just as the safety net provides a sense of reassurance to the performer, your emergency fund offers a financial cushion, offering reassurance that you have a safeguard against the unexpected.

Protection During Uncertainty: How an Emergency Fund Provides Financial Security During Unexpected Events

Life's melodies are known for their unpredictability – a sudden medical expense, an urgent car repair, or an unforeseen job loss can disrupt the rhythm of your financial harmony. This is where your emergency fund takes center stage, playing the role of a guardian against the discord of unexpected events. It ensures that you have funds readily available to meet these financial challenges without missing a beat.

An emergency fund provides you with the financial flexibility to navigate these unexpected twists, much like a talented musician skillfully adapts to changes in a musical composition. Instead of scrambling for funds or resorting to high-interest loans, you can confidently face the unexpected, knowing that your emergency fund has your back.

Peace of Mind: The Emotional Well-Being that Comes from Having a Financial Cushion

The soothing strains of a calming melody can evoke a sense of serenity and peace. Similarly, your emergency fund brings a harmonious sense of tranquility to your financial life. Knowing that you have a safety net allows you to approach life's uncertainties with a composed mind. The peace of mind that accompanies financial security frees you from constant worry and empowers you to focus on the other vibrant elements of your financial composition.

Just as a skilled conductor guides the orchestra with a steady hand, your emergency fund directs your financial decisions, enabling you to make choices based on your long-term well-being rather than immediate financial pressures. With this harmonious presence in your financial symphony, you can confidently navigate the complex interplay of financial notes, secure in the knowledge that you have created a stable and melodious foundation.

In the next section, we will explore how an emergency fund plays a pivotal role in avoiding the strains of debt and how it empowers you to lead a financially independent and fulfilling life.

5.1.2 Avoiding Debt: The Symphony of Prudent Planning

In the grand orchestration of your financial life, the avoidance of debt stands as a crucial movement, creating a symphony of prudent planning. Just as a composer carefully selects each note to create a harmonious composition, your emergency fund orchestrates a debt-free harmony that resonates through your financial endeavors.

A Debt-Free Harmony: How an Emergency Fund Prevents the Need for High-Interest Debt During Emergencies

Imagine a musical piece building to a crescendo, each note building upon the last to create a breathtaking climax. Similarly, your financial journey is a series of notes – some high, some low. In moments of financial urgency, when unexpected expenses arise, you face a pivotal choice. Will you harmonize with the melody of your emergency fund or create a discordant note by turning to high-interest credit cards or loans?

Your emergency fund serves as a conductor, guiding you towards the path of fiscal responsibility. It prevents the need to resort to high-interest debt to cover unforeseen expenses. Just as a skilled musician plays the right notes at the right time, your emergency fund provides you with the right financial resources when you need them the most.

Rhythms of Financial Stress: Exploring the Negative Impact of Relying on Credit Cards and Loans

In the world of music, dissonance can disrupt the entire composition. Similarly, the strains of financial stress, stemming from reliance on credit cards and loans, can create discord in your financial symphony. High-interest debt can accumulate quickly, leading to a crescendo of financial burden that is challenging to overcome.

When you rely on credit cards and loans to address emergencies, you inadvertently introduce a new melody into your financial composition – a melody of interest payments and debt obligations. This dissonance can drown out the harmonious notes of your financial aspirations, making it difficult to achieve your long-term goals.

Financial Empowerment: How an Emergency Fund Empowers You to Face Challenges Without Accumulating Debt

Imagine a conductor guiding an orchestra through a complex piece, ensuring that each instrument contributes to the overall harmony. Your emergency fund plays a similar role in your financial journey, empowering you to navigate challenges without accumulating debt. It provides you with the autonomy to face unexpected events with confidence and without compromising your financial well-being.

An emergency fund is not just a monetary reserve; it is a testament to your commitment to financial prudence and responsible planning. It allows you to maintain the rhythm of your financial life, even when faced with unexpected crescendos. With this financial safety net in place, you can confidently confront the unexpected, knowing that you have the means to address challenges without introducing dissonance into your financial symphony.

In the following section, we will delve into how an emergency fund bestows upon you the gift of flexibility and independence, enabling you to make decisions that align with your financial goals and aspirations.

5.1.3 Flexibility and Independence: The Melodic Freedom

In the grand symphony of your financial journey, an emergency fund serves as the conductor, guiding you through the intricate melodies of life's uncertainties. Just as a composer selects notes to weave together a musical masterpiece, your emergency fund empowers you with flexibility and independence, allowing you to make financial decisions that resonate with harmony and purpose.

Composing Financial Decisions: Drawing Parallels Between Composing Music and Making Financial Choices

Consider the process of composing a musical piece – the careful selection of notes, rhythms, and instruments to create a harmonious whole. Similarly, your financial decisions are like notes on a musical score, contributing to the composition of your financial life. An emergency fund provides you with the freedom to compose these financial decisions with a sense of purpose and intention.

Much like a composer weighs each note's impact on the overall composition, you can weigh your financial choices against the backdrop of your emergency fund. This fund grants you the liberty to make decisions that align with your values and long-term aspirations, creating a symphony of financial freedom.

The Conductor of Your Finances: Discussing How an Emergency Fund Provides Independence and Control

Imagine a conductor guiding an orchestra through a complex musical piece, infusing each movement with direction and intention. Similarly, your emergency fund conducts your financial decisions, allowing you to navigate life's complexities with independence and control.

An emergency fund liberates you from the constraints of financial uncertainty. Just as a conductor dictates the tempo of a musical piece, your emergency fund empowers you to set the tempo of your financial journey. It enables you to make choices based on your own rhythm, ensuring that you're not beholden to external financial pressures or circumstances.

Navigating Life's Variations: Exploring the Ability to Adapt to Unexpected Financial Changes With Confidence

Life is a medley of experiences – some predictable, others unexpected. Just as a musical composition weaves together different themes and variations, your financial journey encounters its share of variations. These may include job changes, health emergencies, or other unforeseen events.

Your emergency fund equips you with the ability to navigate these variations with confidence and grace. Like a skilled musician who adapts to changing musical dynamics, you can adapt to changing financial circumstances without missing a beat. This fund serves as your musical sheet, providing you with the notes to harmonize your financial decisions with the changing rhythms of life.

In the next section, we will explore the process of setting savings goals for your emergency fund, allowing you to establish a clear target and work towards building a robust financial safety net.

5.2 Setting Savings Goals

5.2.1 Identify an Adequate Fund Size: The Baseline Harmony

In the symphony of financial preparedness, the concept of an emergency fund's adequate size serves as the baseline – a fundamental note that grounds the entire composition. Just as a musical piece requires a foundational note to build upon, your emergency fund's size sets the tone for your financial security and readiness.

The Role of Baseline: Comparing the Baseline in Music to the Ideal Fund Size

Think of the baseline in music – a single note that provides a reference point for the entire composition. Similarly, your emergency fund's size acts as a baseline, a reference point for your financial stability. This baseline ensures that you have a firm foundation to navigate unexpected financial challenges without missing a beat.

The ideal fund size is like the baseline note, giving structure and coherence to your financial symphony. It provides a starting point from which you can build your financial security, just as a musical piece develops around its foundational note.

Factors to Consider: Exploring Personal and Financial Factors That Influence Your Fund Size

Just as a musical composition varies based on the genre, mood, and instruments used, the ideal size of your emergency fund is influenced by various personal and financial factors. Consider the following notes that contribute to determining your fund size:

1. **Living Expenses:** Your fund should ideally cover three to six months' worth of living expenses. This ensures that you can maintain your standard of living even if faced with unexpected financial setbacks.
2. **Job Security:** The stability of your job and industry plays a significant role. Those with more stable employment may lean towards the lower end of the range, while those with more variable income or higher risk may prefer a larger fund.
3. **Dependents:** If you have dependents or a family, you might need a larger fund to provide for their needs in case of emergencies.
4. **Health and Insurance:** Consider your health and insurance coverage. A strong insurance safety net may allow you to lean towards the lower end of the fund range.

5. **Debt:** If you have significant debt obligations, you might want a larger fund to avoid disrupting your debt repayment plan during emergencies.

Customizing Your Melody: How Your Unique Circumstances Determine the Appropriate Fund Size

Just as a composer tailors a musical piece to fit a specific occasion or emotion, your emergency fund's size should be customized to your unique circumstances. A one-size-fits-all approach won't suffice, as everyone's financial composition is distinct.

Your fund size is not just a number; it's a reflection of your financial goals, risk tolerance, and comfort level. It's the harmony between your current situation and your future aspirations. By considering the various factors that contribute to your financial melody, you can craft a fund size that resonates with your individual financial symphony.

In the upcoming section, we will delve into the process of setting incremental savings goals, allowing you to gradually build your emergency fund in a way that aligns with your financial rhythm.

5.2.2 Consider Personal Factors: The Individualized Composition

In the grand symphony of financial preparedness, crafting an emergency fund that aligns with your unique circumstances is akin to composing a personalized musical score. Just as a composer tailors every note and melody to create a harmonious piece, your emergency fund's size and structure should be meticulously customized to orchestrate your financial well-being.

Crafting Your Financial Score: Drawing Parallels Between Crafting Music and Tailoring Your Emergency Fund

Imagine yourself as a composer, carefully selecting each musical element to create a masterpiece. Similarly, crafting your emergency fund involves a thoughtful composition. Consider your financial obligations, aspirations, and risk tolerance as the musical notes that come together to form your financial score.

Just as a composer understands the nuances of different instruments to create a balanced arrangement, you must comprehend your personal financial landscape to determine the optimal fund size. This understanding allows you to weave a financial score that resonates with your goals and aspirations.

Your Financial Orchestra: How Personal Factors Dictate the Size and Structure of Your Fund

In an orchestra, each instrument contributes a unique sound, blending together to create harmony. Similarly, your personal factors play distinct roles in shaping your emergency fund. Factors such as income stability, family size, and financial goals form the different instruments in your financial orchestra.

If you have a stable job and minimal dependents, your financial orchestra might emphasize a smaller fund size. On the other hand, if your income is variable and your family's needs are substantial, your orchestra might require a larger and more diverse array of financial instruments.

The Art of Balancing: How to Find the Right Balance Between Risk Tolerance and Fund Size

Balancing your emergency fund's size with your risk tolerance is akin to finding the right balance between melody and harmony in music. A piece of music with too much melody might become overwhelming, while one with too much harmony might lack depth.

Similarly, an emergency fund that is too large might lead to missed investment opportunities, while one that is too small might not provide adequate protection during financial downturns. Striking the right balance ensures that your emergency fund serves its purpose without hindering your financial growth.

Consider your risk tolerance as the conductor of your financial orchestra. It guides the tempo and rhythm of your fund's growth. A conservative approach may lead to a larger fund, providing a stronger safety net. A more aggressive stance might prioritize investment opportunities, with a slightly smaller fund to cover immediate needs.

As you navigate the harmonies of your financial composition, remember that your emergency fund's size is a dynamic element that can be adjusted over time. Life's circumstances change, just as musical pieces evolve. Regularly reassess your personal factors, risk tolerance, and financial goals to ensure that your emergency fund remains in tune with your ever-changing financial symphony.

In the following section, we will explore the concept of setting incremental savings goals as a practical strategy to bring your individualized financial composition to life.

5.2.3 Gradual Increment: The Cadence of Progress

In the intricate tapestry of financial preparedness, the art of saving for an emergency fund is akin to composing a beautiful melody. Just as musical notes progress to form a harmonious composition, your savings gradually build to create a strong and resilient financial foundation.

Musical Progression: Comparing Gradual Savings to the Progression of Musical Notes

Think of the gradual accumulation of your emergency fund as the musical progression within a piece. Just as a melody takes shape note by note, your savings incrementally grow, contributing to the overall financial composition. Each contribution is like a well-placed note that blends seamlessly with the others to create a melodious whole.

Much like a composer carefully arranges musical notes to evoke emotion, you orchestrate your savings journey, crafting a future of financial stability and security. Each small addition to your fund contributes to the overarching theme of preparedness, ensuring that you're ready to face life's unexpected challenges.

Consistency is Key: The Importance of Steady and Sustainable Savings

In music, consistency in tempo and rhythm is crucial for a flawless performance. Similarly, consistent and disciplined savings are essential for building a robust emergency fund. Just as a metronome sets the pace for a musical piece, your dedication to regular contributions sets the tempo for your financial progress.

Consistency is your guide, ensuring that your emergency fund grows steadily over time. It's not about making grand gestures, but rather about the steady cadence of contributions that align with your financial capacity. Small, regular deposits add up over time, creating a fund that resonates with stability and reliability.

Celebrating Small Victories: How Achieving Incremental Milestones Contributes to Your Financial Composition

In music, every accomplished practice session and perfected passage is a small victory that contributes to a flawless performance. Similarly, achieving incremental savings milestones is cause for celebration on your financial journey. Each milestone reached is a testament to your dedication and a harmonious note in the symphony of your financial composition.

Celebrating these small victories not only acknowledges your progress but also reinforces positive financial habits. It's like receiving applause from an audience after a well-played piece. These moments of celebration infuse your savings journey with motivation and enthusiasm, making the path to a fully funded emergency fund an enjoyable and fulfilling one.

As you compose the melody of your emergency fund, remember that gradual increment is the rhythm that propels your financial symphony forward. Just as musical compositions evolve with each note, your emergency fund takes shape with every contribution. In the upcoming section, we will explore practical strategies to accelerate your savings and harmonize your financial composition even further.

5.2.4 Review and Update: The Dynamic Symphony

In the grand symphony of financial planning, the ability to review and update your savings goals is like a conductor fine-tuning the score for a flawless performance. Just as musical compositions evolve with time, your emergency fund goals may need adjustments to stay in perfect harmony with your changing circumstances.

An Evolving Score: Drawing Parallels Between Updating Music Compositions and Adjusting Savings Goals

In the realm of music, composers often revise their compositions to enhance the overall piece. Similarly, your savings goals are not set in stone. They evolve alongside your financial journey. Just as a musical score adapts to achieve the desired sound, your savings goals should adapt to ensure your financial well-being.

Life is a dynamic composition, and your savings goals should reflect this fluidity. As your financial situation, responsibilities, and aspirations change, so too should your emergency fund aspirations. By treating your savings goals as a living composition, you ensure they remain relevant and effective.

Life's Changing Melodies: Exploring Life Events That Warrant a Review and Potential Adjustment of Goals

Life is a series of changing melodies, each presenting unique challenges and opportunities. Just as a musical composition shifts in mood and tone, your financial circumstances can take unexpected turns. Significant life events such as marriage, the birth of a child, a new job, or a career change can impact your financial needs.

Imagine these life events as key changes in a musical piece – they alter the melody and require adjustments to maintain harmony. When such events occur, it's important to review and potentially revise your emergency fund goals. This ensures that your financial symphony continues to resonate with security and stability.

Harmonizing with Life: How to Ensure Your Savings Goals Stay Aligned with Your Ever-Changing Circumstances

In the realm of music, an orchestra adjusts its performance in response to the acoustics of the concert hall. Similarly, your savings goals should harmonize with your evolving circumstances. Regularly reviewing your emergency fund goals is a practice in financial acoustics – ensuring that your savings resonate with your current needs.

When reviewing your goals, consider how changes in your life may impact your financial requirements. Has your family size changed? Have your income or expenses shifted? Are there new milestones on the horizon? These questions guide you in fine-tuning your financial composition.

By embracing the concept of a dynamic symphony, you empower yourself to respond effectively to life's changing melodies. Just as a conductor guides an orchestra through different movements, you guide your financial composition through the various stages of life. The ability to review and adjust your savings goals ensures that your emergency fund remains a steadfast and reliable part of your overall financial harmony.

In the upcoming section, we delve into strategies for building and growing your emergency fund, transforming your financial symphony into a masterpiece of preparedness and security.

5.3 Strategies to Build an Emergency Fund

5.3.1 Automate Savings: The Melody of Regularity

Imagine your emergency fund as a musical piece, with each contribution adding a note to its harmonious composition. Just as a musical composition requires a consistent rhythm to create a captivating melody, automating your savings establishes a reliable beat that steadily builds your emergency fund over time.

Automation in Finances: Comparing Automated Savings to a Consistent Musical Rhythm

In the world of music, rhythm is the heartbeat of a composition, providing structure and consistency. Likewise, automating your savings infuses your financial journey with a rhythmic flow. It transforms sporadic contributions into a steady cadence, ensuring that your emergency fund melody is played flawlessly.

Much like a conductor sets the tempo for a musical piece, you can set the pace for your financial goals through automated savings. This approach eliminates the need for manual transfers and decisions, creating a reliable pattern of contributions that resonate with the harmony of your financial well-being.

Setting the Beat: How Automatic Transfers Ensure Regular Contributions to Your Emergency Fund

Imagine each automated transfer as a musical note, contributing to the symphony of your financial security. By setting up automatic transfers from your main account to your dedicated emergency fund, you establish a rhythmic beat of consistent contributions.

Automated transfers operate as the metronome of your financial composition, ensuring that your savings efforts remain on tempo. Whether it's a weekly, bi-weekly, or monthly transfer, this consistent beat gradually builds the crescendo of your emergency fund, reinforcing your financial stability note by note.

Reliability and Consistency: Discussing the Benefits of Automated Savings in Building Your Fund

In the world of music, consistency is the key to creating a harmonious melody. Similarly, in the realm of finances, consistency paves the way for a secure and stable future. Automated savings provide the reliability needed to fortify your emergency fund and meet your financial goals.

By entrusting automation, you remove the potential for oversight or delay, ensuring that your savings melody plays uninterrupted. Each automated contribution adds to the strength of your financial composition, enhancing your ability to navigate unexpected financial challenges and opportunities.

As we move forward, we'll explore additional strategies to boost your emergency fund's growth and resilience, further enriching the symphony of your financial preparedness.

5.3.2 Reduce Discretionary Spending: The Cadence of Frugality

Picture your financial journey as a musical performance, where every dollar you save plays a crucial role in creating a harmonious composition. Just as harmonious melodies require careful selection and arrangement of musical notes, frugal spending involves conscious choices to create a balanced and sustainable financial tune.

Musical Harmony in Spending: Drawing Parallels Between Frugal Spending and Harmonious Melodies

In the world of music, harmony arises from the thoughtful arrangement of different musical elements. Similarly, financial harmony is achieved by orchestrating your spending in a way that resonates with your goals and values. Frugal spending becomes the underlying rhythm that supports the melody of your financial composition.

Identifying Extravagances: How to Identify and Cut Back on Non-Essential Expenses

Imagine your expenses as musical notes, each contributing to the overall tune of your financial life. To create a harmonious melody, it's essential to identify any discordant notes – unnecessary or extravagant expenses that disrupt your financial harmony.

Conduct a thorough analysis of your spending habits. Are there areas where you could cut back without compromising your well-being? Consider dining out, entertainment, subscriptions, or impulse purchases. By trimming these excesses, you create a clearer, more resonant financial melody.

Directing the Tune: Redirecting Discretionary Spending Towards Your Emergency Fund Composition

Just as a skilled composer directs the flow of a musical piece, you have the power to direct the flow of your financial resources. Instead of letting discretionary spending scatter your financial notes, redirect them toward building your emergency fund.

Visualize each dollar saved as a note in your emergency fund's melody. By consciously allocating discretionary funds to your emergency fund, you transform your spending choices into a harmonious financial composition. This shift in focus not only strengthens your emergency fund but also enhances your overall financial well-being.

As we continue our exploration of building and maintaining an emergency fund, we'll delve into more strategies that contribute to the symphony of your financial security. Remember, just as a well-conducted orchestra produces beautiful music, thoughtful financial decisions lead to a harmonious and stable financial future.

5.3.3 Increase Income: The Crescendo of Earning Potential

Imagine your financial journey as a symphony, with each note representing a source of income. Just as a musical composition builds to a crescendo, increasing your income creates a powerful crescendo of financial potential. This section explores how boosting your earnings contributes to the harmony of your emergency fund composition.

The Symphony of Earnings: Comparing Increased Income to a Musical Crescendo

In the world of music, a crescendo signifies a gradual increase in volume and intensity, adding depth and dimension to a piece. Similarly, increasing your income adds richness and depth to your financial composition. This crescendo allows you to play more notes in your financial symphony, giving you the opportunity to build a stronger and more resilient emergency fund.

Exploring Additional Opportunities: How Side Hustles and Supplementary Income Sources Contribute to Your Fund

Just as a skilled musician might play multiple instruments to enrich a musical composition, you can explore various income streams to enrich your financial composition. Side hustles, freelancing, or part-time gigs can serve as additional instruments in your financial orchestra.

Consider your skills, interests, and available opportunities. Is there a hobby or talent that you could monetize? Are there platforms or marketplaces where you could offer your services? By diversifying your income sources, you create a harmonious blend of financial notes that contribute to the melody of your emergency fund.

Amplifying Your Savings: Discussing the Impact of Higher Earnings on Your Emergency Fund's Growth

Think of your emergency fund as a musical crescendo, growing in intensity and strength. Increasing your income accelerates this crescendo, propelling your emergency fund's growth and ensuring its ability to meet unexpected financial challenges.

As your earnings rise, you can allocate a larger portion of your income to your emergency fund. This not only accelerates your savings but also provides a sense of empowerment and control over your financial narrative. Just as a crescendo adds energy and excitement to a musical piece, the amplified savings from increased income infuse your financial composition with vitality and resilience.

In our ongoing exploration of building and maintaining an emergency fund, we will continue to uncover strategies that contribute to the harmony of your financial well-being. As you embrace the crescendo of earning potential, you create a financial symphony that resonates with security, stability, and a brighter future.

5.3.4 Windfalls and Bonuses: The Unexpected Overture

Imagine your financial journey as a symphony, each note representing your hard-earned income. Now, picture a sudden crescendo, a surge of unexpected music that adds a delightful surprise to the composition. In the world of personal finance, windfalls and bonuses play a similar role, infusing your financial symphony with an unexpected overture of growth. This section explores how utilizing windfalls and bonuses can amplify the harmony of your emergency fund composition.

Windfall as a Musical Surprise: Drawing Parallels Between Unexpected Windfalls and Musical Surprises

In music, surprises often bring excitement and captivation to a composition. Just as an unexpected change in melody can add a fresh layer of intrigue to a musical piece, a windfall injects a similar element of surprise into your financial composition. Windfalls come in various forms – a tax refund, a work bonus, an unexpected inheritance – and, like a sudden musical twist, they enrich your financial narrative.

Utilizing Unexpected Gains: How Tax Refunds, Bonuses, and Unexpected Funds Can Boost Your Fund

Imagine receiving a tax refund – it's akin to stumbling upon a hidden musical treasure. Windfalls provide you with an opportunity to contribute a substantial amount to your emergency fund in one fell swoop. Instead of squandering these unexpected gains on fleeting indulgences, consider channeling them into your financial symphony.

Similarly, work bonuses are like a crescendo that amplifies the overall impact of your efforts. Rather than treating them as disposable income, allocate a significant portion to your emergency fund. This ensures that these unexpected windfalls contribute to the lasting melody of your financial stability.

A Forte in Savings: Exploring the Potential of Windfalls in Accelerating Your Emergency Fund's Growth

In the realm of music, a "forte" signifies a strong and powerful section. Windfalls and unexpected bonuses can serve as the "forte" in your savings strategy. They provide you with the opportunity to make a substantial leap forward in building your emergency fund, amplifying its growth and strengthening its resilience.

Consider this: a well-timed windfall can help you reach your emergency fund goal faster than anticipated. It's like a sudden burst of musical brilliance that elevates the entire performance. By directing windfalls towards your fund, you not only expedite its growth but also create a sense of accomplishment and momentum in your financial journey.

As you orchestrate your financial future, keep an ear out for the unexpected overtures – the windfalls and bonuses that can transform your financial symphony. Embrace these surprises as powerful instruments in your savings composition, playing their unique notes to elevate the harmony of your emergency fund. In our continuing exploration of building and maintaining an emergency fund, we'll uncover more strategies that contribute to the crescendo of your financial well-being.

5.3.5 Minimize Debt: The Symphony of Financial Liberation

Envision your financial landscape as a grand symphony, with each note representing a different financial obligation. Just as a skilled composer carefully balances the notes in a musical piece, managing debt requires a harmonious blend of strategies. This section delves into the parallels between minimizing debt and creating a symphony of financial liberation.

Musical Balance in Debt Management: Comparing Debt Reduction to Creating Harmonious Music

In the world of music, balance is the key to crafting a harmonious composition. The same principle applies to your financial journey, where balancing debt reduction is crucial. Just as a well-composed piece weaves together various melodies, effectively managing debt involves weaving together strategies to achieve financial harmony.

Consider debt as a dissonant note in your financial symphony. By minimizing debt, you resolve this dissonance, allowing the rest of your financial composition to resonate more clearly. Just as a skilled composer eliminates discordant elements, reducing debt creates a clearer, more melodious financial picture.

Allocating Debt Payments: Discussing the Strategy of Reallocating Debt Payments to Your Emergency Fund

Now imagine redirecting the resources previously allocated to debt payments into your emergency fund – it's akin to repurposing musical notes to create a new, captivating melody. As you make progress in reducing your debts, consider channeling a portion of your debt payments towards your emergency fund. This strategic reallocation allows you to shift from a defensive stance – battling debt – to an offensive one, proactively building a financial safety net.

As you orchestrate this reallocation, remember that every dollar redirected towards your emergency fund contributes to the composition of stability and security. It's like composing a new movement in your financial symphony, one that resonates with liberation from the burden of debt.

The Liberation Chorus: How Reduced Debt Contributes to Your Overall Financial Well-Being

Picture a triumphant chorus in a musical performance – the moment of culmination and celebration. Minimizing debt and reallocating funds to your emergency fund creates a similar liberating chorus in your financial journey. With each debt payment redirected, you inch closer to financial liberation and empowerment.

Reduced debt translates into increased financial flexibility and control. It allows you to navigate your financial composition with more ease, unburdened by the weight of excessive obligations. Just as a musical piece gains momentum and energy as it progresses, your financial symphony gains momentum as you reduce debt and contribute to your emergency fund.

As you work towards minimizing debt, remember that every effort contributes to the crescendo of your financial liberation. The act of reallocating debt payments to your emergency fund is akin to introducing a powerful new motif into your composition. It's a melody of freedom, a harmonious movement that brings you closer to financial stability and greater control over your financial future.

In our exploration of building and maintaining an emergency fund, we've explored various techniques that contribute to the harmonious composition of your financial well-being. As we move forward, we'll uncover more strategies to enhance your financial symphony and ensure that you are well-prepared for life's unexpected turns.

5.4 Best Practices for Managing the Fund

5.4.1 Separate Account: The Conductor's Baton

In the intricate composition of your financial orchestra, the concept of a separate account plays a vital role, much like the conductor's baton in a musical performance. Just as a conductor uses the baton to guide and synchronize the musicians, a separate account guides and safeguards your emergency fund, ensuring its distinct purpose and effective management.

Financial Segregation: Drawing Parallels Between a Separate Account and a Conductor's Baton

Consider a conductor skillfully guiding an orchestra with precise gestures of the baton. Each movement has a purpose – to bring out the best in each instrument and create a harmonious whole. Similarly, a separate account serves as your financial conductor's baton, guiding the flow of funds to fulfill the specific purpose of your emergency fund.

Just as a conductor ensures that each instrument contributes to the overall melody, a separate account prevents financial misallocation. It designates a specific space for your emergency fund, preventing it from getting lost in the symphony of daily expenses and transactions. This segregation is as essential as each instrument having its designated part in a musical composition.

Preventing Misallocation: Discussing the Importance of Keeping Your Emergency Fund Distinct From Regular Accounts

Imagine a musical performance where the conductor's baton is accidentally used to direct the wrong section. The result would be a discordant sound, disrupting the entire performance. Similarly, mingling your emergency fund with your regular accounts can lead to confusion and misallocation of funds.

A separate account ensures that your emergency fund remains untouched and readily available for its designated purpose – to provide you with a safety net during unforeseen circumstances. This distinction prevents accidental spending and guarantees that your financial composition remains harmonious, even in the face of unexpected financial crescendos.

Fostering Discipline: How a Separate Account Promotes Disciplined Management of Your Fund

Just as a conductor's baton demands discipline and precision from musicians, a separate account demands disciplined financial management. When your emergency fund is housed in a distinct account, it sends a clear signal that these funds are reserved for emergencies only. This distinctiveness fosters discipline in your financial decisions and spending habits.

Having a separate account acts as a constant reminder of your financial goals and priorities. It's a visual representation of your commitment to financial security and preparedness. Every time you access this account or contribute to it, you're acknowledging the importance of protecting your financial symphony from unexpected dissonance.

In the grand composition of your financial life, a separate account serves as the conductor's baton, guiding the flow of funds and maintaining the integrity of your emergency fund's purpose. It ensures that your financial symphony remains on track, harmonious, and prepared to face any unexpected variations. As we continue our exploration of building and maintaining an emergency fund, we'll delve into further techniques that contribute to the overall harmony of your financial masterpiece.

5.4.2 High Liquidity: The Fluidity of Financial Readiness

In the intricate symphony of financial management, the concept of high liquidity plays a pivotal role, much like the fluidity of musical notes in a composition. Just as musical notes flow seamlessly from one to the next, high liquidity ensures the smooth and efficient movement of funds within your financial composition.

Liquidity in Finances: Comparing High Liquidity to the Fluidity of Musical Notes

Imagine a musical piece where each note seamlessly transitions to the next, creating a harmonious and captivating melody. This fluidity is akin to the concept of high liquidity in finances. High liquidity refers to the ease and speed with which your assets can be converted into cash without significant loss of value. Just as musical notes need to be readily accessible to create a beautiful composition, your emergency fund requires high liquidity to address unexpected financial needs effectively.

Access When Needed: Discussing the Significance of Maintaining Easy Access to Your Emergency Fund

In the realm of music, a skilled musician can effortlessly switch between notes, creating a captivating auditory experience. Similarly, maintaining high liquidity in your emergency fund allows you to swiftly access cash when needed, ensuring that you can transition seamlessly through unexpected financial challenges.

Life's unexpected variations, much like musical improvisations, can require immediate financial adjustments. Whether it's a medical emergency, sudden car repair, or unforeseen job loss, having easy access to your emergency fund allows you to navigate these variations without missing a beat. Just as a musician relies on the availability of each note to create a melodious composition, you rely on the accessibility of your emergency fund to maintain your financial harmony.

Adapting to Financial Surprises: How High Liquidity Ensures You Can Swiftly Address Unexpected Financial Needs

Consider a skilled conductor leading an orchestra through an impromptu musical change. The ability to adapt swiftly ensures that the performance remains flawless, regardless of the surprise. Similarly, high liquidity provides you with the financial flexibility to adapt to unexpected surprises without derailing your overall financial composition.

High liquidity ensures that you can tap into your emergency fund at a moment's notice, allowing you to cover unforeseen expenses and maintain your financial stability. It prevents the need to liquidate other assets at unfavorable terms or resort to high-interest debt. Just as a musician's readiness to adapt ensures a smooth performance, your emergency fund's high liquidity ensures a seamless response to unexpected financial crescendos.

In the grand composition of your financial journey, high liquidity serves as the fluidity that allows your financial notes to transition smoothly from one phase to the next.

As we continue our exploration of building and maintaining an emergency fund, we'll delve into further techniques that contribute to the overall harmony of your financial masterpiece.

In this comprehensive chapter, we'll explore the significance of an emergency fund, strategies for its growth, and best practices for its management. Just as a skilled composer crafts a symphony, building and maintaining an emergency fund requires careful orchestration of your financial resources. By understanding its importance, setting meaningful savings goals, and adopting effective strategies, you'll ensure that your financial composition remains harmonious, even in the face of unexpected challenges.

Chapter 6: Controlling and Reducing Debt

Debt, much like the melodies and harmonies that make up a musical composition, plays a significant role in our financial lives. Just as a skilled composer carefully arranges musical notes to create a harmonious piece, managing debt requires careful orchestration to achieve financial harmony. In this chapter, we delve into the art of controlling and reducing debt, exploring various strategies that parallel the techniques used by musicians to craft beautiful melodies.

6.1 Evaluating Different Types of Debt

Just as a symphony is composed of diverse instruments playing in harmony, your financial composition consists of various types of debt that interact to create your overall financial picture. Much like a conductor bringing different sections of an orchestra together, you must understand and manage these different types of debt to create a harmonious financial future.

Understanding the nature of different debts is the first step in this process. By identifying the distinct characteristics of each type of debt, you can tailor your debt management strategies to achieve the best possible financial outcome. This section will take you on a journey through the different types of debt that you may encounter in your financial symphony. From consumer debt to student loans, mortgage debt, auto loans, and other financial obligations, each type of debt contributes its own melody to your financial composition.

As we explore these various types of debt, think of yourself as both a composer and a conductor. You are crafting a financial symphony that resonates with stability, security, and freedom. Just as a conductor guides the orchestra to create a harmonious masterpiece, you will learn to navigate the nuances of different debts to create a well-balanced and financially sound composition. So, let's dive into the world of debt, where each type of financial obligation plays a crucial role in the overall melody of your financial life.

6.1.1 Consumer Debt: Managing the Crescendo of Credit

Imagine your financial journey as a symphonic composition, where various types of debt take on unique roles in shaping the overall melody. Among these, consumer debt emerges as a powerful crescendo, commanding attention with its high-interest dynamics. This category encompasses credit card debt, personal loans, and retail installment loans, each note contributing to the intricate rhythm of your financial composition.

Understanding Consumer Debt's Impact

Consumer debt, particularly credit card debt, can act as a crescendo that swells unexpectedly. The high-interest rates attached to these debts can quickly amplify your financial burden, creating dissonance within your carefully orchestrated financial composition. Just as a poorly timed crescendo can disrupt the flow of a musical piece, unchecked consumer debt can disrupt your financial harmony.

Crafting a Debt Management Strategy

In the world of music, a skilled conductor guides crescendos to enhance the overall impact of a performance. Similarly, you can guide your consumer debt with a well-crafted strategy. Begin by evaluating each debt instrument – credit cards, personal loans, and retail installment loans – to understand their interest rates, terms, and impact on your financial score.

Symphony of Debt Repayment: Snowball or Avalanche?

Much like a conductor chooses instruments for a crescendo, you must choose a repayment approach that suits your financial composition. The debt snowball method involves paying off smaller debts first, creating a sense of accomplishment. On the other hand, the debt avalanche method prioritizes higher-interest debts, ultimately reducing overall interest payments. Carefully selecting your approach ensures your debt repayment is harmonious and effective.

Rhythm of Responsible Credit Use

In music, a crescendo is balanced within the context of the piece. Similarly, your consumer debt can be balanced through responsible credit use. As you pay down existing debts, consider how you can manage new credit responsibly. This might involve setting a budget, avoiding unnecessary spending, and diligently paying off credit card balances each month to prevent a disruptive debt crescendo.

Conductor of Financial Harmony

Just as a conductor ensures a crescendo enhances a musical performance, you can guide your consumer debt toward harmonious resolution. Craft a well-structured repayment plan, allocate funds strategically, and consider debt consolidation options to orchestrate a smoother debt management process. By conducting your financial symphony with finesse, you can transform the crescendo of consumer debt into a powerful and controlled element within your overall financial composition.

In the sections that follow, we will delve deeper into the strategies and techniques that mirror the conductor's finesse in the world of consumer debt management. From orchestrating the payoff of credit card balances to harmonizing the symphony of your financial stability, you will learn to wield the baton of financial knowledge to achieve a debt-free harmony that resonates with your life's aspirations.

6.1.2 Student Loans: The Melody of Educational Investment

In the grand symphony of your financial life, student loans take center stage as the melodious notes of educational investment. Just as a musical composition features a central theme that captivates the audience, student loans compose the very melody that accompanies your journey towards knowledge and personal growth. These loans, whether obtained from federal sources or private lenders, serve as the orchestral accompaniment to your educational aspirations, each with its unique terms, harmonies, and repayment cadences.

The Educational Crescendo

Imagine your pursuit of education as a crescendo, gradually building to a climactic moment. Student loans, in this metaphor, provide the necessary crescendo, amplifying your potential by granting access to higher education. Just as a crescendo adds depth and intensity to a musical piece, student loans enrich your life's composition by opening the doors to academic and professional opportunities that may have otherwise remained out of reach.

Fine-Tuning Your Repayment Composition

Much like a composer meticulously fine-tunes a melody, managing student loans involves the careful structuring of repayment plans. Each student loan, with its specific terms and conditions, contributes to the intricate composition of your financial future. As you navigate this melodic journey, consider orchestrating a repayment plan that harmonizes with your financial goals, ensuring that the repayment notes seamlessly blend into your overall financial symphony.

The Conductor of Repayment Strategy

A conductor guides an orchestra to create a harmonious arrangement. Similarly, you can be the conductor of your student loan repayment strategy, coordinating the various elements into a coherent and resonant whole. Begin by assessing your student loan portfolio – both federal and private – understanding interest rates, grace periods, and available repayment plans.

Harmonizing with Your Financial Ensemble

Just as a musical composition harmonizes different instruments, your student loan repayment strategy must harmonize with your broader financial ensemble. Consider your income, budget, and financial aspirations when structuring your repayment plan. Explore options such as income-driven repayment plans, loan forgiveness programs, or refinancing to ensure your student loans blend seamlessly with your overall financial composition.

Achieving a Debt-Free Crescendo

In the grand finale of a musical performance, a crescendo may reach its peak, leaving the audience in awe. Similarly, your student loan repayment journey will crescendo towards its culmination – a debt-free finale. As you diligently make payments and strategically manage your student loans, you approach the crescendo of financial liberation, where the harmonious combination of education and responsible debt management leads to a triumphant and debt-free conclusion.

In the upcoming sections, we will delve deeper into the nuances of student loan management, exploring strategies to optimize repayment, navigate available options, and achieve the harmonious blend of education and financial stability. Your student loans, much like the captivating melody in a musical composition, have the power to shape your financial symphony – and with the right approach, you can ensure that this melody is one of achievement, growth, and harmonious financial progress.

6.1.3 Mortgage Debt: Building the Foundation

In the grand orchestration of your financial life, mortgage debt assumes the role of a foundational note – a fundamental bass that sets the tone for the entire composition. Just as a solid and sturdy foundation is essential for a seamless musical performance, mortgage debt forms the bedrock of homeownership, laying the groundwork for your dwelling, your life, and your financial future.

The Symphony of Homeownership

Visualize mortgage debt as the conductor's baton, guiding the rhythm and tempo of your financial symphony. This debt category orchestrates the purchase of your residence, transforming the dream of homeownership into a melodious reality. Just as a conductor shapes the performance of an orchestra, mortgage debt shapes your financial journey by enabling you to acquire the dwelling where life's symphony unfolds.

The Harmonic Structure of Mortgage Debt

Every musical composition has a unique structure – a sequence of harmonies and melodies that create a sense of unity and coherence. Similarly, mortgage debt introduces a structured element into your financial symphony. With varying interest rates, repayment terms, and loan options, mortgage debt crafts the harmonic framework of your homeownership, determining how the notes of your payments will blend into the overall composition of your financial life.

Conducting the Repayment Tempo

Managing mortgage debt is akin to conducting a musical performance – it requires skillful coordination, precision, and an acute sense of timing. Just as a conductor guides the orchestra through tempo changes and transitions, you must navigate through the rhythms of mortgage repayment. Responsible management involves making timely payments, understanding amortization schedules, and considering options for refinancing or accelerating repayment.

Stability and Financial Resonance

Just as a foundation provides stability to a structure, mortgage debt offers financial stability to your life. Owning a home can provide a sense of permanence, a place where memories are created and cherished. Managing mortgage debt ensures that this foundation remains strong and resilient, contributing to the harmonious progression of your financial composition.

Strategies for Harmonious Management

To master the art of managing mortgage debt, consider adopting strategies that harmonize with your financial goals and aspirations:

1. **Strategic Payment Planning:** Much like a musical score requires careful interpretation, develop a strategic payment plan for your mortgage. Explore options such as bi-weekly payments, which can accelerate your debt reduction and save on interest over time.

2. **Refinancing as a Crescendo:** Refinancing is akin to a musical crescendo – a moment of heightened intensity. Just as a crescendo adds depth to a musical piece, refinancing can potentially lower your interest rate, reduce monthly payments, and save you money in the long run.

3. **Extra Payment Overtures:** Similar to a musical overture that introduces themes and motifs, consider making occasional extra payments towards your mortgage principal. These overtures can significantly reduce the overall interest you pay and hasten the final note of full ownership.

4. Harmonizing with Financial Goals: Your mortgage debt should harmonize with your broader financial goals. Consider whether it aligns with your long-term plans and financial well-being. If necessary, explore options to downsize, relocate, or leverage your property for other financial opportunities.

5. Seek Professional Conductors: Just as a conductor guides an orchestra, seek the guidance of financial professionals when managing your mortgage debt. Mortgage advisors and financial planners can help you navigate complex decisions, ensuring your homeownership remains a harmonious part of your overall financial composition.

The Symphony of Ownership

Mortgage debt weaves its melody into the very fabric of your life – it's a symphony of ownership, stability, and financial growth. Just as a musical composition requires balance and harmony among its diverse elements, managing mortgage debt requires thoughtful planning, disciplined payments, and an overarching vision of your financial future. By conducting your mortgage debt with skill and diligence, you contribute a resonant note to the grand composition of your financial symphony.

6.2 Developing a Debt Repayment Plan

In the grand symphony of your financial life, the debt repayment plan takes center stage as the conductor of your fiscal composition. Just as a conductor meticulously guides every instrument in an orchestra to create a harmonious melody, a well-structured debt repayment plan orchestrates your financial instruments to compose a debt-free future. This chapter explores the intricate composition of a debt repayment plan and how it harmonizes with your broader financial goals.

6.2.1 Assess Your Debt: Notating Financial Instruments

In the intricate symphony of your financial life, assessing your debt is akin to the meticulous notations made by a composer to orchestrate a harmonious musical piece. Just as each musical instrument contributes its unique sound to the composition, each debt contributes its own intricacies to your financial ensemble. To create a comprehensive financial score and guide the composition of your debt repayment plan, follow the analogy of notating musical instruments with precision.

The Composition of Debt

Imagine your various debts as distinct musical instruments, each playing a role in the overall composition of your financial melody. To notate these financial instruments, start by listing them in detail. Include the name of the creditor, the outstanding balance, the interest rate, and the minimum monthly payment. This meticulous documentation creates a clear and structured foundation for understanding the components of your financial ensemble.

Creating a Financial Score

Just as a musical score provides a visual representation of musical notes and rhythms, your debt assessment creates a financial score that visually represents the notes of your financial obligations. This score allows you to see the interplay of different debts, their respective interest rates, and their impact on your overall financial harmony.

Clarity and Insight

By notating your debts with precision, you gain clarity and insight into your financial ensemble. You can identify which debts carry the highest interest rates, the total amount of debt you owe, and the monthly obligations you need to meet. This clarity is essential for making informed decisions about how to orchestrate your debt repayment plan effectively.

Guiding the Debt Repayment Composition

Just as a composer uses musical notations to guide musicians in playing their instruments, your debt assessment guides you in orchestrating your debt repayment plan. It provides a roadmap for allocating resources, setting priorities, and making strategic decisions about which debts to tackle first.

Harmonizing Debt Repayment

Just as a conductor ensures that each instrument is in harmony with the rest of the orchestra, your debt repayment plan aims to harmonize your financial obligations. With a well-notated debt assessment, you can allocate your financial resources in a way that optimizes your repayment strategy. You may choose to direct more funds toward higher-interest debts to minimize overall interest payments or focus on paying off smaller debts for a sense of accomplishment – much like a composer strategically directs different sections of an orchestra to achieve a balanced and harmonious performance.

The Art of Financial Composition

In the world of music, precise notations bring forth a masterpiece. Similarly, a detailed debt assessment serves as the notations for your financial composition. By carefully listing and understanding each debt instrument, you empower yourself to create a debt repayment symphony that resonates with financial success. This level of meticulousness ensures that your financial ensemble plays in perfect harmony, leading you toward the crescendo of debt freedom and financial well-being.

As you meticulously notate each debt instrument, you are not just creating a list of numbers; you are composing a financial composition that will guide your path toward debt reduction. Think of this process as the overture to a grand performance – setting the stage for the rest of your debt management journey. In the upcoming sections, we will explore how to prioritize and orchestrate your debt repayment plan based on the intricacies of each "instrument" in your financial ensemble. Just as a skilled conductor brings out the best from each section of an orchestra, your careful assessment of your debts will enable you to conduct a symphony of financial success.

6.2.2 Prioritize Debts: Orchestrating Repayment Strategies

In the intricate orchestration of your financial symphony, your debts play the role of individual musical notes, each contributing to the overall composition. Just as a composer carefully selects and arranges musical notes to create a harmonious masterpiece, you must adopt a debt repayment strategy that resonates with your unique financial melody.

Let us explore two prominent approaches – the "debt snowball" and the "debt avalanche" – each conducting its own rhythm and dynamics in the composition of your debt reduction plan.

The "Debt Snowball" Technique: A Symphony of Small Victories

Imagine a musical composition that gradually builds in intensity and emotion, ultimately reaching a triumphant crescendo. The "debt snowball" technique embraces this crescendo-like progression by focusing on paying off smaller debts first. Just as the increasing intensity of musical notes captivates the listener's attention, the satisfaction of paying off smaller debts creates a sense of accomplishment and momentum in your debt repayment journey.

In the debt snowball approach, you begin by directing extra funds toward the debt with the smallest balance, while continuing to make minimum payments on other debts. As each smaller debt is paid off, the extra funds are then redirected to the next smallest debt. Like a conductor guiding each section of an orchestra to harmonize beautifully, you orchestrate your finances to eliminate debts one by one.

The "Debt Avalanche" Approach: Harmonizing Interest Minimization

In a symphony, each musical instrument contributes to the overall melody. Similarly, your debts contribute their own "interest melodies" to your financial composition. The "debt avalanche" approach aligns with this concept by prioritizing debts with the highest interest rates. Just as a conductor ensures that each note is played at the right time and in the right sequence, you focus on minimizing interest costs to create a harmonious reduction in your overall debt burden.

With the debt avalanche method, you allocate extra funds to the debt carrying the highest interest rate while making minimum payments on other debts. As you pay off the highest-interest debt, you move to the next highest, creating a cascade effect. This approach reduces the total interest paid over time, allowing you to achieve debt freedom more efficiently.

The Conductor's Decision: Choosing Your Repayment Strategy

In a musical composition, the conductor's choice of tempo, dynamics, and emphasis influences the emotional impact of the performance. Similarly, you must carefully select a debt repayment strategy that aligns with your financial goals and circumstances. Consider your financial personality and motivations – if the sense of accomplishment from paying off smaller debts resonates with you, the debt snowball technique may be your symphony of choice. On the other hand, if you are motivated by interest savings and overall financial efficiency, the debt avalanche approach could be your preferred melody.

Ultimately, the decision between the debt snowball and debt avalanche is a personal one, akin to a conductor choosing between different interpretations of a musical piece. Whichever approach you choose, remember that the goal is the same: to create a harmonious and controlled composition of debt reduction. Just as a conductor brings out the best in each section of an orchestra, your chosen strategy will bring out the best in your financial ensemble.

Harmonizing Your Debt Reduction

Just as a skilled conductor blends different sections of an orchestra to create a symphony, your chosen debt repayment strategy harmonizes the diverse notes of your debts into a melodious financial composition. The "debt snowball" celebrates small victories and builds momentum, while the "debt avalanche" orchestrates interest minimization for a grander finale.

In the upcoming sections, we will delve deeper into each approach, providing you with the tools and techniques to execute your chosen debt repayment strategy effectively. Like a conductor guiding a musical performance to perfection, you will guide your financial ensemble toward the harmonious resolution of debt and the crescendo of financial freedom.

6.2.3 Set Repayment Goals: Composing Financial Milestones

Imagine a musical composition with its intricate structure of melodies and rhythms. Within this composition, milestones act as signposts, guiding the listener through the journey of sound. Similarly, in the realm of debt repayment, setting specific and achievable goals serves as your guiding melody, breaking down your larger debt into manageable segments. Just as a composer carefully crafts each note to create a harmonious rhythm, your debt repayment goals create a rhythmic progression toward financial freedom.

Crafting Your Financial Score

In the symphony of debt repayment, your financial goals are akin to musical notes on a staff. Each goal represents a distinct point in your journey, contributing to the overall composition of your debt reduction plan. Much like a composer arranges notes to create an engaging melody, you arrange your goals to create an engaging financial progression.

Your financial milestones should be tailored to your individual circumstances and financial landscape. They should be specific, measurable, achievable, relevant, and time-bound – the hallmark of SMART goals. Consider these principles as the sheet music upon which you write your financial composition.

The Harmonious Rhythm of Progress

Just as a musical piece is made up of sequences of notes, your debt repayment journey is composed of sequences of achievements. Each milestone reached is a note played, contributing to the harmonic rhythm of your financial melody. These milestones not only provide a sense of accomplishment but also help you track your progress and stay motivated.

Imagine composing a symphony without any milestones or pauses. The result would be chaotic and overwhelming. Similarly, without well-defined repayment goals, your debt reduction strategy could lack direction and clarity. By breaking down your debt into smaller, achievable segments, you create a rhythmic progression that resonates with financial harmony.

The Crescendo of Financial Achievement

In a musical composition, a crescendo builds anticipation and excitement, leading to a climactic moment. Your debt repayment milestones serve as these crescendos, leading you toward your ultimate goal of debt freedom. As you reach each milestone, the sense of achievement and progress will build, culminating in the final crescendo of financial liberation.

Picture your debt reduction journey as a symphony in which each financial goal you achieve is a note played, contributing to the crescendo of your financial success. With each milestone, you are composing a harmonious narrative of discipline, determination, and fiscal responsibility.

Conducting Your Financial Ensemble

Just as a conductor guides each section of an orchestra to create a harmonious performance, you must orchestrate your financial ensemble to achieve your debt repayment goals. Your milestones serve as your baton, directing the rhythm and tempo of your financial journey.

As we continue our exploration of debt reduction strategies, remember that your milestones are the rhythmic beats that punctuate your progress. In the upcoming sections, we will delve into strategies and techniques to help you achieve these milestones effectively, ensuring that your financial composition remains on course. Just as a composer refines each note to craft a masterpiece, you will refine your financial milestones to create a symphony of debt reduction and financial empowerment.

6.2.4 Allocate Extra Funds: Enhancing the Financial Score

Imagine a musical composition that gradually builds in complexity and depth as various instruments add their unique elements. Just as a composer strategically adds embellishments to create a richer auditory experience, you have the power to enhance your debt repayment journey by allocating extra funds. This financial harmony is achieved by identifying opportunities to redirect resources from non-essential expenses, seeking additional income sources, and channeling windfalls and bonuses toward debt reduction.

Orchestrating Financial Reallocation

In the orchestra of debt reduction, financial reallocation is your conductor's baton. Just as a conductor guides the ensemble to produce a harmonious performance, you guide your financial resources to achieve a harmonious debt repayment strategy. Take a close look at your budget, much like a composer scrutinizes each musical note, and identify areas where you can trim unnecessary spending.

Consider the rhythm of your daily expenses – are there small, recurring costs that can be reduced or eliminated? Much like a composer selectively adds embellishments to elevate a musical piece, you can selectively reduce discretionary spending to amplify your debt repayment efforts.

Adding New Melodies: Exploring Additional Income

Imagine adding a new instrument to a musical ensemble, enriching the sound and adding depth. Similarly, exploring additional income sources can infuse new energy and resources into your debt repayment composition. Whether it's a part-time job, freelancing, or monetizing a hobby, these additional income streams contribute to the overall harmony of your financial symphony.

Just as a composer seeks out unique instruments to create a captivating auditory experience, you can seek out opportunities to diversify your income sources. This not only accelerates your debt repayment but also strengthens your overall financial composition, making it more resilient and dynamic.

Windfalls and Bonuses: Crescendos of Financial Progress

In a musical composition, a crescendo marks a powerful surge in sound, captivating the listener's attention. Windfalls and bonuses in your financial journey play a similar role – they are unexpected surges that can greatly impact your debt reduction melody. Redirecting these unexpected financial gains toward debt repayment is like strategically placing crescendos to enhance the emotional impact of a musical piece.

As you redirect windfalls and bonuses toward your debt, you're creating moments of heightened financial progress. Just as a composer carefully places crescendos to create a captivating musical narrative, you're crafting a compelling financial story by effectively utilizing these monetary boosts.

Harmonizing Financial Resources

Much like a composer carefully orchestrates each instrument to create a harmonious musical composition, you orchestrate your financial resources to create a harmonious debt repayment strategy. By reallocating funds from non-essential expenses, exploring additional income opportunities, and strategically using windfalls and bonuses, you enrich the melody of your financial journey.

As we move forward in this chapter, remember that you are both the composer and the conductor of your financial symphony. With each allocation of resources, you add depth and resonance to your debt reduction melody. The upcoming sections will explore further strategies to fine-tune your composition, ensuring that every note played contributes to a harmonious and triumphant financial performance.

6.2.5 Negotiate Interest Rates: Refining the Interest Harmonies

Imagine a musical masterpiece, meticulously composed with every note carefully refined to create a harmonious and captivating melody. Just as a composer dedicates time and effort to fine-tune each note, you possess the ability to refine the interest rates on your debts through the art of negotiation. This powerful adjustment has the potential to transform your financial composition, reducing the overall amount you need to repay and enhancing the rhythm of your debt reduction plan.

Conducting a Harmonious Negotiation

In the orchestra of debt reduction, negotiation assumes the role of the conductor's baton. Just as a conductor guides the musicians to achieve a harmonious and synchronized performance, you wield the tool of negotiation to attain a harmonious financial outcome. Initiating open and honest discussions with your creditors about interest rates is akin to conducting a meticulously refined symphony, where each note contributes to the overall beauty and coherence of the composition.

Negotiating interest rates is about striking the right chords with your creditors. It involves presenting your case, demonstrating your unwavering commitment to debt reduction, and skillfully aligning your financial goals with the creditor's interests. This delicate process necessitates effective communication and the ability to harmonize your aspirations with the creditor's perspectives.

Lower Interest Rates: The Key Notes of Debt Reduction

Imagine lower interest rates as the key notes that unlock the true potential of your debt reduction melody. Just as certain musical notes infuse depth and emotion into a composition, lower interest rates infuse depth and efficiency into your debt repayment plan. These adjusted rates serve as the underlying harmony that allows your melody to resound more brightly and melodiously.

By securing lower interest rates on your debts, you create an environment where your debt repayment efforts are optimized. With each payment you make, a greater proportion of your contribution goes directly towards reducing the principal amount rather than being consumed by interest. This refined arrangement ensures that your debt reduction melody is clear, impactful, and resonant.

The Symphony of Savings: The Impact of Refinement

As you embark on negotiations to refine the interest rates on your debts, you are essentially composing a symphony of savings. Much like a composer meticulously arranges various instruments to achieve a balanced and evocative musical piece, you are orchestrating the financial elements of your debt repayment strategy to achieve equilibrium and efficiency.

Lower interest rates contribute significantly to the overall harmony of your financial composition. They alleviate the weight of debt, liberating more resources for repayment, and hastening your journey towards financial liberation. As you continue delving into the chapters ahead, remember that negotiation is a pivotal instrument in your financial orchestra. It refines the interest harmonies, allowing your debt reduction melody to crescendo with power, purpose, and profound impact.

In the upcoming sections, we shall delve deeper into an array of strategies and techniques that will further refine and elevate your debt repayment plan. With negotiation as your guiding baton, each note you play will be an essential element of your harmonious, triumphant, and ultimately successful financial performance.

6.2.6 Consolidate Debt: Harmonizing Financial Instruments

Envision a symphony where various instruments join forces, each playing a distinct role to create a harmonious and impactful musical experience. Similarly, consolidating debt is akin to orchestrating your financial instruments to play in unison, producing a melodious arrangement that simplifies your debt composition. Just as a conductor harmonizes different sections of an orchestra, debt consolidation harmonizes your outstanding balances, streamlining your path towards debt freedom.

The Conductor of Debt Consolidation

In the realm of finances, debt consolidation acts as the conductor that guides the ensemble of your debts. Just as a skilled conductor brings together diverse instruments to create a coherent and captivating performance, debt consolidation unifies your debts under a single arrangement. This consolidation can take various forms, including balance transfers or consolidation loans, and is designed to simplify the intricate composition of multiple debts.

Imagine this process as the conductor bringing the strings, woodwinds, brass, and percussion sections together to create a symphony that is greater than the sum of its parts. Similarly, debt consolidation unifies your debts, allowing you to focus on a single, orchestrated repayment plan rather than juggling multiple accounts and due dates.

The Melody of Simplification and Potential Savings

Just as a musical piece gains clarity when harmonious elements come together, your financial composition gains clarity through debt consolidation. By consolidating your debts, you streamline your financial obligations, making them more manageable and easier to track. This streamlined melody ensures that you no longer feel overwhelmed by the cacophony of multiple payments and varying interest rates.

Additionally, debt consolidation has the potential to introduce a harmonious note of financial relief. For instance, balance transfers to a credit card with a lower interest rate can help reduce the amount of interest you accrue. Similarly, a consolidation loan may offer a more favorable interest rate compared to the collective rates of your existing debts. This newfound harmony translates into potential savings, allowing you to allocate more resources towards the principal amount and accelerate your journey towards debt freedom.

Fine-Tuning Your Debt Repayment Cadence

Just as a conductor refines the tempo and cadence of a musical piece, debt consolidation fine-tunes the rhythm of your debt repayment. It allows you to establish a structured plan with a clear beginning, middle, and end. This organized arrangement empowers you to monitor your progress and make adjustments as needed, ensuring that your debt repayment melody is on track and harmonious.

However, it's important to approach debt consolidation with a composed and well-informed strategy. Consider the terms, fees, and potential impact on your credit score before proceeding. Just as a conductor carefully selects the instruments to create the desired sound, you should carefully evaluate consolidation options to ensure they align with your financial goals and aspirations.

As you venture into the following sections, keep in mind the analogy of a harmonious orchestra. Debt consolidation serves as the conductor that unites your debts into a synchronized composition, allowing you to create a clear and resonant financial melody. By taking control of your financial instruments and harmonizing their elements, you are poised to conduct a debt reduction performance that is both empowering and melodious.

6.3 Strategies for Reducing Debt

Imagine your financial life as a composition—an intricate symphony that plays out over time. Just as a symphony is carefully orchestrated, your approach to managing and reducing debt requires a well-composed strategy. This chapter delves into the art of harmonizing your financial symphony through effective debt reduction strategies.

6.3.1 Budgeting and Expense Tracking: The Rhythmic Harmony

Creating the Financial Score: Crafting Your Budget Sheet

In the grand orchestra of your financial journey, budgeting and expense tracking function as the rhythm section, establishing the cadence for effective debt reduction. Much like a conductor's baton guides musicians through a complex musical piece, your budget serves as the guiding force behind your financial decisions and behaviors. It ensures that your debt repayment melody resonates in perfect harmony, orchestrating the various financial instruments at your disposal.

Crafting a Symphony of Financial Well-being

Crafting a budget is akin to composing the sheet music for your financial symphony. Just as a composer carefully arranges notes and instruments to create a harmonious composition, you meticulously outline your income sources and meticulously detail every expense. This process results in a structured and organized composition that vividly outlines the destination of each dollar in your possession.

Similar to how a conductor painstakingly ensures that each musician plays their note at the right time and intensity, your budget meticulously allocates resources to each aspect of your financial life. Each dollar finds its purpose, contributing to the overall rhythm and flow of your financial symphony.

The Conductor of Financial Choices

A conductor's role extends beyond guiding musicians; it involves interpreting the composer's intentions and bringing the musical piece to life. Similarly, your budget interprets your financial goals and aspirations, infusing life into your fiscal aspirations. It serves as the conductor that directs your financial choices, ensuring that every decision resonates with the overarching melody of debt reduction and financial stability.

Harmony Through Thoughtful Allocation

Much like a conductor ensures that no instrument overwhelms the others, your budget prevents any one expense from dominating your financial composition. It allocates funds thoughtfully, considering the needs of each category while maintaining the harmony of your financial symphony. This careful distribution of resources prevents disharmony, allowing your debt reduction melody to shine through without undue strain.

In essence, your budget becomes the guardian of fiscal discipline, curating a harmonious arrangement that accommodates your needs, obligations, and aspirations. By harmonizing income and expenses, your budget ensures that your financial symphony resonates with clarity and purpose.

Final Notes on Crafting Your Budget

Just as a musical composition may require adjustments during rehearsals, your budget may also undergo refinement. Regular reviews and adjustments ensure that your budget remains in tune with your evolving financial circumstances. As life introduces new variations and melodies, your budget adapts accordingly, maintaining the harmonious progression of your debt reduction symphony.

As we delve further into this chapter, you will encounter an array of strategies that complement the rhythm set by your budget. Each of these strategies will play a unique instrument in your financial orchestra, contributing to the harmonious arrangement of debt reduction. But it all begins with the crafting of your budget—the foundational sheet music that guides your financial symphony towards the crescendo of debt freedom.

Fine-Tuning and Rehearsal: Regular Expense Tracking

Just as a composer continually refines a musical composition to achieve perfection, a budget is a living entity that requires ongoing attention and adjustment. A budget isn't merely a static blueprint; it's a dynamic process, much like the conductor's role in guiding a performance. In this ongoing financial symphony, regular expense tracking assumes the role of a vigilant ear, attuned to every note, ensuring that your financial melody remains harmonious and aligned with your debt reduction goals.

Conducting a Continuous Financial Performance

A budget is not a one-time creation; it's a tool for orchestrating a perpetual performance of financial prudence. Just as a conductor adapts the tempo of a musical piece to match the mood and context, your budget needs periodic adjustments to align with changing financial circumstances. Regularly revisiting and fine-tuning your budget ensures that it continues to direct your financial decisions effectively.

Listening to the Rhythms of Spending Habits

As you engage in meticulous tracking of your financial transactions, you immerse yourself in the intricate rhythms of your spending habits. Each transaction becomes a musical note, contributing to the overall composition of your financial symphony. This process reveals patterns, revealing both harmonious melodies and dissonant notes that may be disrupting the flow of your financial composition.

By examining these patterns, you can identify areas of overspending or unnecessary dissonance. These financial "off-key" notes represent expenses that are out of tune with your debt reduction goals. Just as a conductor refines a musical performance through rigorous rehearsal, your regular expense tracking allows you to pinpoint these discordant elements within your financial score.

Fine-Tuning Your Financial Performance

Imagine a conductor guiding an orchestra through repeated rehearsals to enhance the quality of a musical performance. Similarly, your budget, coupled with consistent expense tracking, empowers you to refine and enhance your financial performance. By making necessary adjustments, you replace these discordant financial elements with harmonious choices that resonate with your debt reduction objectives.

Perhaps you identify an expense category where you consistently overspend, akin to a section of instruments that occasionally overpower the melody in a musical piece. Through vigilant expense tracking, you can correct this imbalance, reallocating funds to ensure a harmonious progression towards your debt reduction goals.

A Symphony of Financial Progress

The process of regular expense tracking and budget refinement is akin to rehearsing for a grand symphony. Each iteration fine-tunes your financial performance, enhancing the overall composition. By paying attention to the nuances of your spending, you bring your financial symphony closer to the crescendo of debt freedom.

Just as a conductor meticulously listens to every instrument, ensuring they blend seamlessly, your expense tracking allows you to create a cohesive and harmonious financial composition. With each adjustment, you harmonize your financial choices, orchestrating a symphony of progress that resonates with the melody of debt reduction and financial well-being.

As you proceed through this chapter, remember that while budgeting sets the initial tempo, consistent expense tracking and adjustment maintain the rhythm of your financial performance. With your budget as the conductor's baton and expense tracking as the attentive ear, you're poised to create a symphony of financial success that's in perfect harmony with your debt reduction goals.

Maintaining the Rhythm: Directing Resources Towards Debt Reduction

In the grand symphony of your financial journey, budgeting and expense tracking are the rhythm section that sets the tempo and beat for your debt reduction composition. Just as a conductor guides the orchestra with precise rhythm and timing, your budget and expense tracking direct your financial resources toward the symphony of debt repayment goals, ensuring a steady and consistent progression. This rhythmic harmony serves as the foundation for a powerful and resonant debt reduction symphony, where every note of financial control and freedom rings true.

The Rhythmic Dance of Budgeting and Expense Tracking

Think of your budget as the sheet music that outlines the rhythm and notes of your financial composition. It details your income sources, orchestrates your expenses, and assigns each dollar a specific purpose. In harmony with your budget, expense tracking acts as the vigilant conductor, ensuring that every financial move is in line with the established rhythm.

With every expense tracked, every financial decision guided, you maintain the rhythm of your debt reduction symphony. This rhythm is not only about managing day-to-day spending but also about strategically allocating resources toward your debt repayment goals. Just as a conductor keeps the orchestra in sync, your budget and expense tracking keep your financial resources aligned with the goal of reducing debt.

Creating the Foundation for Harmonious Debt Reduction

Much like a strong rhythm section is essential for a captivating musical performance, a well-structured budget and diligent expense tracking are vital for effective debt reduction. The rhythm and beat they provide ensure that you are not only making consistent payments towards your debts but also making informed and intentional financial choices.

By maintaining this rhythm, you lay the groundwork for a harmonious debt reduction symphony. Your financial resources flow seamlessly, contributing to the overall composition of reducing debt and achieving financial freedom. With every budgeted dollar, with every tracked expense, you're conducting a masterpiece of financial discipline and responsibility.

Charting the Path Forward

As you progress through the chapters ahead, you will explore various strategies and techniques that build upon this rhythmic foundation. Each section of this financial symphony contributes to the overall harmony of debt reduction. From negotiating interest rates to exploring debt repayment methods, you'll orchestrate a comprehensive approach that resonates with your unique financial situation.

In the upcoming sections, we will delve deeper into the orchestration of your debt reduction strategies. We will begin by exploring the rhythmic harmony of budgeting and expense tracking. Just as a composer meticulously crafts each note, you will learn to craft a financial composition that leads you towards the crescendo of debt reduction and ultimately, financial liberation.

6.3.2 Debt Snowball or Debt Avalanche: Crafting Musical Strategies

In the grand orchestration of debt reduction, envision two distinct musical compositions – the Debt Snowball and the Debt Avalanche. Each approach carries its own melody and rhythm, creating contrasting yet harmonious pathways towards your goal of financial liberation. Just as a composer carefully selects notes to create a masterpiece, you must carefully choose between these two strategies to craft a debt reduction symphony that resonates with your financial journey.

The Crescendo of the Debt Snowball

Imagine the Debt Snowball as a musical composition that begins with a soft, almost imperceptible note – a whisper that sets the tone for a remarkable journey. This approach orchestrates a crescendo of financial progress, gradually building momentum until it reaches a triumphant and resounding peak. Just as a conductor guides an orchestra through a meticulously crafted piece, you will orchestrate your debt reduction symphony with the Debt Snowball technique.

Picture yourself standing at the conductor's podium, ready to lead your financial ensemble. The Debt Snowball strategy prompts you to focus on paying off your smaller debts first, creating a delicate yet empowering opening sequence. These smaller debts, akin to the opening notes of a melodious composition, are addressed with unwavering determination and fervor.

As each modest debt is met and conquered, the tempo of your financial symphony quickens. The melody gains depth, and the rhythm becomes more pronounced, echoing the heartbeat of your financial journey. This method isn't solely about the monetary value of these smaller debts; it's about the emotional resonance they hold. With every debt settled, a harmonious sense of accomplishment and motivation fills the air.

The Debt Snowball technique harnesses the psychological power of quick wins. Similar to a series of beautifully harmonized notes, the satisfaction of eliminating these smaller debts one by one creates a symphony of fulfilling resolutions. Each debt paid off adds to the chorus of accomplishments, creating a harmonious composition that resonates with your determination and willpower.

This symphony of progress does more than just reduce your debt load; it uplifts your financial spirit. Just as a rising crescendo in a musical piece evokes powerful emotions, your journey through the Debt Snowball method kindles a sense of achievement, propelling you forward in your debt reduction odyssey.

The Debt Snowball isn't just a strategy; it's a symphonic arrangement of financial empowerment. It is the delicate opening movement that transforms into a majestic finale. With every smaller debt vanquished, the melody of your financial composition intensifies, creating an uplifting and inspiring experience. As the conductor of this financial symphony, you wield the baton of determination, crafting a masterpiece that harmonizes with your pursuit of debt freedom.

The Harmonious Reduction of the Debt Avalanche

In the symphony of debt reduction, the Debt Avalanche emerges as a distinct composition – one characterized by precision, strategy, and meticulous attention to detail. Envision this approach as a seasoned conductor guiding a symphony through intricate harmonies, each note meticulously placed to create a masterpiece. The Debt Avalanche strategy directs your financial efforts like the conductor's baton, channeling your energy towards the most resonant and impactful notes.

Imagine yourself at the helm of this symphonic endeavor, leading your financial ensemble with a steady hand. The Debt Avalanche is akin to crafting a symphony where each note is chosen deliberately, each instrument playing its part with purpose. In this composition, your focus is directed towards debts with the highest interest rates – the sharpest and most dominant notes in your financial score.

Picture the Debt Avalanche conductor, guiding the orchestra's precision as they navigate complex harmonies. Similarly, you orchestrate your financial resources towards the most resonant debts, those that accrue the highest interest costs. This strategic focus isn't just about settling debts; it's about creating a harmonious reduction in overall interest expenses.

With every high-interest debt that succumbs to your efforts, the symphony of the Debt Avalanche gains momentum. As the crescendo builds, the reduction in interest charges adds a profound depth to the composition. The resulting financial melody becomes smoother, resonating with the strategic symphony you've conducted. While the Debt Avalanche may not provide the immediate gratification of the Debt Snowball, it cultivates a symphonic progression that optimizes your financial resources.

Unlike the quick crescendo of the Debt Snowball, the Debt Avalanche is a gradual composition that requires meticulous attention. It may not provide the same instant gratification, but it creates a calculated and strategic progression towards debt freedom. Each payment made towards high-interest debts adds another layer of harmonious reduction to the symphony, refining the financial composition with each passing note.

As the maestro of your financial symphony, the Debt Avalanche conductor guides your efforts towards a crescendo of debt reduction. With each high-interest debt that is vanquished, the symphony gains clarity and depth. The meticulous focus on interest rates and strategic repayment builds a resonant and impactful composition, ultimately leading to a symphonic climax of debt reduction. Just as a conductor shapes the unique sound of an orchestra, you shape the cadence of your financial future with the strategic precision of the Debt Avalanche.

Choosing Your Musical Path

As you find yourself standing at the crossroads of debt reduction, envision yourself as a composer selecting the perfect melody for your financial symphony. Just as a composer carefully chooses notes to create a harmonious piece, you have the opportunity to select the debt reduction composition that resonates most with your financial goals and personality.

On one side of the musical spectrum is the Debt Snowball, a composition that offers a series of melodic victories, each note contributing to a crescendo of accomplishments. Envision this path as a musical journey filled with quick wins and triumphant resolutions. Much like the opening notes of a melody, the Debt Snowball method focuses on paying off smaller debts first. This approach provides a psychological boost as you experience a string of victories, each debt paid off adding to the harmony of your financial composition. If you're seeking emotional gratification and motivation through rapid achievements, the Debt Snowball is your chosen melody.

On the other side of the spectrum, the Debt Avalanche stands as a composition characterized by calculated efficiency. Imagine this path as a symphony guided by precision and strategic focus. In the world of financial melodies, the Debt Avalanche directs your efforts towards debts with the highest interest rates. It's like channeling your energy into the most resonant and impactful notes, crafting a symphonic reduction in overall interest costs. While the immediate gratification of the Debt Snowball might be absent, the Debt Avalanche offers an optimized approach that ultimately reduces the financial dissonance caused by high-interest debts. If you're seeking a meticulously crafted symphony that strategically minimizes interest expenses, the Debt Avalanche is your chosen composition.

Your choice between these two debt reduction melodies hinges on your financial aspirations and the tune that resonates most with your personality. Are you drawn to the crescendo of quick wins and the emotional reward they bring? Or do you find harmony in the precision of strategic efficiency, where interest reduction is the paramount note? Your financial composition is uniquely yours, and the path you select will influence the symphony of your debt reduction journey.

Just as a composer's choice shapes the character of a musical piece, your decision between the Debt Snowball and Debt Avalanche shapes the rhythm of your financial composition. Consider your goals, preferences, and the harmonies you wish to create within your financial symphony. Whether you opt for the crescendo of victories or the calculated efficiency of interest reduction, your chosen melody will lead you toward the harmonious debt reduction composition that aligns with your financial aspirations.

Just as a conductor tailors a performance to the music at hand, select the strategy that harmonizes with your financial symphony. Whether you opt for the crescendo of the Debt Snowball or the harmonious reduction of the Debt Avalanche, remember that both approaches contribute to the overall composition of debt reduction. With careful crafting and intentional choice, you will conduct a debt reduction symphony that resonates with financial success.

6.3.3 Lifestyle Adjustments: Adjusting the Financial Dynamics

In the symphony of your financial journey, sometimes a change in dynamics is needed to create the desired harmony. Just as a conductor adjusts musical dynamics to evoke different emotions, you can make temporary lifestyle adjustments to fine-tune your financial composition. These adaptations involve altering certain aspects of your day-to-day life, ultimately contributing to a more balanced and harmonious financial melody.

Downsizing Living Arrangements: Softening the Financial Crescendo

In the intricate composition of your financial journey, the concept of downsizing living arrangements plays a pivotal role, much like a composer modulating the volume of a musical piece. Just as a skilled conductor guides the orchestra to achieve a balanced and harmonious performance, you have the opportunity to explore the option of downsizing your living space, orchestrating a reduction in financial strain and allowing for a more harmonious debt reduction symphony.

Imagine this adjustment as a deliberate shift from a forte to a pianissimo, creating a softer and more controlled financial crescendo. This could involve considering a move to a smaller, more affordable home or exploring alternative housing options that align with your current financial objectives. By harmonizing your living arrangements with your debt reduction goals, you craft a smoother rhythm within your financial composition.

The impact of this choice is profound. By reducing housing expenses, you effectively adjust the volume of your financial obligations, allowing other instruments, such as debt repayment, to take the spotlight. This strategic maneuver introduces a gentler and more manageable tempo to your financial composition. With fewer financial obligations resonating at a high volume, you can redirect your resources towards your debt reduction melody, amplifying your progress and moving closer to your desired financial harmony.

Much like a masterful composer who understands the nuances of modulation, you too can control the financial modulation of your life by carefully considering the option of downsizing living arrangements. By orchestrating this adjustment, you take control of the financial dynamics, ensuring that your composition remains in tune with your aspirations and objectives. In doing so, you create a financial melody that is not only pleasing to the ear but also aligned with your ultimate goal of achieving a debt-free and harmonious future.

Curbing Discretionary Spending: Transitioning from Forte to Pianissimo

In the symphony of your financial journey, the concept of curbing discretionary spending resembles a skilled musician's transition from a resonant forte to a gentle pianissimo. Just as a musician skillfully adjusts the intensity of their performance to convey different emotions, you have the power to transition from extravagant spending to more mindful choices, thus creating a harmonious balance within your financial composition.

Imagine this transition as a deliberate change in musical dynamics, where the extravagance of a forte is replaced by the subtlety of a pianissimo. This involves a thoughtful evaluation of your discretionary expenses, including activities such as dining out, entertainment, and non-essential purchases. By consciously curbing these expenditures, you orchestrate a shift in the tempo of your financial composition, allowing for a more moderate and controlled rhythm.

Much like a skilled musician's ability to seamlessly transition between different musical dynamics, you too can navigate the ebb and flow of your financial choices. By reducing discretionary spending, you effectively adjust the volume of your financial commitments, creating a space for other financial elements to take center stage. This intentional shift introduces a sense of balance and restraint, allowing your financial composition to breathe and harmonize more effectively.

The impact of this adjustment is significant. By curbing discretionary spending, you create a financial melody that is characterized by prudent and mindful choices. This deliberate transition from a loud forte to a gentle pianissimo ensures that your financial composition is not overwhelmed by unnecessary expenses. Instead, it allows the underlying themes of financial flexibility and debt reduction to shine through, contributing to a more harmonious and resonant composition.

In the grand orchestration of your financial journey, curbing discretionary spending becomes a powerful instrument in your repertoire. By deftly managing this aspect of your financial dynamics, you craft a composition that is not only melodious but also aligned with your overarching goal of achieving greater financial control and debt reduction. Just as a musician's mastery lies in their ability to interpret and adjust their performance, your financial finesse shines through as you transition from extravagant spending to the artful restraint of prudent choices.

Innovative Utility and Transportation Practices: Introducing Fresh Harmonies

In the symphony of your financial journey, the notion of innovative utility and transportation practices serves as a creative crescendo, introducing fresh harmonies that elevate your financial composition. Just as a composer experiments with innovative techniques to infuse a musical piece with unique melodies, you too have the opportunity to explore inventive ways to reduce utility and transportation costs, creating a symphony of sustainability and fiscal responsibility.

Imagine this exploration as a musician's quest for novel sounds, where innovative practices lead to the discovery of fresh harmonies. This entails adopting energy-efficient habits, such as conserving electricity and water, and seeking out eco-friendly alternatives. Additionally, it involves reimagining your transportation routines by embracing carpooling, utilizing public transportation, or even incorporating biking and walking into your daily routine. As these innovative strategies find their place within your financial composition, they create a distinctive rhythm that harmonizes with your debt reduction goals.

Just as a composer introduces unexpected elements to captivate the audience's attention, your incorporation of innovative practices introduces a captivating rhythm to your financial composition. This rhythm is marked by conscious choices that not only reduce your ecological footprint but also liberate funds that can be redirected towards your debt repayment endeavors. The result is a symphony of financial responsibility and environmental mindfulness, where the harmonies of sustainable practices blend seamlessly with the overarching melody of debt reduction.

The impact of these innovative practices reverberates throughout your financial composition. By embracing energy-efficient habits, you reduce the discordant notes of excessive utility costs, creating a smoother and more harmonious financial melody. Likewise, by adopting alternative transportation methods, you enhance the fluidity of your financial rhythms, ensuring that resources flow efficiently towards your debt reduction goals. This orchestration of innovative utility and transportation practices introduces a dynamic interplay of elements, enlivening your financial composition with a vibrant and forward-moving tempo.

In the grand symphony of your financial journey, the inclusion of innovative utility and transportation practices is akin to introducing a captivating new theme that enhances the overall composition. By embracing these harmonious techniques, you not only contribute to the preservation of both financial and environmental resources but also infuse your debt reduction melody with a renewed sense of purpose and vitality. As a conductor of your financial destiny, your thoughtful incorporation of innovative practices creates a symphony that resonates with sustainable fiscal harmony.

These lifestyle adjustments are like subtle changes in musical dynamics that enhance the overall composition. By carefully orchestrating downsizing, curbing spending, and embracing innovative practices, you create a financial melody that is not only pleasing but also aligned with your debt reduction goals. Just as a conductor guides musicians to achieve a balanced and harmonious performance, these adjustments guide you towards a more symphonic and debt-free financial future.

6.3.4 Additional Income Sources: Enriching the Financial Orchestra

Exploring New Crescendos: The Symphony of Additional Income

Harmonizing Part-Time Pursuits: A Melodic Approach

In the grand orchestration of your financial journey, the concept of seeking additional income sources serves as a captivating crescendo that enriches the overall composition. Just as a composer introduces new instruments to breathe life into a musical piece, you too have the opportunity to explore diverse avenues that contribute fresh notes to your financial melody. By engaging in part-time work, freelancing, or transforming a personal passion into a lucrative venture, you amplify the harmonious progression of your debt reduction opus.

Embracing a Duet of Opportunities. Envision your pursuit of part-time work as a harmonious duet, with your primary occupation serving as the main melody and your additional income source creating an intricate counterpoint. Similar to how a musical duet involves two distinct voices melding together, your part-time endeavor harmonizes with your main income, enhancing the depth and resonance of your financial composition.

Conducting a Symphony of Flexibility. Just as a conductor skillfully orchestrates various sections of an ensemble, your involvement in part-time work requires a symphony of flexibility. You seamlessly integrate this pursuit into your schedule, ensuring it complements your primary responsibilities. This flexibility allows you to strike a harmonious balance between your main occupation and your additional income, generating an ensemble of financial stability and growth.

Freelancing: Crafting Unique Melodies

Imagine freelancing as crafting unique musical melodies that add complexity and depth to a composition. In a similar fashion, freelancing introduces a distinctive financial melody that intertwines with your main income. Your freelancing pursuits may involve your professional skills, creative talents, or even a hobby you're passionate about. This multifaceted approach adds layers of harmonious financial progression, contributing to your debt reduction symphony.

Transforming Passion into Profit: A Crescendo of Innovation

Consider the transformative power of transforming a personal passion into a profitable venture. Just as a composer infuses emotion into a musical piece, you infuse your passions into a revenue-generating enterprise. This creative endeavor adds a crescendo of innovation to your financial composition. Whether you're selling crafts, offering consulting services, or conducting workshops, your venture becomes a key player in your debt reduction orchestra.

The Harmonious Ensemble: A Flourishing Financial Composition

As each instrument in an orchestra contributes to a harmonious ensemble, your pursuit of part-time work, freelancing, or entrepreneurial ventures enriches the symphony of your financial journey. Each note played by your additional income sources resonates with purpose, enhancing the overall melody of debt reduction. Your financial composition gains depth, texture, and resilience, creating a harmonious ensemble that conducts you toward your debt-free finale.

Symphonic Freelancing: A Concerto of Financial Growth

Envision this pursuit of additional income as a composer's quest to integrate new instruments, each contributing its unique timbre to the composition. Similarly, you can embark on symphonic endeavors such as taking on a part-time job or freelancing in your area of expertise. These endeavors introduce new financial notes that seamlessly blend with the existing melody, creating a richer and more intricate arrangement. Just as each instrument enhances the overall sound of a musical piece, each additional income source enhances your financial composition, allowing for a more robust and resonant progression.

Turning Passion into Profit: The Overture of Personal Ventures

Furthermore, consider the transformative potential of turning a personal passion into a revenue-generating endeavor. Much like a composer infuses a musical piece with emotion and meaning, your hobbies and talents can be harnessed to generate income. Whether it's photography, writing, crafting, or any other skill, these pursuits have the potential to add depth and variety to your financial symphony. By exploring these creative avenues, you not only enhance your financial resources but also infuse your debt reduction journey with a newfound sense of purpose and enthusiasm.

Harmonious Financial Arrangement: A Multifaceted Melody

The impact of these additional income sources reverberates throughout your financial composition. Just as the introduction of new instruments adds layers of complexity to a musical arrangement, the integration of additional income streams enriches the depth and texture of your financial melody. The increased funds generated through these pursuits provide a harmonious counterpoint to your debt reduction efforts, allowing for a more robust and efficient progression toward your financial goals.

Conducting the Financial Symphony: Empowering the Melody

In the grand symphony of your financial journey, the pursuit of additional income sources serves as a dynamic movement that elevates the overall composition. By embracing part-time work, freelancing, or capitalizing on your passions, you infuse your financial opus with an empowered tempo. This enrichment of your financial orchestra not only accelerates your debt reduction but also transforms your financial landscape into a multifaceted and harmonious masterpiece. As a conductor of your financial destiny, your orchestration of additional income sources adds depth and resonance to your debt reduction symphony.

6.3.5 Debt Counseling and Consolidation: Seeking Professional Conductors

The Role of Debt Counseling: Guiding Your Financial Symphony

6.3.5 Debt Counseling and Consolidation: Professional Guidance for Debt Management

Debt counseling and consolidation services play a significant role in helping you effectively manage and reduce your debts. These professional resources offer guidance and support to navigate the complexities of debt, ensuring a smoother path towards financial stability.

Expert Insights and Strategies

Debt counselors bring expert insights and strategies to your debt reduction journey. They assess your financial situation, analyze your debts, and develop personalized plans tailored to your specific needs. Their expertise helps you make informed decisions and craft a clear pathway towards debt reduction and eventual financial freedom.

Negotiation and Coordination

Debt counselors also engage in negotiations with your creditors on your behalf. Through these negotiations, they aim to secure favorable terms such as reduced interest rates or waived fees. This process not only helps in decreasing the overall debt burden but also contributes to a more manageable and structured repayment plan.

Consolidation for Clarity

Debt consolidation is another facet of debt management. It involves combining multiple debts into a single payment, simplifying your financial obligations. This can make it easier to keep track of payments, avoid missed deadlines, and create a more organized approach to debt reduction.

Creating a Structured Plan

Both debt counseling and consolidation assist you in creating a structured plan to tackle your debts. This plan serves as a roadmap, outlining the steps you need to take and the timeline for achieving your debt reduction goals. Having a well-defined plan in place provides a sense of direction and control over your financial situation.

Support Throughout the Journey

Perhaps most importantly, debt counseling and consolidation services offer ongoing support throughout your debt reduction journey. They act as partners who are invested in your financial success, providing guidance, answering your questions, and offering solutions if unexpected challenges arise.

A Clearer Financial Path

In essence, debt counseling and consolidation provide you with a clearer financial path forward. They help you navigate the complexities of debt, provide expert guidance, and offer practical strategies to overcome your financial challenges. With their assistance, you can approach debt reduction with confidence and work towards a more secure and stable financial future.

Negotiating with Creditor Harmonies

Debt negotiation is a key aspect of debt management, akin to a harmonious collaboration between a conductor and an orchestra. Debt counselors take on the role of negotiators, working closely with your creditors to create more favorable terms for debt repayment. This collaborative effort is instrumental in orchestrating a smoother path toward reducing your debts and achieving financial stability.

Effective Communication

Much like a conductor communicates with musicians to bring out the best performance, debt counselors engage in effective communication with your creditors. They articulate your financial situation, your commitment to resolving the debt, and your willingness to cooperate. This open line of communication sets the stage for productive negotiations.

Seeking Favorable Terms

Debt negotiation is all about seeking favorable terms that can ease your debt burden. Debt counselors strive to lower high-interest rates that often contribute to the escalation of debt. They also aim to have fees and penalties waived or reduced, which can significantly reduce the overall amount you owe.

Structuring Feasible Repayment Plans

Just as a conductor arranges musical notes to create a harmonious composition, debt counselors work to structure feasible repayment plans. These plans are designed to align with your financial capacity and resources. By collaborating with creditors, debt counselors help design repayment schedules that you can realistically adhere to, ensuring consistent progress toward debt reduction.

Minimizing Stress and Conflict

Negotiating with creditors can be stressful and daunting, similar to maintaining harmony within a complex musical arrangement. Debt counselors take on this burden, acting as intermediaries to minimize potential conflicts and disputes. Their expertise and experience allow for smoother negotiations and more successful outcomes.

The Conductor of Debt Resolution

In many ways, debt counselors function as conductors in the symphony of debt resolution. They orchestrate negotiations, harmonize the interests of both parties, and guide the process toward a positive resolution. Just as a conductor shapes the music's emotional journey, debt counselors shape the course of debt repayment, striving for a more manageable and harmonious financial future.

A Harmonious Resolution

In conclusion, debt negotiation through debt counselors creates a harmonious resolution to the challenge of debt management. Their skills in communication, negotiation, and compromise ensure that your debt repayment arrangements are conducive to your financial well-being. Through collaborative efforts, debt negotiation paves the way for a more balanced and harmonious financial composition, leading you closer to a debt-free future.

The Unified Composition of Debt Consolidation

Debt consolidation stands as a unified approach to managing multiple debts, akin to the harmonious blending of musical instruments in an orchestra. Just as various instruments with different tones and timbres create a unified sound, debt consolidation brings together multiple debts into a single, manageable entity. This financial strategy simplifies the repayment process, allowing you to focus on a unified and structured plan, rather than juggling various financial obligations.

Creating a Consolidated Ensemble

Imagine debt consolidation as a conductor skillfully assembling an orchestra, where each instrument contributes to a cohesive performance. Similarly, debt consolidation assembles your outstanding debts – credit card balances, personal loans, and other obligations – into a single debt instrument. This consolidated approach streamlines the repayment process, making it more convenient to manage.

Simplifying Repayment

Much like a conductor directs musicians to play in harmony, debt consolidation directs your debts into a single monthly payment. This simplifies your financial score, making it easier to keep track of payments and deadlines.

Rather than managing multiple due dates and payment amounts, you have one clear rhythm of repayment.

Potential Interest Savings

Debt consolidation, like the careful arrangement of musical notes, can lead to potential interest savings. By consolidating high-interest debts into a single lower-interest loan or credit option, you may reduce the overall interest you pay. This creates a harmonious financial outcome – less interest paid over time, allowing more of your funds to contribute to the principal balance.

Enhanced Financial Management

Just as a conductor guides the orchestra to a synchronized performance, debt consolidation guides your debts toward a more synchronized resolution. It enhances your financial management by offering a clearer overview of your debt landscape. This holistic perspective enables you to make informed decisions and adjustments as needed, creating a harmonious path to debt reduction.

Choosing the Right Conductor

Selecting the right conductor is vital for a successful orchestral performance. Similarly, choosing the right debt consolidation method is crucial for a successful financial composition. You have options like balance transfer, debt consolidation loans, or debt management programs. Each serves as a different conductor, guiding your debts toward unified harmony. It's essential to research and determine which approach best aligns with your financial goals and circumstances.

The Harmonic Outcome

In sum, debt consolidation orchestrates a harmonious financial outcome. By merging multiple debts into a single entity, it simplifies repayment, potentially reduces interest costs, and enhances overall financial management. Just as a conductor's expertise shapes a musical performance, debt consolidation shapes your journey toward debt reduction, leading you closer to a financially harmonious future.

Crafting Structured Repayment Arrangements

Structured repayment plans, akin to a well-composed musical sequence, are the heart of effective debt consolidation. Just as a composer arranges musical notes to create a harmonious melody, debt consolidation experts design repayment plans tailored to your unique financial situation. These plans establish the tempo and rhythm for your debt reduction journey, offering a clear and organized route toward achieving your debt-free goals.

Customized Composition

Imagine a structured repayment plan as a customized musical composition, meticulously crafted to resonate with your financial capabilities. Debt consolidation professionals take into account your income, expenses, and debt obligations to design a plan that suits your financial melody. This tailored approach ensures that your repayment plan is neither too fast nor too slow – it's a tempo that aligns with your current financial rhythm.

Setting the Tempo

Much like a composer sets the tempo of a musical piece, a structured repayment plan sets the pace of your debt reduction journey. This established tempo ensures that you make consistent, manageable payments toward your consolidated debt. It prevents the financial equivalent of rushing through complex musical passages or lagging behind, creating a balanced and sustainable repayment rhythm.

Rhythmic Progression

A well-crafted repayment plan orchestrates a rhythmic progression toward your debt-free destination. Each payment contributes to the overall composition, much like each note contributes to a musical piece. As you follow the plan, you experience a sense of steady advancement, moving closer to your goal with every payment made. This consistent rhythm builds a foundation of discipline and determination.

Harmonious Alignment

Just as musical arrangements are tailored to suit the performers and the occasion, structured repayment plans are aligned with your unique financial circumstances. The plan harmonizes with your income, ensuring that monthly payments are manageable and sustainable. This harmonious alignment prevents financial strains and ensures that your debt reduction composition is melodious and balanced.

Conductor of Your Debt Repayment Symphony

In the realm of debt consolidation, you are the conductor guiding your debt repayment symphony. With a structured repayment plan, you wield the baton that directs your financial choices and actions. Each payment is a note in your composition, playing a vital role in the harmonious progression toward becoming debt-free.

The Crescendo of Debt Freedom

As your structured repayment plan unfolds, it builds toward a crescendo of debt freedom. The steady rhythm of payments, like the progression of musical notes, culminates in a triumphant resolution – the complete repayment of your consolidated debt. This harmonious culmination reflects your dedication, financial discipline, and the power of a well-orchestrated debt reduction plan.

Conclusion: A Harmonious Debt Composition

In conclusion, structured repayment plans compose a harmonious debt reduction composition. Much like a musical masterpiece, these plans are carefully designed to resonate with your financial abilities and aspirations. They set the tempo, guide your rhythm, and lead you on a journey toward debt freedom. As you follow this financial score, you orchestrate a symphony of disciplined payments, steady progress, and ultimately, the harmonious resolution of your debts.

The Resonance of Professional Guidance

In the symphony of debt management, the resonance of professional guidance plays a pivotal role. Debt counseling and consolidation professionals bring a wealth of expertise that finely tunes your financial composition. Their guidance ensures a harmonious alignment of your debt management efforts, smoothing out discordant notes and creating a cohesive financial melody. Much like a skilled conductor leads an orchestra to a harmonious performance, seeking the guidance of these professionals orchestrates a synchronized approach to your debt reduction journey.

Expert Conductor of Your Financial Orchestra

Imagine debt counseling and consolidation professionals as expert conductors of your financial orchestra. Their knowledge and experience guide each section of your financial ensemble to play in perfect unison. Just as a conductor interprets the nuances of a musical piece, these professionals interpret the intricacies of your financial situation. They lead with precision, ensuring that every element of your debt management strategy harmonizes flawlessly.

Harmonizing Your Debt Management Efforts

Debt counseling and consolidation professionals have a unique ability to harmonize your debt management efforts. Like a conductor who balances the sound of different instruments, these experts balance the various aspects of your financial situation. They analyze your debts, income, expenses, and goals, creating a well-orchestrated plan that resonates with your financial aspirations.

Resolving Discordant Financial Notes

In the realm of debt management, discordant financial notes can disrupt the harmony of your financial composition. These may include high-interest rates, overwhelming debt obligations, or uncertain repayment strategies. Debt counseling and consolidation professionals act as skilled troubleshooters, identifying these discordant elements and resolving them through strategic negotiation and planning. Their intervention transforms your financial composition into a melodious arrangement.

Creating a Cohesive Financial Melody

Much like a composer weaves different musical themes into a cohesive melody, debt counseling and consolidation professionals weave together various financial elements into a cohesive strategy. They bring clarity to complex financial situations, crafting a comprehensive plan that guides your debt reduction journey. This cohesive financial melody not only simplifies your approach but also enhances your understanding of the path ahead.

Guiding You Toward Financial Symphony

Enlisting the expertise of debt counseling and consolidation professionals is akin to having a seasoned conductor who leads your financial symphony. They provide direction, insight, and guidance, ensuring that each instrument of your financial ensemble contributes to a harmonious performance. Their involvement lends an air of confidence to your debt reduction journey, allowing you to navigate challenges with a sense of assurance.

Conclusion: A Harmonious Financial Performance

In conclusion, the resonance of professional guidance in debt counseling and consolidation orchestrates a harmonious financial performance. Just as a conductor shapes the sound of an orchestra, these professionals shape the trajectory of your debt management efforts. Their expertise resolves dissonance, aligns financial elements, and creates a symphony of disciplined debt reduction. By entrusting your financial composition to their skilled hands, you set the stage for a melodious journey toward debt freedom.

The Climactic Resolution: A Debt-Free Future

In the grand symphony of your financial life, the climactic resolution emerges as a debt-free overture, marking the culmination of your debt reduction journey under the guidance of debt counseling and consolidation. Just as a symphony crescendos to its grand finale, your path to debt freedom crescendos to a harmonious resolution – a future unburdened by debt. The expertise and strategic orchestration provided by these professionals lead you to this momentous finale, where financial challenges are conquered and a harmonious economic composition is achieved.

Guided by Expert Baton Holders

Imagine the debt counseling and consolidation professionals as expert baton holders, conducting your financial composition to its peak performance. With their skilled guidance, they lead you through intricate financial arrangements and strategic negotiations, ensuring that every note of your debt management journey is played to perfection. Their expertise is the guiding force that directs your symphony of debt reduction toward its resounding conclusion.

The Crescendo of Financial Resilience

Similar to the crescendo that builds anticipation in a musical piece, your journey guided by debt counseling and consolidation builds a crescendo of financial resilience. As you progress through their well-designed strategies, your ability to navigate economic challenges strengthens. The financial harmony they introduce paves the way for a triumphant climax – a debt-free future that resonates with stability, confidence, and a newfound sense of control.

Harmony of Stability, Freedom, and Peace of Mind

Just as the harmonious blend of musical notes creates an enchanting melody, the orchestration of debt counseling and consolidation professionals leads to a blend of stability, freedom, and peace of mind in your financial composition. The culmination of their guidance paints a picture of a debt-free future where the dissonance of debt is replaced by the serene harmony of financial stability. This harmony extends beyond mere numbers, encompassing the tranquility that comes from knowing your financial symphony is finally in tune.

A Symphony of Achievement

In essence, your debt reduction journey, harmonized by the expertise of debt counseling and consolidation professionals, becomes a symphony of achievement. Just as a symphony is composed of various movements, each contributing to the overall masterpiece, your financial journey is composed of various steps, each conducted with precision and purpose. The climactic resolution, a debt-free future, is the grand crescendo that resonates with the notes of your diligence, determination, and the skilled guidance of financial professionals.

Conclusion: The Echoes of Financial Freedom

As the final notes of a symphony linger in the air, so do the echoes of your debt-free future. The harmonious resolution brought about by debt counseling and consolidation reverberates through your financial landscape, creating a lasting impact. The symphony of your debt reduction journey, guided by these professionals, leaves behind a melody of accomplishment, resilience, and the sweet sound of financial freedom.

6.4 Dealing with Creditors and Negotiating Debt

6.4.1 Contact Creditors: The Open Communication Overture

In the symphony of debt management, open communication with your creditors sets the keynote for a harmonious resolution. Just as a conductor guides an orchestra through a musical piece, initiating proactive discussions with your creditors orchestrates an atmosphere of collaboration and understanding. This overture of communication creates the foundation upon which the rest of your debt reduction symphony can be built.

Harmonizing Financial Dialogue

In the realm of debt settlement, envision a process akin to composing a harmonious compromise between different sections of an orchestra. Here, negotiation takes the spotlight, as both creditors and debtors collaborate to create a resolution that finds balance in the composition of debt repayment. This negotiation mirrors the role of a conductor who guides diverse instruments to produce a unified and satisfactory musical performance.

Visualize yourself as the conductor of this negotiation, leading the elements of your debt structure towards a harmonious compromise. Just as a conductor controls the orchestra's instruments, you navigate the negotiation process, orchestrating an agreement that resonates well with both parties. Your objective is to ensure that the resultant settlement produces a coherent and equitable financial arrangement.

Think of debt settlement as crafting a well-balanced musical composition. Much like musical compositions blend different notes and tones to create an appealing auditory experience, debt settlement harmonizes various financial aspects to achieve a mutually advantageous result. Through adept negotiation, the aim is to strike a chord of compromise that adequately addresses your financial limitations while also meeting the expectations of your creditors.

In the context of debt settlement, the negotiation process itself can be compared to harmonizing financial chords. Just as musical chords are meticulously arranged to create harmonious progressions, your negotiations seek to align the interests of creditors and debtors, moving the melody of debt reduction forward in a coordinated manner. This harmonious endeavor involves finding common ground and sculpting a settlement that resonates with the themes of financial stability and practical repayment.

Ultimately, the culmination of debt settlement resembles the conclusion of a musical piece, wherein a melodic resolution is reached. Your negotiation skills function as the conductor's baton, gracefully guiding the negotiation process to a harmonious close. The outcome is a finely orchestrated agreement that achieves a satisfactory resolution to your debt-related challenges, enabling you to move ahead with a more harmonious financial future.

A Prelude to Negotiation

Much like the opening notes of a musical prelude set the tone for a symphony, initiating contact with your creditors serves as the prelude to negotiation in the realm of debt resolution. This preliminary step can be likened to the initial chords of a musical piece, laying the foundation for the harmonious composition of productive discussions and effective debt management strategies.

Just as a prelude introduces the key themes and melodies of a musical composition, reaching out to your creditors provides an opportunity to introduce your financial situation and express your sincere intentions. This initial communication functions as a prelude to the negotiation process, signaling your willingness to engage in a collaborative dialogue to find mutually beneficial solutions.

Imagine this stage as the overture of a grand opera, where the main themes of the performance are announced and the mood is set. Similarly, by sharing essential information about your financial challenges, clarifying your goals, and proposing a proactive approach, you create a harmonious atmosphere for forthcoming negotiations. This prelude establishes a rhythm of transparency and cooperation that can resonate throughout the negotiation process.

Just as a musical prelude creates anticipation for what is to come, initiating contact with creditors generates a sense of expectation and readiness for the negotiation phase. It is the initial chord progression that prepares the audience for the symphonic journey ahead. Through this prelude, you signal your readiness to engage in a thoughtful discussion, aiming for a harmonious resolution that aligns with your financial circumstances.

In the grand composition of debt resolution, this prelude to negotiation functions as the introductory movement, setting the tempo and rhythm for the upcoming performance. By taking this proactive step, you open the door to productive discussions, collaborative problem-solving, and the harmonious orchestration of debt management strategies that can lead to a more stable and controlled financial future. Just as a prelude captures the essence of a musical masterpiece, your initial contact with creditors encapsulates the essence of your commitment to finding harmonious resolutions in the world of debt management.

Creating a Melody of Understanding

In the intricate symphony of debt management, your communication with creditors functions much like a weaving melody that adds depth and meaning to the composition. Just as a melody threads its way through a musical piece, your dialogue with creditors threads understanding and clarity into your debt management journey. This communication serves as a unifying theme, connecting different elements and creating a harmonious flow within your debt repayment plan.

Imagine your communication with creditors as the melodic thread that ties together the various sections of an orchestra. It carries the essence of your sincerity, commitment, and intention to fulfill your financial responsibilities. Similar to how a melody conveys emotions and themes in a musical composition, your open dialogue expresses your willingness to engage and collaborate in finding suitable solutions.

This melodic communication is akin to a recurring motif in a musical work, appearing in different variations but always maintaining its core essence. Every interaction with creditors, every exchange of information, and every effort to address your financial situation contributes to this ongoing melody of understanding. It's a rhythm of discourse that resonates with honesty and responsibility, enhancing the overall harmony of your debt management composition.

Just as a skilled composer crafts a melody to evoke specific feelings and responses, your communication with creditors is carefully composed to evoke understanding and cooperation. It sets the tempo for productive negotiations and creates an environment where both parties can work together to find resolutions. This harmonious exchange of information builds a bridge of understanding, allowing you to navigate the complexities of debt management more effectively.

As the melody of understanding weaves through your debt management journey, it transforms what could be a disjointed cacophony of financial challenges into a harmonious arrangement of solutions. Your willingness to communicate openly, coupled with your commitment to addressing your debts, forms a captivating and meaningful composition that guides you towards a more stable and secure financial future. Just as a well-crafted melody can bring a musical composition to life, your communication with creditors breathes life into your debt management strategy, creating a symphony of financial responsibility and progress.

The Conductor of Your Financial Journey

Within the realm of debt management, you assume the pivotal role of a conductor, orchestrating the flow of communication with your creditors. In this symphony of financial responsibilities, you wield the baton that guides the orchestra of negotiation. By proactively initiating discussions surrounding your financial challenges, you embrace the conductor's mantle, leading the ensemble towards a harmonious resolution. This conductorship embodies your unwavering dedication to achieving a seamless accord, conducting your financial symphony with precision, determination, and purpose.

Much like a conductor shapes the tempo and dynamics of a musical performance, you mold the rhythm of communication with your creditors. Your proactive approach sets the pace for constructive dialogue and fosters an environment of mutual understanding. By stepping into this conductor's role, you establish a clear direction for the negotiations, ensuring that the harmonies of cooperation and resolution resonate throughout the process.

As the conductor of your financial journey, you not only initiate conversations but also guide their progression. Just as a conductor interprets a musical score, you interpret your financial situation and convey it to your creditors. Your ability to effectively communicate challenges, aspirations, and commitments serves as the symphonic interpretation that harmonizes your objectives with the realities of your debt management.

Consider the conductor's responsibility to lead musicians through intricate passages, blending diverse instruments into a cohesive whole. Similarly, you harmonize the intricate components of your financial arrangement by conducting dialogues that lead to feasible solutions. Your conductorship ensures that every note of communication contributes to the overall melody of debt resolution.

Furthermore, the conductor's baton is a symbol of authority, directing the musicians' actions with purpose and clarity. Similarly, your initiative to communicate with creditors demonstrates your authority over your financial journey. By taking the lead in these conversations, you exert control over the direction of your debt management strategy, steering it towards a harmonious and successful outcome.

Just as a conductor's gestures evoke specific nuances from each instrument, your communication evokes understanding, empathy, and cooperation from your creditors. Your role as the conductor of your financial symphony exemplifies your commitment to conducting negotiations with skill and finesse. Through your proactive engagement, you ensure that the dialogue is in tune, the rhythm is steady, and the ultimate resolution is harmonious.

In the grand orchestration of debt management, your role as the conductor signifies your dedication to harmonizing the elements of communication, negotiation, and resolution. With your steady baton, you guide the ensemble of financial interactions towards a crescendo of understanding and cooperation. As you conduct your financial symphony, you infuse each note of communication with purpose, leading to an ultimately harmonious resolution that echoes with the sound of financial stability and success.

Conclusion: A Prelude to Harmony

Just as the opening notes of a musical piece set the tone for what's to come, your open communication with creditors becomes a prelude to the harmonious resolution of your debt management symphony. This initial overture of dialogue establishes the themes of collaboration, understanding, and determination. As the conductor of your financial composition, you ensure that the symphony of debt reduction is guided by the harmonious rhythm of open communication.

6.4.2 Debt Settlement: The Art of Harmonious Compromise

In the symphony of debt resolution, debt settlement emerges as the art of harmonious compromise. Just as a composer weaves together different musical sections to create a unified piece, you engage in negotiations with creditors to reach a mutually agreeable settlement. This orchestrated agreement forms a harmonious resolution to the complex composition of your debt.

Creating a Compelling Arrangement

Visualize debt settlement as the art of crafting a compelling arrangement within the intricate score of your financial composition. Much like a composer skillfully arranges musical sections to form a harmonious melody, you engage with your creditors to design a unique repayment plan. This arrangement, analogous to a well-orchestrated symphony, involves the payment of a reduced lump sum to settle the debt. It emerges as the result of a collaborative negotiation, where both parties work in concert to achieve a final harmonious compromise.

In this financial symphony, you assume the role of a composer, carefully selecting and arranging the elements of the settlement agreement. Just as a composer balances various musical components to evoke specific emotions, you strive to strike a chord of balance and agreement in your negotiations. The composition of the settlement arrangement is a delicate process, requiring meticulous attention to detail and a keen understanding of both your financial capacity and the creditor's expectations.

As you negotiate with your creditors, you act as both conductor and soloist, leading the conversation while harmonizing divergent interests. Through open dialogue and careful negotiation, you compose the terms of the settlement arrangement, shaping it into a composition that resonates with both your financial needs and the creditor's requirements. Like a composer crafting a musical piece that captivates its audience, you create a settlement arrangement that captures the essence of compromise and cooperation.

Just as a musical arrangement progresses through distinct movements, your negotiations with creditors evolve through stages of discussion, counteroffers, and mutual understanding. The symphony of negotiation builds towards a climactic resolution—a moment where the arrangement is finalized and the agreement is reached. This resolution signifies the culmination of your artistic negotiation skills, resulting in a harmonious compromise that harmonizes with your financial goals.

The creation of a compelling debt settlement arrangement echoes the artistry of musical composition. It involves weaving together different elements—your financial situation, the creditor's expectations, and the terms of repayment—into a coherent and balanced whole. This financial arrangement is the crescendo of your negotiation symphony, where diverse notes of compromise and collaboration come together to form a powerful chord of resolution.

In this financial composition, you hold the baton, guiding the negotiations with skill and purpose. Through your efforts, you harmonize conflicting interests, bridge gaps, and forge a path towards an agreement that resonates with both sides. The final arrangement is not merely a transaction but a finely crafted piece of financial orchestration that contributes to the larger composition of your debt management journey.

As you finalize the settlement arrangement, you mark the end of a symphonic negotiation process—a journey that parallels the crafting of a musical masterpiece. Just as a well-composed piece leaves a lasting impression on its audience, your compelling debt settlement arrangement leaves an indelible mark on your financial landscape. It stands as a testament to your ability to navigate complexities, find common ground, and create a harmonious arrangement that moves your financial symphony towards a triumphant resolution.

The Negotiation Symphony

In the grand orchestration of debt settlement, negotiation emerges as the symphony that gracefully guides the entire process. Much like a masterful conductor adeptly navigates diverse musical elements to craft a harmonious performance, you, too, conduct the delicate conversations with creditors to seek a harmonious resolution. This negotiation symphony is a meticulous composition, where each note of discussion and compromise contributes to the overall harmony of your financial arrangement.

Just as a conductor meticulously directs each section of the orchestra to produce a coherent and beautiful sound, you engage in negotiation with creditors, orchestrating the interaction to reach a mutually beneficial agreement. The negotiation symphony demands a keen ear, attentive listening, and a strategic approach to align the terms and conditions of the settlement with your unique financial capabilities.

Throughout the negotiation symphony, you serve as both conductor and soloist. As conductor, you guide the pace and rhythm of the discussions, ensuring that each note of communication resonates with clarity and purpose. You harmonize differing viewpoints and steer the dialogue towards a crescendo of understanding. Through this orchestration, you set the stage for a harmonious resolution that strikes a chord between your financial situation and the creditor's expectations.

Just as a symphony progresses through various movements, your negotiation journey evolves through stages of proposal, counterproposal, and compromise. The negotiation symphony requires a delicate balance, where you adapt and refine your approach in response to each note of discussion. With finesse and finesse, you navigate the ebb and flow of negotiations, working towards a harmonious blend of terms that will lead to a satisfactory resolution.

Similar to how a symphony unifies a diverse array of instruments, your negotiation symphony harmonizes diverse interests and objectives. Through strategic dialogue and artful communication, you find common ground and weave a tapestry of compromise that seamlessly integrates your financial constraints and the creditor's requirements. This harmonization results in an arrangement that is pleasing to both parties, much like the harmonious chords produced by a well-coordinated orchestra.

As the negotiation symphony nears its final movement, you anticipate the climactic resolution—a moment where the collective notes of discussion culminate in a harmonious agreement. The harmonies of compromise and collaboration resound, signifying the successful completion of your negotiation composition. This resolution is not merely a transactional conclusion but a symphonic achievement that reverberates with your skillful negotiation and determination.

In the grand score of your financial journey, the negotiation symphony is a crucial movement—a melody of dialogue and compromise that shapes the contours of your debt settlement. Just as a symphony leaves a lasting impression on its audience, your negotiation symphony leaves an indelible mark on your financial landscape. It stands as a testament to your ability to orchestrate discussions, harmonize conflicting interests, and create a melodious resolution that brings your debt management journey to a harmonious and triumphant close.

A Crescendo of Resolution

Envision the path of debt settlement as a crescendo within the symphony of your financial composition. Much like the gradual intensification of musical dynamics, the process of negotiation progresses, with harmonies of compromise steadily rising to form a powerful crescendo of resolution. This climactic point signifies the culmination of your dedicated efforts – a harmonious agreement that harmonizes both your financial circumstances and the interests of your creditors.

As negotiations unfold, the harmonies of discussion and compromise evolve, much like the intricate weaving of musical themes in a symphony. With each exchanged note of communication, the intensity of the composition builds, creating a sense of anticipation and forward momentum. Just as a musical crescendo adds depth and drama to a piece, the crescendo of debt settlement infuses your financial journey with a heightened sense of resolution and closure.

The crescendo of debt settlement is a transformative movement within your financial opus. It embodies the collaborative spirit of negotiation, where each note of conversation contributes to the overall harmony of the agreement. This crescendo mirrors the skillful craftsmanship of a composer, who carefully crafts each note to create a powerful and resonant moment within the music.

As the crescendo reaches its zenith, you find yourself at the precipice of resolution – a moment where the harmonious convergence of interests comes to fruition. This resolution is more than a transactional endpoint; it is a crescendo of mutual understanding, compromise, and alignment. It represents the symphonic blend of your determination to manage your debts and the willingness of your creditors to find common ground.

In the crescendo of resolution, the symphony of debt settlement reaches its grand finale. The harmonies of negotiation coalesce into a triumphant chord, signaling the successful conclusion of your efforts. This moment echoes the emotional impact of a musical climax, evoking a sense of satisfaction, relief, and accomplishment.

Just as a well-executed crescendo leaves a lasting impression on an audience, the crescendo of debt settlement leaves an enduring mark on your financial landscape. It showcases your ability to navigate challenging conversations, harmonize differing perspectives, and compose a harmonious resolution that echoes through your financial journey. With the crescendo of resolution, your debt settlement process finds its place in the grand symphony of your financial composition, adding depth, richness, and a sense of closure to your debt management efforts.

The Orchestra of Financial Compromise

Visualize the intricate dynamics of debt resolution as an orchestra, with each component playing a unique role in the grand composition of your financial journey. Within this symphony, debt settlement emerges as a distinctive section that adds depth and resonance to the overall performance. Much like the diverse instruments of an orchestra blending together in harmony, your negotiations with creditors create a symphony of compromise and understanding, producing a harmonious resolution that resonates throughout your financial landscape.

Every instrument within an orchestra contributes its distinct timbre and melody, enriching the composition as a whole. Similarly, the process of debt settlement introduces a unique melodic line to your financial score. Through thoughtful negotiation and dialogue, you orchestrate an arrangement that aligns with your financial capabilities and aspirations. This harmonious negotiation becomes a powerful instrument that can transform discord into resolution, turning the dissonance of debt challenges into a harmonious chord of compromise.

In this financial orchestra, your role as the conductor is pivotal. Your skilled direction guides the negotiation process, ensuring that the various sections – you and your creditors – play in sync and harmony. The ebb and flow of discussion mirror the dynamic crescendos and decrescendos of a musical performance, creating a rhythm that moves towards a resounding conclusion.

As the negotiation symphony reaches its finale, the orchestra of financial compromise reaches its peak. The collective efforts, much like the blending of musical instruments, culminate in a harmonious resolution that reverberates throughout your financial landscape. This resolution not only addresses your debt challenges but also enables you to regain control over the melody of your finances.

Just as a musical composition leaves an indelible mark on its listeners, the orchestra of financial compromise leaves a lasting imprint on your financial journey. The harmonious resolution achieved through debt settlement becomes a defining moment – a turning point where challenges are met with strategic negotiation, and dissonance transforms into harmony. This harmonious arrangement allows you to carry forward a newfound sense of financial equilibrium and empowerment, resonating with stability and control as you continue to compose your financial symphony.

Conclusion: The Harmony of Resolution

Debt settlement, as the art of harmonious compromise, adds a unique and vital note to your debt management symphony. Through skillful negotiation and collaboration, you craft an arrangement that harmonizes with your financial needs and goals. This resolution is not just the end of a challenging movement but the beginning of a new harmonious phase in your overall financial composition.

6.4.3 Repayment Plans: Crafting Structured Harmonies

Harmonizing Financial Arrangements

In the grand symphony of debt resolution, the crafting of structured repayment plans takes center stage as a harmonious composition. Just as a composer intricately weaves melodies together to create a musical masterpiece, you collaborate with your creditors to design repayment arrangements that harmonize with your financial capabilities and aspirations.

Akin to Musical Harmonies

Much like musical harmonies blend diverse notes into a seamless melody, repayment plans combine various elements of debt reduction into a cohesive arrangement. Through constructive communication and negotiation, you and your creditors orchestrate a plan that not only satisfies your debt obligations but also aligns with your financial rhythm. This cooperative effort resembles the coordination of instruments in an orchestra, each contributing to the overall harmony of the composition.

Fine-Tuning the Financial Score

Just as a conductor refines a musical performance, you fine-tune the terms of repayment plans to create a harmonious financial score. Lowering interest rates, extending repayment periods, or waiving fees become the notes that compose this melody of debt reduction. This meticulous adjustment ensures that the arrangement resonates with your financial melody, allowing you to navigate the path toward financial stability with confidence.

Navigating the Negotiation Symphony

Similar to a conductor guiding musicians through intricate passages, you navigate the negotiation symphony with your creditors. Your adept management of this dialogue ensures that the proposed repayment terms blend smoothly with your financial harmony. Through this orchestration, you transform the negotiation process into a harmonious collaboration that produces solutions attuned to your financial composition.

A Crescendo of Structured Solutions

As the negotiation symphony reaches its crescendo, the structured harmonies of repayment plans crescendo to a resolution. This orchestrated effort culminates in a clear and organized path forward – a financial composition that aligns with your goals and abilities. These harmonious arrangements not only alleviate your debt burden but also serve as a testament to your dedication and skill in conducting a financially stable future.

Enriching the Symphony of Debt Reduction

Within the intricate tapestry of debt resolution, the creation of structured repayment plans enriches the overall symphony. Through collaboration, negotiation, and careful orchestration, you bring together the diverse instruments of debt management into a harmonious ensemble. This melodious effort resonates with financial progress, empowering you to continue composing your financial opus with assurance and optimism.

Akin to Musical Harmonies

Just as musical harmonies blend diverse notes into a seamless melody, the creation of structured repayment plans orchestrates various elements of debt reduction into a cohesive arrangement. This financial composition emerges from the collaborative process of constructive communication and negotiation between you and your creditors.

Crafting a Harmonious Arrangement

Imagine the process of crafting a structured repayment plan as akin to a composer intricately weaving melodies together. Each element, whether it's a lowered interest rate, extended repayment term, or waived fees, contributes a distinct note to the arrangement. These notes combine to form a harmonious composition that resonates with your financial situation and goals.

The Symphony of Cooperation

In this endeavor, you and your creditors function as a harmonious ensemble, much like the coordination of instruments in an orchestra. Each party plays a vital role, contributing their expertise and flexibility to ensure that the arrangement aligns with your unique financial rhythm. The result is a coordinated effort that produces a financial arrangement where all components work in concert.

Balancing Debt Obligations and Financial Realities

Just as a musical arrangement must strike a balance between different musical elements, your repayment plan balances your debt obligations with your financial realities. The negotiation process fine-tunes this balance, ensuring that the terms and conditions of the plan harmonize with your ability to pay. This equilibrium mirrors the intricate balance that a conductor maintains in guiding various sections of an orchestra.

A Symphony of Financial Harmony

As the structured repayment plan takes shape, it forms a symphony of financial harmony. The diverse elements – the negotiated terms, the strategic adjustments, and the cooperative spirit – come together to create a composition that resonates with your journey toward debt reduction. This symphony represents not only the reduction of your debt burden but also the culmination of your dedicated efforts to regain financial control.

Harmonizing a Debt-Free Future

Ultimately, the creation of structured repayment plans plays a pivotal role in harmonizing your path toward a debt-free future. This orchestrated effort embodies your commitment to resolving financial challenges and conducting your financial symphony with skill and determination. Just as a well-composed musical harmony leaves a lasting impression, your harmonious repayment arrangement sets the stage for a future where your financial composition is one of stability, freedom, and accomplishment.

Fine-Tuning the Financial Score

Much like a conductor painstakingly refines a musical performance, you assume the role of a conductor in fine-tuning the intricate details of your repayment plans to craft a harmonious financial score. Within this score, the elements of debt reduction – such as lowered interest rates, extended repayment periods, or waived fees – form the notes that create a unique and personalized melody.

Crafting a Harmonious Arrangement

Imagine the process of fine-tuning repayment terms as a composer meticulously adjusting musical notes. Each element represents a distinct note in your financial composition, contributing to the overall harmony. By carefully negotiating and modifying these elements, you compose an arrangement that resonates with your financial circumstances and aspirations.

The Symphony of Adjustments

In this symphony of adjustments, you hold the baton, guiding the negotiation process to create a financial arrangement that suits your needs. Just as a conductor carefully balances the volume and tone of different instruments, you balance the components of your repayment plan to achieve a harmonious composition that aligns with your ability to pay.

Creating a Melodic Repayment Plan

The result is a melodic repayment plan, carefully composed to reflect your financial capabilities and goals. Lowered interest rates act as the soothing tones that reduce the burden of repayment, while extended periods provide the spaciousness needed to maneuver through your financial journey. Waived fees add a lightness to the composition, freeing you from unnecessary encumbrances.

Navigating the Path to Financial Stability

Much like a conductor guides a musical piece toward its crescendo, your fine-tuned repayment arrangement steers you toward a crescendo of financial stability. Every adjustment made to the terms of your plan contributes to the rhythm and tempo of your debt reduction journey. As you continue to conduct this financial symphony, you gain a sense of control and confidence, knowing that your arrangement is harmonized with your unique circumstances.

A Melody of Confidence

In the end, fine-tuning the financial score is about creating a melody of confidence. The carefully orchestrated arrangement serves as the backdrop to your financial journey, providing you with the structure and support needed to navigate challenges and reach your debt reduction goals. Just as a well-conducted musical piece leaves an indelible impression, your harmonious financial score sets the stage for a future where your debt burden is lightened, and your financial melody plays in perfect harmony.

Navigating the Negotiation Symphony

Much like a skilled conductor guiding a group of musicians through a complex musical composition, you assume the role of the conductor in navigating the negotiation symphony with your creditors. This intricate process involves harmonizing your financial needs and capabilities with the proposed repayment terms, creating a collaborative and melodious resolution to your debt challenges.

Conducting the Dialogue

Imagine yourself on the conductor's podium, directing each aspect of the negotiation process. Just as a conductor ensures that every instrument plays in harmony, you ensure that the proposed terms align seamlessly with your financial circumstances. Your adept management of this dialogue is key to orchestrating a successful negotiation, where both parties find common ground.

Blending Financial Notes

Much like a conductor blends different musical notes to create a harmonious piece, you blend the elements of negotiation – interest rates, repayment periods, and other terms – to compose a balanced and harmonious arrangement. Your careful orchestration ensures that the financial notes resonate with your unique financial melody, creating a repayment plan that you can confidently follow.

Creating a Collaborative Melody

The negotiation symphony is not a solo performance; it's a collaborative effort between you and your creditors. You collaborate to create a melodious arrangement that not only satisfies your debt obligations but also respects your financial rhythm. The back-and-forth exchange of proposals and counteroffers resembles the interplay of instruments in an orchestra, each contributing to the overall harmony.

A Harmonious Resolution

As you navigate this negotiation symphony, you lead the way toward a harmonious resolution. The final agreement is akin to the final notes of a well-conducted musical piece – it resonates, satisfies, and leaves both parties in agreement. Your ability to guide the negotiation process ensures that the financial composition that emerges is in sync with your goals and capabilities.

Orchestrating Financial Solutions

In essence, your role in navigating the negotiation symphony is that of a skilled conductor who orchestrates financial solutions. Your careful guidance transforms what could be a discordant negotiation into a symphony of collaboration and understanding. With each skillful maneuver, you guide the negotiation towards a resolution that complements your financial composition and moves you closer to your desired outcome.

A Symphony of Resolution

Ultimately, the negotiation symphony you conduct with your creditors results in a symphony of resolution. Through your adept navigation, the discordant notes of financial uncertainty transform into a harmonious arrangement that paves the way for a more stable and debt-free future. Just as a conductor shapes the musical narrative, you shape the financial narrative, leading it towards a crescendo of successful debt management.

A Crescendo of Structured Solutions

Much like a carefully composed piece of music building to an impactful peak, the negotiation process with your creditors reaches a similar point of culmination. This orchestrated effort results in well-structured and harmonious repayment solutions. These agreements form a clear and organized path forward, tailored to align with your goals and capabilities.

The Harmony of Repayment Plans

Consider the process of negotiation as a collaborative effort, akin to different instruments blending together in a harmonious composition. Just as musical harmonies create a pleasing sound, the negotiation process harmonizes your financial needs and the proposed terms from your creditors. This synergy leads to cohesive repayment plans that resonate with your financial rhythm, guiding your debt reduction journey.

Culmination and Resolution

The negotiation process comes to a meaningful culmination as structured repayment plans take precedence. This significant juncture signifies not only a resolution to your debt challenges but also the victory of your strategic financial orchestration. These well-designed arrangements showcase your dedication and adeptness in steering toward a financially responsible future.

A Path Forward

The structured solutions resulting from this negotiation process illuminate a clear path forward, much like a roadmap guiding you toward financial stability. These thoughtfully arranged agreements provide you with actionable strategies to navigate your debt reduction journey confidently and with precision.

A Testimony to Your Skill

In a manner similar to a conductor receiving recognition for a finely directed performance, your adept negotiation skills are applauded in the arena of debt management. These structured solutions not only ease your debt burden but also stand as a testament to your capability in harmonizing the complexities of your financial situation. Your commitment to conducting a financially stable future is evident in every aspect of these well-orchestrated agreements.

A Resounding Melody of Success

In conclusion, the negotiation process culminates in a resounding melody of success. The structured solutions that emerge are more than just financial agreements; they signify a symphony of stability and progress. Your skillful navigation through this negotiation journey harmonizes your financial composition, leading to a future marked by financial harmony and the promising notes of a debt-free life.

Enriching the Symphony of Debt Reduction

Within the intricate tapestry of debt resolution, where the notes of financial challenges and aspirations interweave, the creation of structured repayment plans emerges as a masterful conductor, orchestrating a harmonious ensemble. This composition, achieved through collaboration, negotiation, and the skilled artistry of orchestration, serves to unify the diverse instruments of debt management, producing a resonant and unified sound that reverberates with financial progress.

Imagine the process of crafting structured repayment plans as a symphonic performance, with you at the helm, skillfully guiding each section of instruments towards a unified crescendo. Through harmonious collaboration with creditors, you craft arrangements that harmonize the various components of debt reduction, blending the notes of lowered interest rates, extended repayment periods, and waived fees. Just as a composer meticulously adjusts harmonies and tones to evoke desired emotions, you fine-tune these repayment arrangements to resonate with your unique financial composition.

The negotiation table becomes your conductor's podium, where the dialogue dances to the rhythm of compromise and understanding. Your adept management of this symphony ensures that the proposed terms blend seamlessly with your financial melody, creating a seamless progression from challenge to resolution. The symphony swells as these negotiations reach their zenith, and the structured harmonies of repayment plans crescendo to a resolution.

This harmonious ensemble of structured repayment plans is more than a financial arrangement; it's a testament to your dedication and financial acumen. It underscores your commitment to the composition of a financially secure future, where the notes of debt reduction and fiscal stability blend seamlessly. Each repayment plan becomes a note in your financial score, a note that symbolizes another step towards liberation from debt's discordant strains.

As the symphony of debt reduction swells and reaches its harmonious resolution, it adds a layer of resonance to your financial journey. The structured arrangements you've crafted serve as a guiding melody, leading you towards a more stable and promising future. With each payment made, with each milestone reached, the melody becomes stronger, the symphony richer, until the triumphant finale of a debt-free existence.

In the grand composition of your financial opus, the enrichment brought by structured repayment plans is a defining movement. It harmonizes the dissonance, creates a rhythm of progress, and empowers you to continue composing with a renewed sense of assurance and optimism. As you navigate the complexities of debt resolution, remember that you are not only the conductor of this symphony but also its composer, shaping a masterpiece of financial well-being, one harmonious note at a time.

6.4.4 Seek Professional Assistance: Enlisting Skilled Conductors

Maestros of Legal Harmonies: Debt Attorneys

In the intricate composition of debt negotiation, the role of a debt attorney parallels that of a maestro leading an orchestra through a complex musical score. When the harmonies of negotiation become intricate and challenging, enlisting the assistance of a skilled debt attorney emerges as a pivotal decision. With their profound understanding of financial laws and debt dynamics, debt attorneys step onto the stage as expert conductors, directing each movement of the negotiation symphony with precision.

Guiding the Performance: Debt Attorneys as Skilled Orchestration

Just as a conductor molds the musical performance, debt attorneys mold the negotiation process. Their legal acumen and experience become the baton that guides the rhythm of discussions with creditors. Much like a conductor ensures seamless coordination among musicians, debt attorneys ensure seamless coordination between you and your creditors, fostering an environment conducive to productive negotiation.

Enhancing the Financial Sonata: Legal Protection and Harmonious Strategies

The presence of debt attorneys enriches the overall financial sonata of debt management. Their expertise in legal harmonies not only provides you with essential legal protection but also elevates the symphony of debt resolution to new heights. They harmonize the negotiation process, orchestrating strategies that align with your financial goals. Their involvement ensures that every note of negotiation resonates within the legal framework, crafting a symphony of debt management that is both effective and legally sound.

Composing Resonant Solutions: The Debt Attorney's Baton

As a maestro crafts resonant musical solutions, debt attorneys wield their legal baton to compose financial resolutions. Their orchestration navigates the intricacies of negotiation, bringing forth harmonious agreements that strike a chord with both parties. The symphony of debt management becomes a collaborative endeavor, with debt attorneys fine-tuning each detail to create a composition that rings true to your financial needs.

Harmony Amid Complexity: The Debt Attorney's Crescendo

In the grand crescendo of debt negotiation, debt attorneys lead the symphony towards resolution. Like a maestro who steers an orchestra through challenging passages, debt attorneys guide you through the complexities of negotiation. Their involvement brings clarity and harmony to the process, ensuring that the final composition of debt resolution is both melodious and legally harmonious.

Conductors of Comprehensive Debt Management: Credit Counseling Agencies

Maestros of Financial Harmony: Credit Counseling Agencies as Guiding Conductors

In the intricate composition of debt management, credit counseling agencies emerge as maestros of financial harmony, leading your financial symphony with expertise and finesse. Just as a conductor guides an orchestra through a complex musical piece, these agencies conduct your debt management journey, orchestrating a comprehensive approach that encompasses structured repayment plans, creditor negotiations, and a harmonious alignment of your financial instruments.

Crafting Melodic Strategies: Credit Counseling Agencies as Expert Orchestrators

Credit counseling agencies possess the skills of expert orchestrators, much like conductors who craft melodic strategies for musical performances. Their deep understanding of debt dynamics enables them to weave together different elements of debt management into a harmonious composition. With your financial goals as the focal point, credit counseling agencies design a symphony of strategies that resonate with your unique situation, ensuring that each note of debt management blends seamlessly into the next.

Symphony of Unity: Unifying Financial Instruments Through Credit Counseling

Just as a conductor blends various musical sections into a unified and harmonious performance, credit counseling agencies blend the diverse aspects of debt management into a coherent and effective strategy. They act as the guiding conductor that unifies your financial instruments, ensuring that every element of debt reduction – from repayment plans to creditor negotiations – works together harmoniously towards a common goal.

Harmonizing Financial Goals: Credit Counseling Agencies as Symphony Conductors

Credit counseling agencies serve as symphony conductors for your financial aspirations. Just as a conductor aligns the musicians' efforts with the musical score, these agencies align your financial efforts with your goals. They listen to your financial narrative, interpret your aspirations, and then lead the orchestra of debt management towards a harmonious composition that resonates with your desired financial future.

Conducting Financial Success: Credit Counseling Agencies' Baton of Expertise

In the grand performance of debt management, credit counseling agencies wield their baton of expertise to conduct your financial success. Like a maestro who guides musicians through intricate passages, these agencies guide you through the complexities of debt management. Their orchestration ensures that each note of negotiation, repayment, and financial strategy blends seamlessly, creating a symphony of debt management that leads to a harmonious financial future.

Fine-Tuning Your Financial Composition

The Maestro's Touch: Bringing Skilled Conductors into Your Debt Management Symphony

In the intricate orchestration of your debt management journey, enlisting professional assistance is comparable to inviting a masterful conductor to lead a symphony. Just as a conductor navigates intricate musical passages, these skilled professionals navigate the complexities of debt negotiation and strategy. With their guidance, every note of your financial composition is played with precision and expertise, adding a layer of sophistication to your debt reduction journey.

Elevating Your Financial Symphony: Professional Assistance as an Artful Conductor

Professional debt assistance professionals function as artful conductors in your financial symphony. Much like a conductor who shapes and refines musical performances, these experts shape and refine your debt management strategy. With their involvement, your debt reduction composition gains depth, resonance, and balance, transforming it from a solo performance into a symphonic masterpiece.

Harmonizing Complex Passages: Conductors of Strategic Debt Management

Similar to conductors who harmonize the interplay of musical instruments, professional debt assistance experts harmonize the complex dynamics of debt management. They carefully orchestrate negotiation techniques, repayment plans, and financial strategies, ensuring that each component works in harmony to achieve your desired goals. Their involvement ensures that your financial composition flows seamlessly, producing a harmonious and impactful result.

The Symphony of Expertise: Crafting a Refined Debt Management Score

Just as a conductor brings out the best in each musician, professional debt assistance brings out the best in your debt management efforts. Their expertise acts as a guiding baton, directing your financial choices with finesse and insight. By integrating their knowledge, you create a refined debt management score that not only addresses your immediate challenges but also sets the stage for a future of financial stability and harmony.

A Masterpiece in the Making: Professional Assistance as the Final Flourish

In the grand masterpiece of your debt reduction journey, professional assistance adds the final flourish, much like a conductor's finishing touch to a musical performance. Their involvement completes your financial composition, ensuring that every note, every strategy, and every negotiation align seamlessly to produce a symphony of debt reduction success. With their guidance, your debt management opus reaches its crescendo, echoing with the harmonious tones of financial achievement and stability.

Harmonizing Every Element: Expertise in Sync

Fine-Tuning Your Financial Composition: The Expert Conductor's Touch

When you enlist the assistance of skilled conductors, such as debt attorneys and credit counseling agencies, you infuse your debt management symphony with a new level of precision and harmony. Their expertise becomes a vital instrument, adding depth and nuance to every element of your financial composition. With their guidance, each movement, negotiation note, and strategy are synchronized to resonate perfectly with the rhythm of your financial aspirations.

The Symphony of Expertise: Conducting Mastery in Debt Management

Much like a seasoned conductor who coordinates each instrument in an orchestra, these expert conductors coordinate every aspect of your debt management journey. Debt attorneys and credit counseling agencies lend their mastery to ensure that your financial composition unfolds seamlessly. Each note of negotiation is played with finesse, every strategy is orchestrated with skill, and the entire ensemble of your debt management symphony performs in harmonious synchrony.

Crafting a Harmonious Score: Precision in Negotiation and Strategy

Enlisting expert conductors ensures that your debt management score is meticulously crafted. Debt attorneys and credit counseling agencies refine each movement within your financial composition. They bring precision to negotiation, ensuring that your interests are well represented, and they expertly craft strategies that align with your unique situation. With their assistance, your debt management symphony achieves a level of refinement that resonates with financial success.

Reaching the Crescendo: Expert Guidance in Your Financial Symphony

As your debt management symphony reaches its crescendo, the expertise of debt attorneys and credit counseling agencies shines brilliantly. Their guidance elevates your composition to its highest point, much like a conductor who leads an orchestra to its climactic finale. With their assistance, your financial composition achieves a harmonious and satisfying resolution, marking the completion of a journey conducted with skill, precision, and expertise.

Remember, just as a conductor steers an orchestra to a harmonious performance, your proactive approach, open communication, and strategic negotiation can lead to a harmonious resolution of your debt composition. Stay attuned to the rhythm of negotiation and strive for a symphony of financial freedom.

Chapter 7: Investing for Growth

7.1 Importance of Investing for Financial Growth

Investing plays a pivotal role in achieving long-term financial growth and building wealth. Recognizing its significance can shape your financial journey, with key reasons underscoring its importance.

7.1.1 Wealth Accumulation

Investing: The Conductor of Financial Growth

In the realm of financial orchestration, investing takes center stage as the conductor that guides the symphony of wealth accumulation. Much like a skilled maestro guiding a musical composition to perfection, investing empowers individuals to cultivate their financial resources, potentially outpacing the erosive effects of inflation and generating substantial returns.

The Crescendo of Compounding: Building Wealth Over Time

At the heart of wealth accumulation through investing lies the concept of compounding. This financial phenomenon can be likened to a gradual crescendo in a musical piece, starting softly but gaining momentum as time progresses. When you invest, your money has the potential to earn returns. Over time, these returns not only generate additional earnings but also reinvest themselves, further amplifying growth. This compounding effect is akin to the increasing intensity of a musical composition, transforming your initial investments into a harmonious symphony of wealth.

A Symphony of Returns: Unveiling the Potential for Prosperity

While all investments carry inherent risks, a well-structured and diversified investment portfolio offers the potential for substantial returns. This potential for growth can significantly enhance your financial well-being. Historical data showcases the resilience of various investment markets and their ability to yield prosperity over extended periods. Just as a symphony evolves through different movements, your investment portfolio can evolve and adapt, aligning with your changing financial goals and life aspirations.

Harmonizing Dreams and Reality: Investing for Financial Goals

Wealth accumulation through investing takes on a profound role in the realization of your financial aspirations. Whether your dreams involve a comfortable retirement, a new home, quality education for your children, or the pursuit of entrepreneurial endeavors, investing provides the means to bring these goals to fruition. A meticulously conducted investment strategy harmonizes your financial efforts with your life ambitions, ensuring that you have the financial resources necessary to orchestrate your dreams.

Resilience in Harmony: Building Financial Security

Beyond the pursuit of dreams, wealth accumulation through investing adds a layer of financial security to your life composition. Economic landscapes are prone to fluctuations, and unexpected expenses can arise without warning. By nurturing a diversified investment portfolio, you create a financial buffer that can withstand unforeseen challenges. This buffer acts as the steady rhythm in your financial symphony, allowing you to navigate through uncertainties with confidence and poise.

Crafting the Composition: Planning for Success

Just as a composer meticulously crafts a musical composition, your approach to wealth accumulation through investing demands careful planning, discipline, and understanding. Evaluating your risk tolerance, establishing clear investment objectives, and defining your time horizon are the essential notes that shape your investment melody. Seeking guidance from financial professionals acts as the harmonious chord progression that ensures your investment decisions are attuned to your unique circumstances and objectives.

In the grand symphony of wealth accumulation, investing emerges as the guiding conductor of financial growth. Through strategic decisions, thoughtful asset allocation, and a steadfast long-term perspective, you have the opportunity to compose a financial composition that resonates with stability, prosperity, and the realization of your dreams. Just as a symphony builds harmonious layers of music, your investment portfolio can build harmonious layers of wealth that amplify your financial well-being over time.

7.1.2 Retirement Planning

Investing: The Melodic Prelude to Retirement

In the grand score of your financial journey, investing takes on a profound role as the melodic prelude to retirement planning. Similar to how a composer carefully crafts the beginning of a musical piece to set the tone, initiating investments early in your career establishes the foundation for a harmonious retirement melody. The interplay of time, contributions, and compounding transforms your investment efforts into a symphony of financial security during your non-working years.

The Rhythmic Dance of Time: Leveraging Early Investments

Much like a musical composition evolves over time, your retirement savings thrive when nurtured from the early stages of your professional journey. The power of time is your ally, allowing your investments to undergo the gradual crescendo of growth. By starting early, even modest contributions can experience the symphonic effects of compounding, amplifying your retirement fund's potential to crescendo into a substantial nest egg.

Harmonizing Effort and Consistency: Building a Resilient Retirement Fund

Retirement planning necessitates a harmonious blend of effort and consistency. Just as a well-conducted symphony requires every instrument to play its part, consistently contributing to your retirement investments ensures a steady rhythm of financial progress. This harmonization of contributions over time orchestrates a resilient retirement fund that harmonizes with your aspirations for a comfortable and fulfilling retirement lifestyle.

The Orchestration of Lifestyle: Sustaining Non-Working Years

Retirement represents a distinct movement within your life's composition, a time to transition from the bustling tempo of work to the more serene notes of relaxation and self-enjoyment. Investing in your retirement ensures that this movement is gracefully orchestrated. The symphony of consistent investments shapes your retirement composition, providing the financial instruments necessary to sustain your desired lifestyle, pursue new interests, and savor the fruits of your labor.

A Symphony of Security: Safeguarding Against Uncertainties

Life's journey, much like a musical composition, carries its own twists and turns. Investing for retirement acts as a harmonious counterpoint to life's uncertainties. While unforeseen events may arise, a well-crafted retirement plan with thoughtful investments offers a harmonious chord of financial security. This chord resonates with the assurance that you've taken proactive steps to safeguard your non-working years against the unpredictable harmonies of life.

Conducting Your Retirement Symphony: Crafting a Tailored Score

Just as a conductor shapes the nuances of a musical performance, your approach to retirement planning requires careful consideration and direction. Assessing your financial situation, determining your retirement goals, and mapping out an investment strategy are essential notes that form your retirement symphony. Seeking guidance from financial experts serves as the harmonious orchestration that ensures your retirement composition aligns with your unique circumstances, allowing you to confidently conduct your symphony of retirement with grace and financial harmony.

In the grand symphony of your financial life, investing takes the lead as the melodic prelude to retirement planning. Through early initiation, consistent contributions, and prudent investment decisions, you compose a retirement symphony that resonates with financial security, freedom, and the fulfillment of your post-work dreams. As the conductor of your financial journey, you wield the baton that guides your retirement symphony, ensuring that each note of investment leads to a harmonious crescendo of retirement well-being.

7.1.3 Beating Inflation

Investing: A Harmonious Counterbalance to Inflation

In the symphony of financial management, investing emerges as a powerful composition that counterbalances the erosive impact of inflation. Much like a conductor directs the orchestra to create a harmonious melody, investing allows you to orchestrate a proactive strategy to preserve your money's value and purchasing power over time. This harmonious interplay between investments and inflation ensures that your financial composition remains in tune with the rhythms of economic change.

The Discordant Effects of Inflation: Eroding Purchasing Power

Inflation, like a dissonant note in a musical piece, has the potential to disrupt the harmonious progression of your financial composition. Over time, the value of money gradually erodes, causing each dollar to play a slightly different tune in the economic symphony. This discordant effect can undermine your ability to maintain your desired lifestyle and achieve your financial goals.

The Crescendo of Investment Returns: A Harmonious Response

Investing acts as a crescendo in your financial composition, responding harmoniously to the challenge posed by inflation. Through strategic allocation, diversified investments, and thoughtful decision-making, you can harness returns that outpace the pace of inflation. This harmonious response ensures that your financial melody doesn't fall out of tune with rising prices, allowing you to maintain the value of your money and preserve your purchasing power.

Orchestrating a Harmonic Preservation: Investing in Appreciating Assets

Just as a composer selects specific instruments to achieve desired musical effects, you can choose investment vehicles that appreciate in value over time. Assets such as stocks, real estate, and commodities can act as harmonious notes in your portfolio, appreciating in value and effectively countering the erosive effects of inflation. By strategically composing your investment portfolio, you harmonize your financial symphony, ensuring that your money's value remains resilient against the passage of time.

The Harmonious Echo of Compound Growth: Amplifying Inflation-Beating Potential

In the financial overture of investing, compound growth emerges as a dominant theme. Similar to how a repeated musical motif gains intensity, compound growth amplifies the potential of your investments to outpace inflation. The reinvestment of earnings and gains adds depth to your financial melody, allowing your investment composition to rise above the dissonance of inflation and resonate with a harmonious appreciation of wealth over time.

A Conductor of Financial Resilience: Navigating Economic Changes

In the grand symphony of your financial journey, investing takes on the role of a skilled conductor, guiding your composition through the changing dynamics of the economic landscape. By proactively investing to beat inflation, you harmonize your financial melody with the evolving rhythms of the economy. This orchestration ensures that your money's value remains strong, preserving your ability to achieve your goals, fulfill your aspirations, and compose a prosperous financial future.

As you compose the financial symphony of your life, investing stands as a powerful note that harmonizes with the challenge of inflation. Through strategic investment choices, compound growth, and a proactive approach, you craft a melody that resonates with the harmonious preservation of your money's value and purchasing power. With investing as your guiding conductor, your financial composition remains in tune with the changing economic dynamics, ensuring a resilient and harmonious financial journey.

7.1.4 Meeting Financial Goals

Investing: A Harmonious Pathway to Achievement

In the symphony of financial aspirations, investing emerges as a harmonious conductor that orchestrates the path to meeting your financial goals. Just as a composer carefully selects each note to create a melodious masterpiece, you have the opportunity to select and nurture investments that generate the funds necessary to achieve significant life milestones. This harmonious interplay between investments and goals ensures that your financial composition resonates with accomplishment and success.

The Crescendo of Financial Aspirations: Setting the Stage

Like the opening notes of a musical piece that set the stage for a grand performance, your financial goals define the direction of your life's composition. Whether it's purchasing a home, funding education, or embarking on a business venture, these goals add depth and meaning to your financial symphony. However, just as a melody requires harmony to create a pleasing sound, your goals require a harmonious alignment with your financial resources.

Investing as a Harmonious Melody: Generating Funds for Milestones

Investing becomes the harmonious melody that supports your financial aspirations. Much like a skilled musician who practices diligently to master their instrument, you allocate your resources strategically to investments that have the potential to yield substantial returns. These returns gradually compose the funds needed to turn your milestones into realities, creating a symphony of financial progress that harmonizes with your life's objectives.

The Harmonic Flow of Capital: Cultivating Resources

In the orchestra of financial growth, investments act as the steady rhythm that cultivates the resources required for your goals. Through a carefully composed investment strategy, you contribute regular investments that harmoniously accumulate over time. This symphonic flow of capital nurtures your financial composition, allowing you to watch your investments grow and your aspirations come within reach.

Composing a Resonant Financial Path: Strategic Investment Choices

Just as a composer selects specific musical elements to create an emotive experience, you choose investments that align with your goals. Some investments may yield steady income, while others may offer the potential for significant capital appreciation. By thoughtfully composing your investment portfolio, you create a harmonious balance that resonates with your aspirations, ensuring that the financial melody of your life moves steadily toward accomplishment.

The Symphony of Achievement: Your Financial Composition

As you navigate the intricate movements of your financial journey, investing emerges as the conductor that guides your composition toward achievement. By carefully selecting investments, nurturing growth, and maintaining a harmonious balance between goals and resources, you craft a symphony of financial success. Each investment note contributes to the harmonious progression of your goals, creating a composition that resonates with accomplishment, prosperity, and the fulfillment of your dreams.

Just as a composer shapes a musical masterpiece through careful selection and arrangement, you too shape your financial masterpiece through strategic investments and harmonious goal alignment. With investing as your guiding conductor, your financial composition reaches a crescendo of achievement, turning your aspirations into reality and creating a symphony of success that echoes throughout your life.

7.2 Assessing Risk Tolerance and Investment Objectives

Before embarking on your investment journey, an essential prelude involves assessing your risk tolerance and delineating clear investment objectives.

7.2.1 Risk Tolerance

The Conductor of Investment Comfort

In the intricate symphony of investment decisions, understanding your risk tolerance emerges as the conductor that shapes the harmony of your portfolio. Just as a skilled conductor navigates the tempo and dynamics of a musical composition, your comprehension of risk tolerance guides the rhythm of your investment choices, ensuring that your portfolio's melody resonates harmoniously with your comfort level.

The Prelude to Investment Harmony: Defining Risk Tolerance

Before embarking on your investment journey, take a moment to define your risk tolerance. Picture it as the initial notes of a musical piece that set the tone for the entire composition. Understanding how comfortable you are with market fluctuations and potential losses becomes the prelude to a harmonious investment strategy. This self-awareness serves as a guiding star, allowing you to select investments that align with your individual temperament.

Investment Harmony in Action: Guiding Decision-Making

Much like a conductor fine-tunes each musical note to create a captivating performance, your awareness of risk tolerance fine-tunes your investment decisions. It serves as a compass that navigates you through the vast landscape of investment options. When selecting investment vehicles, you can now evaluate them in relation to your risk threshold. This assessment shapes the tempo of your investment choices, ensuring that each note strikes a harmonious chord with your comfort level.

Crafting a Harmonic Portfolio: Aligning with Comfort

Just as a composer selects instruments that blend seamlessly to create a pleasing arrangement, you select investments that blend harmoniously with your risk tolerance. Some investments may offer potentially higher returns but come with greater volatility, while others may provide stability with more modest growth. By aligning your portfolio's composition with your risk comfort, you create a symphony of investments that resonates with your unique temperament and goals.

Fine-Tuning Investment Dynamics: Adapting to Fluctuations

Investment harmony extends beyond the initial selection. Like a conductor adjusting the orchestra's dynamics to fit different sections of a composition, you continuously monitor and adjust your investments to maintain alignment with your risk tolerance. Market fluctuations may introduce crescendos of uncertainty, but your awareness of risk tolerance guides you in making strategic decisions that keep your investment melody in tune.

A Resonant Investment Symphony: Navigating with Confidence

As you journey through the investment landscape, risk tolerance acts as your unwavering conductor, ensuring that your portfolio's melody remains steady and harmonious. By understanding your aptitude for risk, you infuse your investment composition with confidence and purpose. This symphony of investment decisions is finely tuned to your preferences, allowing you to navigate market fluctuations with a sense of assurance and an unwavering commitment to your financial goals.

Just as a conductor guides an orchestra to create a symphony of captivating melodies, your comprehension of risk tolerance guides your investment decisions to create a harmonious composition that resonates with your comfort, confidence, and long-term aspirations.

7.2.2 Investment Objectives

Composing Investment Objectives: The Heartbeat of Your Portfolio

In the intricate composition of investment decisions, defining your investment objectives is akin to establishing the heartbeat of your portfolio. Just as a rhythmic pulse sets the tempo and mood of a musical piece, your investment goals lay the foundation for a harmonious strategy, guiding the flow and direction of your financial symphony.

The Prelude to Investment Harmony: Unveiling Your Objectives

Picture the process of defining investment objectives as the opening notes of a musical overture. It introduces the themes and motifs that will weave through your investment journey. By clearly articulating your goals, whether focused on capital appreciation, income generation, or a fusion of both, you set the stage for a composition that resonates with your financial aspirations.

Investment Harmony in Action: Guiding the Composition

Much like a composer crafts a symphony to evoke specific emotions, your investment objectives craft the composition of your portfolio. They serve as the guiding light, illuminating the path through the vast landscape of investment options. With your goals at the forefront, you can make informed decisions that align with the melodies of your financial aspirations.

Harmonizing Portfolio Dynamics: Asset Allocation in Tune

Imagine investment objectives as the conductor that harmonizes the different sections of an orchestra. In the same way, your goals harmonize the various components of your investment strategy. They influence your asset allocation, determining the balance between higher-growth but potentially riskier investments and more stable, income-generating options. This harmonious blend ensures that your portfolio's melody is attuned to your desired financial outcomes.

Crafting a Symphonic Strategy: Blending Melodies

Just as a composer blends different instruments to create a harmonious arrangement, you blend various investment instruments to craft a symphonic strategy. Your objectives guide you in selecting investments that align with your goals. Whether you seek the soaring crescendo of capital appreciation or the steady rhythm of income generation, your portfolio's composition echoes your aspirations.

Adapting to the Financial Symphony: Flexibility and Evolution

Investment harmony is a dynamic process, much like a conductor adjusting the orchestra's performance based on audience reactions. Your investment objectives provide flexibility, allowing your portfolio to evolve as your financial journey progresses. Whether your goals shift over time or external factors introduce new melodies, your investment strategy can adapt while remaining harmoniously aligned with your objectives.

A Resonant Investment Symphony: Achieving Financial Crescendos

As you compose your investment symphony, remember that your objectives serve as the guiding conductor, ensuring that each note of your portfolio resonates harmoniously with your aspirations. By defining your investment goals, you infuse purpose into your financial composition, creating a melody that harmonizes with your unique ambitions. This symphony of investment decisions is finely tuned to your preferences, propelling you toward financial crescendos and a harmonious future.

Just as a conductor shapes a musical performance, your investment objectives shape your portfolio, guiding it toward a harmonious and resonant composition that echoes your financial aspirations and sets the stage for a successful and fulfilling investment journey.

7.2.3 Time Horizon

The Melodic Sweep of Time: Crafting Investment Symphonies

In the symphony of investment decision-making, the concept of time horizon functions as the conductor, orchestrating the tempo and rhythm of your financial composition. Much like a composer weaving melodies across time, your consideration of the timeframe you intend to invest over creates a harmonious sweep that guides your investment choices and sets the stage for potential crescendos of financial growth.

A Prelude to Investment Harmony: Defining Time Horizons

Imagine the concept of time horizon as the opening notes of a musical piece – a prelude that sets the tone for the entire composition. By contemplating the span of time you are willing to commit to your investments, you establish the foundational structure for your financial symphony. Longer time horizons, akin to extended musical passages, provide ample room for the development of harmonious investment strategies.

Time's Role in Investment Dynamics: A Musical Tempo

Much like the tempo in a musical piece dictates its pace, your chosen time horizon dictates the pace of your investment journey. A longer time horizon creates a slower and more deliberate tempo, allowing you to weather the ebbs and flows of the market with greater resilience. Conversely, a shorter time horizon sets a brisker pace, necessitating a more immediate and potentially more risk-averse approach to investment decision-making.

Harmonizing Risk and Reward: The Time-Risk Melody

Visualize time horizon as the melody that harmonizes risk and reward in your investment composition. Just as certain musical passages evoke different emotions, different time horizons evoke different risk and return profiles. Longer time horizons offer the potential for greater returns, as they allow for compounding to work its magic, while also affording you the flexibility to recover from market downturns.

The Investment Sonata: Adapting Time Horizon

Consider your investment journey as a sonata, with distinct movements that unfold over time. Each movement represents a phase of your financial life – from early accumulation to mid-life growth and, finally, to retirement harmony. Your chosen time horizon influences how you compose each movement, adapting your strategies and asset allocation to ensure that your financial symphony maintains its harmonious melody.

The Crescendo of Potential: Extended Time Horizons

Envision extended time horizons as the crescendo in your investment symphony. The longer you hold your investments, the more potential for a climactic build-up of returns. This crescendo is marked by the virtuoso performance of compounding, where your money earns returns on its returns, creating a harmonious swell of financial growth over time.

Harmonious Investment Crescendos: The Result of Time

As you harmonize your investment decisions with your chosen time horizon, you create the potential for multiple crescendos of financial growth. Each period of patient holding and strategic decision-making contributes to the symphonic rise of your investment portfolio. Just as a composer crafts climactic moments in a musical piece, you craft crescendos of wealth accumulation that resonate with your long-term financial aspirations.

Composing a Timeless Symphony: Your Investment Journey

In the grand symphony of investment, time horizon is the conductor that guides your financial composition. With its sweeping melodies and evolving rhythms, time horizon shapes each note of your investment decisions. By considering the interplay of time, risk, and reward, you create a symphony that harmonizes with your financial goals, allowing you to navigate the complex and beautiful world of investments with skill and purpose.

7.2.4 Financial Situation

The Financial Score: A Prelude to Investment Harmony

In the grand composition of investment decision-making, your financial situation functions as the opening notes of a symphony, setting the stage for the harmonious interplay of risk, reward, and strategy. Just as a composer carefully chooses the initial notes to create a captivating melody, your comprehensive evaluation of your financial landscape forms the foundation upon which your investment symphony unfolds.

A Conductor's Assessment: Mapping Your Financial Landscape

Imagine your evaluation of your financial situation as the conductor's assessment before the first note is played. This meticulous examination delves into the intricate details of your financial score – your income, expenses, outstanding debts, and liquidity requirements. Like a conductor analyzing the strengths and nuances of each instrument, you assess the strengths and vulnerabilities of your financial resources.

Crafting Financial Melodies: The Interplay of Factors

Consider your financial situation as the interplay of different musical elements. Your income becomes the melody, setting the tone for what you can contribute to your investment endeavors. Expenses and debts act as the accompanying harmonies, influencing the resources available for investment. Liquidity requirements serve as the rhythm, dictating the flexibility you have in allocating funds.

Harmonizing Allocation and Risk: A Financial Overture

Visualize your financial situation as the overture that introduces the themes of allocation and risk in your investment symphony. Just as a musical overture prepares the audience for the themes that will unfold, your financial evaluation prepares you for the choices you will make in allocating funds toward investments and determining your risk tolerance.

The Composition of Allocation: Financial Crescendos

Think of your allocation decisions as musical crescendos in your investment symphony. Based on your financial situation, you determine how much of your resources can be directed toward different investment vehicles. These crescendos represent the moments of decision, where you choose the instruments that will play the leading roles in your investment composition.

Risk as a Harmonious Element: Aligning with Resources

Envision risk as an element that needs to harmonize with the resources revealed by your financial assessment. Just as a musician selects notes that fit within the musical composition, you select investment strategies and vehicles that align with your financial capabilities. This harmony between risk and resources ensures that your investment symphony plays out without discord.

The Financial Symphony Unveiled: Your Investment Path

As the conductor unveils the symphony, you unveil your investment path based on your financial situation. Your evaluation serves as the guiding sheet music, dictating the tempo, tone, and rhythm of your investment decisions. By conducting this assessment, you ensure that your investment symphony is composed in a way that resonates with your unique financial melody.

Harmonious Investment Crescendos: The Result of Assessment

Just as a well-conducted orchestra produces harmonious music, a well-conducted financial assessment produces harmonious investment decisions. The crescendos of allocation, the harmonies of risk, and the melodies of strategy all blend seamlessly together, creating a symphony of financial growth and opportunity.

Composing a Financial Opus: Your Investment Overture

In the grand opus of investment, your financial situation is the overture that introduces the themes and motifs of your investment symphony. With its careful evaluation and comprehensive understanding, you set the stage for a composition that harmonizes with your financial goals. By allowing your financial situation to guide your investment decisions, you embark on a journey that transforms your resources into a melodious and prosperous financial future.

7.3 Exploring Different Investment Options

A realm of diverse investment options awaits exploration, each imbued with distinct attributes, risk profiles, and potential returns.

7.3.1 Stocks

Harmonizing Ownership and Risk

Within the investment symphony, individual company stocks emerge as a distinct musical score – one that harmonizes the allure of ownership with the crescendo of risk. Imagine each stock as a unique musical note, contributing to the composition of your investment portfolio. Just as a composer carefully selects notes to create a melody, you choose stocks to craft a harmonious financial arrangement.

Owning a Melodic Stake: Becoming a Shareholder

Consider investing in stocks as taking on the role of a shareholder in a musical ensemble. With each stock you invest in, you acquire a share of ownership in the corresponding company. This ownership is akin to a musical instrument playing in harmony with others, contributing to the overall sound of the orchestra. Just as each instrument adds depth to a musical piece, each stock adds depth to your investment portfolio.

The Symphony of Growth and Profitability: A Harmonious Tune

Visualize the growth and profitability of a company as the symphony that each stock participates in. As the company flourishes, this symphony swells into a harmonious tune of increasing value and potential returns. Your role as a shareholder is akin to being part of the orchestra, playing your instrument to contribute to this symphony of financial growth.

A Crescendo of Returns: Tempting Rewards

Think of the tantalizing returns offered by stocks as a crescendo in the investment composition. Just as a musical crescendo adds intensity and excitement to a piece, the potential returns from stocks can add excitement to your investment journey. This crescendo lures you with the promise of amplified financial gains, creating a thrilling harmony of opportunity.

Harmonizing with Volatility: Navigating Risk

Envision risk as an integral part of the stock investment composition. Similar to the ebb and flow of musical dynamics, stocks can exhibit fluctuations in value – a characteristic known as volatility. While volatility adds a layer of unpredictability, it is also what contributes to the potential for higher returns. Like a skilled musician navigating complex passages, you navigate market fluctuations while seeking to maintain harmony in your investment performance.

The Conductor of Strategy: Aligning with Goals

Imagine your role as the conductor of your stock investment strategy. Just as a conductor directs musicians to play in harmony, you direct your investments to align with your financial goals. You may choose growth stocks for a more aggressive approach, value stocks for stability, or a mix of both for a harmonious blend. Your conductor's baton guides the symphony of your investment choices, ensuring they resonate with your overall financial composition.

A Harmonious Duet: Combining Stocks and Diversification

Consider the interplay between stocks and diversification as a harmonious duet within your investment composition. Diversification, like a second musical instrument, tempers the intensity of individual stocks. By spreading your investments across various stocks, industries, and sectors, you create a harmonious blend that reduces the impact of any single stock's performance on your overall portfolio.

Crafting Your Stock Symphony: A Personalized Overture

In the grand opus of investment, stocks create a personalized overture that adds depth, intensity, and potential to your financial composition. Each stock represents a note, a melody, and a harmony within the larger symphony of your portfolio. By carefully selecting and harmonizing these notes, you craft a stock symphony that resonates with your financial goals and aspirations.

7.3.2 Bonds

Crafting Financial Cadence

Within the investment ensemble, bonds emerge as a composed cadence – a harmonious blend of stability and income generation. Imagine bonds as the structured rhythm section of your investment portfolio, providing a steady beat of returns. Just as a musical cadence creates a sense of resolution in a piece, bonds offer a sense of financial reassurance and consistency.

The Melody of Fixed-Income Securities: Notes of Stability

Consider bonds as individual musical notes contributing to the melody of your investment composition. Each bond, whether issued by a government, municipality, or corporation, represents a distinct note of stability. This stability is akin to the consistent, soothing notes of a well-played musical melody, adding a layer of comfort to your financial symphony.

A Symphonic Dance of Regular Payments: The Interest Tune

Visualize the regular interest payments from bonds as a symphonic dance of financial reward. Just as a musical dance combines various steps into a cohesive performance, bonds combine regular interest payments to create a harmonious tune of income generation. Your role as an investor is to join this dance, enjoying the rhythm of consistent returns over time.

The Principal Resonance: A Promised Refrain

Think of the reimbursement of principal upon bond maturity as a resonant refrain in the investment melody. This refrain, like a recurring musical theme, brings a sense of closure and completion to the bond investment. When a bond matures, you receive the principal amount back, underscoring the reliability and predictability of this investment instrument.

A Counterpoint to Volatility: Embracing Lower Risk

Envision bonds as a counterpoint to the volatility often associated with stocks. Similar to a musical counterpoint that contrasts with the main melody, bonds provide a contrasting element of lower risk within your investment composition. While stocks may experience fluctuations, bonds offer a stable and consistent performance, contributing a sense of harmony and balance to your portfolio.

The Conductor of Diversification: Blending Notes of Stability

Imagine yourself as the conductor blending the notes of stability within your investment composition. Just as a conductor brings together different musical sections to create a harmonious performance, you bring together bonds to create a balanced and diversified portfolio. The conductor's baton guides the symphony of your investments, ensuring a harmonious blend of risk and reward.

Harmonizing Income and Preservation: A Dual Tune

Consider the harmonious interplay between income generation and capital preservation as a dual tune within your investment composition. Bonds provide the melody of income, offering regular interest payments, while also preserving your capital through their stability. This dual tune creates a harmonious balance that resonates with both short-term financial needs and long-term goals.

Crafting Your Bond Symphony: An Ensemble of Stability

In the grand orchestration of your investment journey, bonds create an ensemble of stability, producing a symphony of reliable returns and consistent performance. Each bond contributes a note of certainty to the composition, creating a melody that harmonizes with your financial objectives. By carefully selecting and blending these notes, you craft a bond symphony that complements and enriches the overall sound of your investment portfolio.

7.3.3 Mutual Funds

Orchestrating Investment Harmony

In the symphony of investment choices, mutual funds emerge as a harmonious ensemble – a well-tuned orchestra of financial opportunities. Envision mutual funds as a conductor's baton, expertly blending the diverse notes of stocks, bonds, and other assets into a cohesive and balanced composition.

A Symphony of Pooling Resources: Uniting Investors

Imagine mutual funds as the conductor that unites individual investors, pooling their resources to create a harmonious financial performance. Just as an orchestra's conductor guides musicians to play in harmony, mutual funds bring together resources from multiple individuals to invest in a diversified portfolio. This pooling of resources amplifies the potential for growth and returns.

The Composition of Diversification: Blending Musical Elements

Consider mutual funds as skilled composers, crafting a composition of diversification. Each mutual fund represents a carefully selected combination of stocks, bonds, or other assets, similar to a musical composition blending different instruments to create a balanced melody. This diversification reduces the impact of any single investment's performance on your overall portfolio.

Conducted by Professionals: The Maestros of Management

Visualize mutual fund managers as the maestros conducting this financial symphony. Their expertise and experience guide the performance of the fund, making real-time decisions to maximize returns and manage risk. Like a conductor shaping the interpretation of a musical piece, mutual fund managers make crucial choices to enhance the fund's performance.

Harmonizing Convenience and Expertise: A Seamless Performance

Imagine mutual funds as a seamless musical performance, where convenience and expertise harmonize. By investing in a mutual fund, you delegate the intricate decisions to skilled professionals, allowing you to focus on other aspects of your financial journey. This harmonious collaboration between expertise and convenience creates a symphony of financial growth.

Diversification in Every Note: Notes of Opportunity

Envision each mutual fund as a unique note within your investment composition. Each note contributes to the overall harmony by offering exposure to different asset classes, sectors, and regions. Just as a musical note contributes to the depth of a composition, each mutual fund adds a layer of diversification to your portfolio, enhancing its potential for growth.

A Harmonious Balance: Creating Your Portfolio Ensemble

Think of yourself as the composer, selecting mutual funds to create a balanced and harmonious portfolio ensemble. Just as a composer chooses instruments to create a well-rounded musical piece, you choose mutual funds to achieve a diversified investment strategy. The goal is to create a symphony of growth and stability that aligns with your financial goals.

The Conductor of Growth: Leading the Performance

Consider yourself the conductor of your investment journey, leading the performance of your mutual fund ensemble. Like a conductor guiding an orchestra to play in harmony, you shape your portfolio by selecting funds that resonate with your risk tolerance and investment objectives. Your role as a conductor ensures that your investment composition produces a harmonious and rewarding financial symphony.

7.3.4 Exchange-Traded Funds (ETFs)

Harmonizing Flexibility and Diversification

In the intricate composition of investment options, Exchange-Traded Funds (ETFs) emerge as versatile notes that add depth and harmony to your portfolio. Imagine ETFs as skillful musicians, seamlessly blending liquidity, diversification, and strategic potential into a harmonious financial melody.

A Symphony of Exchange: The Trading Orchestra

Visualize ETFs as a trading orchestra performing on the grand stage of stock exchanges. Just as a conductor guides musicians through a musical piece, ETFs offer a conductor-like role in your investment journey. They mirror specific market indices or sectors, providing a synchronized performance that aligns with your strategic investment goals.

The Melody of Liquidity: Harmonious Accessibility

Consider ETFs as a melodious note of liquidity in your investment composition. Much like a well-practiced musician effortlessly transitioning between notes, ETFs allow you to buy and sell shares throughout market hours. This liquidity provides you with the flexibility to adapt your investment strategy in response to changing market conditions.

Diversification in Harmony: Blending Asset Notes

Imagine ETFs as skillful composers, blending different asset notes into a harmonious composition. Each ETF represents a diversified portfolio of assets, similar to a musical arrangement combining various instruments. This diversification minimizes risk by spreading your investment across multiple holdings, creating a well-balanced and harmonious performance.

Flexibility as the Conductor: Shaping Your Investment Composition

Envision yourself as the conductor of your investment ensemble, wielding the flexibility of ETFs to shape your portfolio's performance. Like a conductor guiding the tempo and mood of a musical piece, you can adjust your investment mix by selecting specific ETFs that align with your goals. This flexibility allows you to compose a personalized and harmonious investment melody.

Harmonizing Strategic Exposure: Notes of Market Indices

Consider ETFs as the notes that provide strategic exposure to market indices or sectors. Just as different musical notes contribute to the richness of a composition, each ETF adds a layer of market exposure to your portfolio. Whether you seek growth, income, or a specific market theme, ETFs allow you to harmonize your investment strategy with precision.

The Composition of Convenience: Seamless Performance

Imagine your investment journey as a seamless performance, facilitated by the convenience of ETFs. Like a well-orchestrated musical piece, ETFs combine ease of access with strategic intent. Their exchange-traded nature allows you to invest in a wide range of assets without the complexities of individual stock selection.

A Harmonious Blend: Your ETF Symphony

Think of your portfolio as a symphony of ETFs, each playing a unique role in the composition. Just as different musical instruments create a balanced melody, different ETFs create a harmonious investment blend. Your role as the composer involves selecting ETFs that align with your investment objectives, creating a symphony of growth, diversification, and strategic opportunity.

7.3.5 Real Estate

Constructing Wealth Through Property

In the vast orchestration of investment options, real estate emerges as a foundational note that adds depth and resonance to your portfolio. Imagine real estate as the architectural blueprint of your investment symphony, where each property contributes a unique harmony to your financial composition.

The Melody of Rental Income: A Harmonious Cash Flow

Visualize real estate as a melodious tune of rental income, a continuous stream of financial notes that harmonize with your investment goals. Just as a musician plays different notes to create a melody, your real estate properties generate rental income, creating a harmonious rhythm of cash flow that contributes to your financial composition.

Capital Appreciation: The Crescendo of Value

Consider capital appreciation as the crescendo of your real estate investment melody. Like a musical piece that builds to a climactic point, real estate properties can appreciate in value over time, potentially yielding substantial returns when you decide to sell. This appreciation adds a layer of depth and dimension to your investment symphony.

Diversification in the Ensemble: A Blend of Assets

Imagine real estate as a skilled conductor, orchestrating a diversified ensemble of assets within your investment portfolio. Just as a conductor blends different musical instruments to create a harmonious composition, real estate properties blend with other investment notes to create a well-balanced and diversified performance. This diversification helps mitigate risk and adds stability to your financial melody.

Inflation Hedging: A Note of Protection

Consider real estate as a note of protection against the eroding impact of inflation. Like a shield that guards against external forces, real estate properties have the potential to appreciate in value during inflationary periods, acting as a hedge against the rising cost of living. This protective note adds a layer of stability to your investment composition.

Your Role as the Composer: Crafting the Real Estate Symphony

Envision yourself as the composer of your real estate symphony, selecting properties that align with your investment goals and risk tolerance. Like a composer carefully selecting musical elements to create a masterpiece, you choose real estate assets that contribute to the harmonious performance of your financial composition.

Leveraging Leverage: Amplifying Investment Impact

Think of leverage as the amplifier that enhances the impact of your real estate investment melody. Just as a musician uses amplification to increase the volume of their performance, leveraging allows you to magnify your real estate returns by using borrowed funds. This amplification can lead to greater wealth accumulation and a more resonant financial composition.

A Symphony of Potential: Your Real Estate Investment

Consider your real estate portfolio as a symphony of potential, where each property plays a distinct róle in the overall composition. Just as different musical sections contribute to the richness of a symphony, different real estate properties contribute to the richness of your investment strategy. Your role as the conductor involves selecting, managing, and fine-tuning each property to create a harmonious and rewarding investment symphony.

7.3.6 Commodities and Precious Metals

Harmonizing Diversification and Protection

In the grand composition of your investment portfolio, commodities and precious metals emerge as distinctive notes that add both diversification and resilience. Imagine these assets as the harmonious chords that enhance the depth and stability of your financial melody.

Commodities: The Versatile Notes of the Market

Visualize commodities as the versatile notes of the investment world, each representing a unique aspect of global markets. Just as different musical instruments contribute to the richness of a symphony, commodities like oil, gold, and agricultural products contribute to the richness of your investment strategy, offering exposure to diverse sectors and industries.

Protection Against Uncertainty: The Shield of Precious Metals

Consider precious metals as the shield against uncertainty in the investment landscape. Like a protective armor that safeguards your portfolio, assets such as gold and silver have historically served as a hedge against inflation and geopolitical upheavals. These precious notes add a layer of security and stability to your financial composition.

Inflation Hedging: The Timeless Tune of Preservation

Imagine commodities and precious metals as the timeless tune of preservation against the erosive impact of inflation. Just as a classic melody transcends time, these assets have the potential to preserve their value during inflationary periods, safeguarding your purchasing power and maintaining the resonance of your financial symphony.

Diversification: Blending Harmonious Elements

Visualize commodities and precious metals as the skilled conductor of diversification within your investment orchestra. Like a conductor blending different musical elements to create a harmonious performance, these assets blend with other investment notes to create a well-balanced and diversified composition. This diversification helps reduce risk and enhances the overall harmony of your financial melody.

A Note of Caution: The Complex Composition

Consider commodities and precious metals as intricate notes that require careful consideration and understanding. Just as a complex musical composition demands attention to detail, these assets require research and insight to navigate effectively. While they can contribute to the symphony of your portfolio, it's important to approach them with knowledge and a clear investment strategy.

Your Role as the Composer: Crafting a Balanced Composition

Envision yourself as the composer of your investment symphony, strategically incorporating commodities and precious metals to create a balanced and harmonious composition. Like a composer selecting the right musical elements to evoke a specific mood, you choose these assets to evoke resilience, diversification, and protection within your portfolio.

The Harmonious Blend: Your Investment Composition

Consider your investment portfolio as a harmonious blend of different notes, with commodities and precious metals adding unique tones to the overall composition. Just as a blend of musical notes creates a captivating melody, the blend of assets in your portfolio creates a captivating investment strategy. Your role as the conductor involves orchestrating this blend to create a resilient and harmonious financial symphony.

7.3.7 Index Funds

Harmonizing with Market Trends

In the realm of investment instruments, index funds emerge as a melodious reflection of market dynamics. Imagine these funds as a mirror that perfectly captures the rhythm and tempo of market indices, creating a harmonious and simplified approach to investing.

Market Mirroring: A Symphonic Replica

Visualize index funds as the symphonic replica of market indices. Just as a mirror faithfully reflects an image, these funds faithfully replicate the performance of specific market benchmarks. This replication ensures that your investment composition resonates with the broader movements of the market, creating a harmonious and synchronized financial melody.

Broad Market Exposure: A Full-Spectrum Sonata

Consider index funds as a full-spectrum sonata that captures the essence of diverse market segments. Like a musical piece that spans different musical themes, these funds offer exposure to a wide range of industries, sectors, and companies. This comprehensive coverage enhances the richness and depth of your investment portfolio.

Lower Fees: The Echo of Efficiency

Imagine lower fees as the echo of efficiency within index funds. Similar to the efficiency of a well-conducted orchestra, these funds are designed to operate with minimal management costs. This cost-effectiveness translates into higher returns for investors, creating a harmonious balance between performance and expenses.

Long-Term Melody: The Promise of Consistency

Visualize index funds as the promise of a consistent and enduring melody in your investment journey. Just as a timeless melody remains relevant over the years, these funds offer a long-term investment strategy that aims to deliver sustained and reliable returns. Their focus on market replication and low fees contributes to the stability and continuity of your financial composition.

The Composer's Choice: Crafting a Simplified Composition

Envision yourself as the composer of your investment symphony, choosing index funds to craft a simplified and harmonious composition. Like a composer selecting specific musical elements to convey a specific mood, you select index funds to convey the mood of consistency, diversification, and market alignment within your portfolio.

Harmonizing with Strategy: Your Investment Composition

Consider your investment portfolio as a harmonious blend of strategies, with index funds harmonizing with other instruments to create a well-rounded composition. Just as different musical instruments blend to create a pleasing arrangement, index funds blend with other assets to create a pleasing investment strategy. Your role as the conductor involves orchestrating this blend to create a harmonious and synchronized financial symphony.

7.4 Portfolio Diversification and Asset Allocation

Central to risk management and optimizing returns, portfolio diversification and asset allocation are key principles to uphold.

7.4.1 Diversification

Harmonizing Investment Resilience

In the realm of investment strategies, diversification emerges as the symphony of risk mitigation. Imagine this strategy as a conductor skillfully orchestrating various instruments to create a harmonious and resilient financial composition.

The Maestro's Approach: A Balanced Ensemble

Picture diversification as the practiced touch of a seasoned maestro, crafting a harmonious investment ensemble. In this symphony of financial composition, much like a conductor's deliberate choice of instruments to achieve a harmonious sound, diversification is the art of selecting a carefully curated blend of asset classes, sectors, and regions. Just as the conductor's careful selection of each instrument contributes to the symphony's overall balance, your diversification strategy aims to create a portfolio that resonates with equilibrium and resilience.

Imagine the conductor's discerning eye as you consider your investment choices. Each asset class, akin to a musical instrument, plays its unique role in your financial orchestra. Just as a conductor balances the presence of strings, winds, and brass, you, too, aim to balance the presence of stocks, bonds, real estate, and other asset categories. This intricate balance not only creates a harmonious and well-rounded portfolio but also guards against the vulnerabilities of a single-note composition.

Similarly, sectors within the market can be likened to the various sections of an orchestra. Just as a conductor skillfully blends the melodies of woodwinds, strings, and percussion, you weave together sectors like technology, healthcare, and energy to create a diversified blend that can weather the shifts and fluctuations of the economic landscape.

Just as a conductor may draw inspiration from different musical traditions to craft a unique performance, your diversification extends its reach to different regions. Just as the sounds of different cultures enrich the musical experience, investing across various geographic regions provides exposure to diverse economic conditions and opportunities. This international presence within your portfolio enhances its adaptability and stability, much like the way a diverse range of musical influences adds depth and character to a symphony.

In essence, the maestro's approach to diversification is not merely about selecting assets – it's about curating a balanced and resilient ensemble that performs harmoniously across various economic stages. Just as a conductor ensures that no single instrument overwhelms the others, your diversification strategy aims to prevent any one investment from exerting undue influence on your financial composition.

As you stand in the role of the maestro, envision your diversification strategy as the conductor's baton, skillfully guiding the performance of your investment ensemble. With each investment choice you make, you harmonize the components of your portfolio, creating a masterpiece that resounds with equilibrium, adaptability, and the potential for lasting financial crescendos.

A Melodic Buffer: Shielding from Volatility

Think of diversification as a soothing melodic buffer that offers protection against the tumultuous winds of market volatility. Just as the walls of an orchestra pit shield musicians from external disturbances, diversification acts as a protective barrier, insulating your investment portfolio from the potential impact of underperforming assets. This metaphorical cushioning effect creates a sense of stability and resilience within your financial composition, resulting in a smoother and more harmonious investment journey.

In the world of investments, market volatility is akin to the unpredictable shifts in musical tempo and dynamics. Just as sudden changes in music can disrupt the listener's experience, sharp market fluctuations can unsettle your financial performance. Diversification steps in as the conductor of your financial orchestra, moderating the impact of these market variations. Just as the orchestra pit absorbs sound and enhances the auditory experience, diversification absorbs the shocks of market turbulence, minimizing the negative effects of any single investment's poor performance.

Imagine your investment portfolio as a musical score that includes both high and low notes. Just as a skilled composer strategically places contrasting musical elements to create a harmonious piece, diversification strategically places a mix of assets within your portfolio. This arrangement ensures that the underperformance of one investment doesn't overshadow the positive contributions of others, maintaining a balanced and melodious financial composition.

By buffering your portfolio against volatility, diversification offers you a more enjoyable and seamless investment experience. Just as the audience relishes a smooth and continuous musical performance, you can navigate market fluctuations with greater confidence, knowing that your diversified holdings are working in harmony to minimize the impact of any individual setback.

So, envision diversification as the protective embrace of a melodic buffer that envelops your investments, shielding them from the abrupt gusts of market changes. Just as the walls of an orchestra pit cocoon musicians in a controlled environment, diversification cocoons your investments in a well-structured mix of assets. This protective layer allows you to enjoy a financial journey that is both melodious and resilient, where the harmonious balance of your diversified portfolio cushions you from the cacophony of market turbulence.

The Ensemble Effect: Enhancing Performance

Picture the ensemble effect of diversification as a captivating performance by a symphony orchestra, where various sections seamlessly intertwine their melodies to create a mesmerizing and unified sound. In much the same way, diversified investments harmonize within your portfolio, generating a harmonious interplay that has the potential to elevate your overall financial performance.

Each section of an orchestra contributes its unique timbre and resonance to the collective piece. Similarly, diverse investments, such as stocks, bonds, real estate, and commodities, each bring their own attributes and potential returns to your investment mix. This symphony of assets collaborates to create a balanced and well-rounded financial composition.

Just as a conductor carefully guides musicians to synchronize their rhythms and dynamics, your diversified portfolio is guided by your strategic asset allocation. By selecting a mix of investments with varying risk profiles and growth potentials, you orchestrate a performance where each element plays its part in enhancing the overall harmony of your financial symphony.

The beauty of the ensemble effect is that it can lead to a more stable and potentially higher-performing portfolio. Just as a well-rehearsed orchestra produces a breathtaking musical experience, a diversified portfolio that effectively blends different asset classes and sectors can produce a financially rewarding experience over the long term.

Consider the impact of diversification during times of market turbulence. Just as a skilled conductor can guide an orchestra through challenging passages, a well-diversified portfolio can weather market downturns more effectively. When one investment faces a temporary setback, the collaborative strength of other investments can help mitigate losses and maintain the overall rhythm of your financial performance.

Moreover, the ensemble effect has the potential to enhance your risk-adjusted returns. By combining assets with varying levels of risk and return potential, you create a balanced and harmonious financial score that aims to deliver steady growth while minimizing the impact of market fluctuations.

In essence, the ensemble effect of diversification is like watching a symphony orchestra perform a masterpiece. The individual instruments, each contributing their unique sound, come together in perfect harmony to create a memorable and moving performance. Similarly, your diversified investments, when harmonized effectively, can create a financial composition that resonates with stability, growth, and the potential for a higher-performing portfolio. Just as an ensemble elevates a musical piece to new heights, diversification can elevate your financial journey to new levels of success and prosperity.

Reducing Single-Note Impact: Minimizing Risk

Visualize diversification as a carefully orchestrated composition, where each investment note plays its part in a harmonious arrangement. Just as a skilled composer blends different musical elements to create a balanced melody, diversification blends various investments to reduce the prominence of any single note within your portfolio.

Consider a musical performance where no single note overwhelms the entire piece. Similarly, a well-diversified portfolio ensures that the poor performance of a single investment doesn't overshadow your entire financial composition. This concept acts as a protective layer, guarding your portfolio against the potential negative impact of a single underperforming asset.

In the realm of finance, the value of diversification shines particularly bright during periods of market volatility. Just as an unexpected dissonant note can momentarily disrupt a musical performance, market fluctuations can affect the performance of individual investments. However, the strength of a diversified portfolio lies in its ability to absorb these fluctuations without causing significant disruption to your overall financial harmony.

Imagine a scenario where a single investment experiences a decline in value due to unforeseen market conditions. In a non-diversified portfolio heavily reliant on that investment, the impact would be substantial and potentially detrimental to your financial goals. However, in a diversified portfolio, the influence of that single investment is minimized, much like a single note blending into the larger musical composition.

Diversification, in this sense, acts as a form of risk management. By spreading your investments across different asset classes, sectors, and regions, you reduce the vulnerability of your portfolio to the unpredictable performance of any individual investment. This balanced approach helps maintain the overall rhythm of your financial journey, even when faced with discordant market movements.

Just as a composer carefully arranges each note to create a pleasing musical arrangement, you can carefully arrange your investments to create a pleasing financial composition. Diversification ensures that no single investment note becomes so dominant that it disrupts the harmonious flow of your portfolio. Instead, each investment contributes its own unique contribution to your financial performance, resulting in a resilient and well-rounded composition that can weather the challenges of the financial landscape.

Global Symphony: Embracing Geographical Variety

Picture your investment portfolio as a grand symphony, where the notes are not limited to a single instrument or section. Diversification, in its essence, is like composing a global symphony that draws inspiration from various musical traditions. Just as a captivating musical performance weaves together melodies from different cultures, diversification weaves together investments from diverse geographical regions, creating a harmonious and well-rounded financial composition.

In this symphony of investments, each geographical region represents a distinct section of the orchestra, contributing its own unique sound to the overall performance. Just as different sections of an orchestra come together to create a rich and layered sound, diverse geographical investments come together to create a balanced and resilient portfolio.

Imagine a musical piece that seamlessly transitions from one cultural melody to another, creating a captivating and dynamic experience. Similarly, a diversified portfolio that embraces geographical variety allows you to transition smoothly through different economic conditions and opportunities across the globe.

The concept of a "global symphony" in your portfolio means that you're not reliant on the performance of a single economy or market. Just as a musical symphony benefits from the interplay of different instruments, your portfolio benefits from the interplay of investments across regions. If one region experiences economic challenges or market fluctuations, the performance of your portfolio can still remain melodious because of the presence of investments from other, more stable regions.

Diversification across different geographical areas also taps into the potential for growth in emerging markets. Like discovering a new musical genre, investing in regions with untapped potential can lead to exciting opportunities and a more diverse range of returns.

Moreover, just as a musical performance is enriched by the introduction of new sounds and rhythms, a globally diversified portfolio is enriched by the introduction of different economic cycles and trends. This diversity helps to smooth out the overall performance and reduce the impact of downturns in any single region.

As the conductor of your global investment symphony, you have the power to create a composition that resonates with stability, growth, and resilience. By embracing geographical variety, you are crafting a financial masterpiece that can adapt and flourish in the ever-changing global landscape, ensuring that your portfolio's symphony is one of enduring success.

The Conductor's Role: Crafting Harmonious Blend

In the realm of investment strategies, you are the conductor of an intricate and captivating orchestra. Envision yourself on the podium, holding the baton of financial wisdom, and directing the harmonious blend of different asset classes and sectors. Just as a conductor shapes the musical arrangement, you have the power to shape your portfolio's composition, aiming for a harmonious and well-balanced financial symphony.

In this role, you are not merely a passive participant, but an active architect of your financial future. Just as a conductor carefully selects which instruments will shine at different moments in a musical piece, you strategically allocate and balance your investments to achieve optimal results. The strings of stocks, the brass of bonds, the woodwinds of real estate, and the percussion of commodities all come together under your guidance to form a symphony of potential growth and stability.

As the conductor of your investment orchestra, you determine the tempo and rhythm of your financial performance. You have the ability to adjust the allocation of your assets based on market conditions, economic trends, and your own risk tolerance. Just as a conductor may speed up or slow down a musical passage, you can make informed decisions to capitalize on opportunities or mitigate risks within your portfolio.

Your role also involves maintaining harmony among different sections of your investment orchestra. Just as a conductor ensures that no single instrument overpowers the others, you strive to achieve a balanced allocation that minimizes the dominance of any one asset class. This balanced approach helps create a more stable and resilient portfolio, capable of weathering market fluctuations and economic challenges.

In the midst of this financial symphony, you must also listen keenly to the notes of your own financial goals and aspirations. Just as a conductor interprets the composer's intentions, you interpret your own financial aspirations and adjust the composition of your portfolio accordingly. Whether your goal is to achieve steady income, long-term growth, or a combination of both, your conductor's role involves crafting a portfolio that aligns with your unique financial melody.

Ultimately, envisioning yourself as the conductor of your investment orchestra empowers you to create a composition that resonates with your financial aspirations. Your ability to blend different asset classes, sectors, and regions harmoniously is the key to orchestrating a well-balanced and harmonious financial symphony. By embracing this role and conducting your investment orchestra with skill and diligence, you can strive for a performance that crescendos toward your desired financial outcomes.

Harmonizing with Stability: Your Diversified Score

Picture your diversified investment portfolio as a finely tuned musical score, resonating with a symphony of stability and resilience. Just as a well-composed musical piece transitions seamlessly from one movement to the next, your diversified portfolio moves harmoniously through the ebbs and flows of market fluctuations, ensuring the safeguarding of your financial melody with its well-structured harmony.

In this analogy, each asset class, sector, and region within your portfolio plays a unique role, much like different musical instruments contributing to the overall composition. Just as a composer carefully arranges musical notes to create a captivating rhythm, you strategically allocate your investments to create a balanced and harmonious financial rhythm. This orchestrated arrangement allows your portfolio to weather the unpredictable variations of the financial market, much like a masterful composition that remains resilient across different movements.

Just as a conductor guides a musical score, you guide your portfolio with a steady hand, making necessary adjustments to maintain its harmonious structure. As market conditions shift, you may decide to reallocate your assets, much like a conductor directing the flow of music in response to changes in tempo. This proactive approach ensures that your financial melody remains in tune and aligned with your long-term goals.

As you listen to the melodies and counter-melodies of the financial markets, you make informed decisions to preserve the balance and integrity of your portfolio. Just as a conductor's attentive ear detects nuances in sound, your financial acumen enables you to detect shifts in market trends and adjust your investments accordingly, maintaining the overall harmony of your diversified score.

And just as a musical score creates an emotional impact on its audience, your diversified portfolio aims to create a sense of financial security and peace of mind. The careful composition of your investments allows you to navigate market volatility with a sense of calm, knowing that your portfolio is designed to harmonize with stability and resilience, no matter the financial movements around you.

In the grand performance of your financial journey, your diversified portfolio is the score that plays in the background, supporting and enhancing your overall financial composition. By considering your portfolio as a harmonious and well-structured score, you can navigate the complex financial landscape with confidence, ensuring that your financial melody remains strong, vibrant, and enduring.

7.4.2 Asset Allocation

Composing a Balanced Financial Composition

In the realm of investment orchestration, asset allocation emerges as the conductor's baton, guiding the creation of a harmonious financial symphony. Visualize this process as a composer skillfully blending different musical elements to create a balanced and resonant piece.

The Conductor's Baton: Guiding Investment Harmony

Visualize asset allocation as the conductor's baton gracefully guiding the symphony of your investments. Just as a conductor wields the baton to shape the tempo, dynamics, and emotions of a musical performance, asset allocation wields its influence over the distribution of your investment funds, dictating the cadence and resonance of your financial performance.

In this orchestral analogy, each section of the orchestra represents a different asset class within your investment portfolio. Just as the conductor carefully assigns musical themes to various sections of instruments, you allocate your funds across asset classes such as stocks, bonds, real estate, and more. The conductor's baton, akin to your asset allocation strategy, ensures that each section plays its part harmoniously, creating a balanced and cohesive composition.

The baton's movement guides the orchestra through transitions – from soft and subtle passages to bold and dramatic crescendos. Similarly, your asset allocation strategy guides your portfolio through market fluctuations, adjusting the balance of investments to adapt to changing economic conditions and your own financial goals. Just as a conductor maintains a delicate equilibrium between different instruments, you balance risk and reward, seeking optimal performance within your risk tolerance.

As a conductor uses the baton to emphasize certain sections of the orchestra, you may adjust your asset allocation to emphasize certain asset classes based on market trends or your investment objectives. This strategic guidance shapes the overall tone of your financial performance, aligning your portfolio with your long-term aspirations.

The conductor's baton also communicates intent and vision to the orchestra, guiding them towards a unified artistic expression. Likewise, your asset allocation strategy communicates your financial vision and guides your investments towards a unified and coherent financial outcome. With each movement of the baton, you orchestrate a harmonious blend of investments that work in concert to achieve your financial goals.

Just as a conductor's baton commands attention and respect, your asset allocation strategy demands careful consideration and strategic thinking. It is the tool through which you shape the very essence of your investment symphony, ensuring that your financial performance resonates with purpose, balance, and harmony.

So, take up the conductor's baton of asset allocation and lead your investment orchestra towards a crescendo of financial success. Just as a conductor's skill shapes the destiny of a musical performance, your mastery of asset allocation shapes the destiny of your financial journey, creating a symphony of prosperity that echoes through time.

The Palette of Asset Classes: Painted Investment Landscape

Imagine asset allocation as the artist's palette, each color representing a different asset class that together paints your investment landscape. Just as an artist carefully selects and blends colors to create a visually captivating masterpiece, you strategically allocate your funds across asset classes – stocks, bonds, real estate, and cash – to craft a balanced and harmonious financial composition.

Each asset class can be likened to a distinct color on your palette. Stocks, with their potential for growth, may be the vibrant reds and oranges that infuse energy into your portfolio. Bonds, known for stability, could be the calming blues and greens that provide a sense of tranquility. Real estate, offering diversification, might resemble the earthy browns that ground your composition. Cash, with its liquidity and safety, acts as the pure white that illuminates and accentuates the overall picture.

Just as an artist balances colors to evoke emotions and convey meaning, you balance asset classes to achieve financial goals and manage risk. The composition's beauty lies in the intricate interplay of these colors, each contributing to the overall impact. Your asset allocation decisions, like the artist's brushstrokes, shape the texture and depth of your investment landscape.

Just as an artist adjusts the blend of colors to capture different lighting and perspectives, you adjust your asset allocation to adapt to changing market conditions and your evolving financial situation. Like a skilled painter, you continuously refine your masterpiece, ensuring that it remains relevant and aligned with your objectives.

As you step back to admire a painting, you take in the entirety of the artist's vision. Similarly, when you review your asset allocation, you consider the holistic impact on your portfolio. Each asset class plays a role, harmonizing to create a well-rounded and aesthetically pleasing financial picture.

In both art and finance, the right balance leads to a symphony of beauty and harmony. Your asset allocation is your artistic expression, reflecting your unique financial goals and risk tolerance. With every brushstroke of asset allocation, you bring your investment landscape to life, creating a masterpiece that tells the story of your financial journey. Just as an artist's palette transforms a blank canvas into art, your thoughtful asset allocation transforms your funds into a masterpiece of financial possibility.

Harmonizing with Objectives: Aligning Goals and Allocation

Envision asset allocation as the intricate bridge that spans the divide between your investment goals and the actual makeup of your portfolio. Much like a bridge connects two shores of a river, asset allocation seamlessly links your financial aspirations with the tangible allocation of your investment resources. This harmonious connection is the linchpin that ensures your investments are meticulously aligned with your overarching objectives. It's the conduit through which your dreams are transformed into a tangible investment strategy.

Your asset allocation strategy is the manifestation of your goals and aspirations, translated into a mix of assets that reflect your risk tolerance, time horizon, and desired outcomes. Just as an architect designs a bridge to withstand the forces of nature and support safe passage, you craft your asset allocation to withstand market fluctuations and guide you safely toward your financial destination. This alignment between objectives and allocation forms the backbone of a robust and purpose-driven investment approach.

Risk and Reward Ballet: Balancing the Performance

Imagine asset allocation as an elegant ballet, a graceful dance between risk and reward. Just as dancers move in harmony across a stage, you delicately choreograph the interplay between higher-risk, higher-reward investments and lower-risk, more stable ones. This dynamic choreography gives rise to a finely balanced financial performance that resonates with both growth potential and stability.

In this ballet of risk and reward, each asset class represents a different dance move – some daring and bold, others steady and reliable. Just as a ballet dancer seamlessly transitions from one move to the next, you transition between asset classes to navigate changing market conditions and optimize your portfolio's performance. The result is a symphony of returns that dances to the rhythm of your financial objectives.

Diversified Ensemble: Weaving Asset Classes

Consider asset allocation as the skilled composer weaving a symphony from different musical instruments. Each asset class is akin to an instrument contributing a unique note to the overall composition. The harmonious interplay of these asset classes creates a diversified ensemble, where the strengths of one offset the weaknesses of another, enhancing your portfolio's resilience to market fluctuations.

Much like a composer carefully selects instruments to create a harmonious melody, you thoughtfully allocate your investment resources across asset classes to create a harmonious financial composition. Just as the combination of different instruments enriches a musical piece, the combination of diverse asset classes enriches your portfolio's performance potential.

Rhythm of Goals: Shaping Allocation Strategy

Visualize asset allocation as the rhythmic pulse that shapes the tempo of your allocation strategy. Just as different musical rhythms evoke distinct moods in a composition, your allocation rhythm sets the tone for your investment portfolio. Whether your goal is capital appreciation, income generation, or a blend of both, your asset allocation rhythm dictates the pace at which your portfolio moves toward your desired outcomes.

Your allocation rhythm is a reflection of your investment philosophy and your unique financial situation. It guides the ebb and flow of your portfolio's composition, adjusting as your circumstances evolve. Just as a skilled conductor uses tempo changes to evoke different emotions in a musical piece, you use allocation adjustments to navigate the ever-changing financial landscape.

The Composer's Vision: Designing Allocation Structure

Envision yourself as the composer crafting the intricate structure of your asset allocation. Like a composer who arranges musical sections to create a balanced piece, you strategically arrange your investment funds across asset classes to produce a harmonious and well-orchestrated financial composition.

Each section of your asset allocation serves a purpose, much like the different movements of a musical piece. Some sections may emphasize growth, while others prioritize stability. Just as a composer's vision shapes the arrangement of musical elements, your vision shapes the allocation structure that underpins your investment strategy.

Harmonious Crescendo: Your Asset Allocation Symphony

Consider your asset allocation as a symphony building toward a harmonious crescendo – a climactic peak that aligns with your financial goals. Like a musical piece that gradually intensifies, your asset allocation strategy gradually amplifies your investment potential. With each carefully timed adjustment to your allocation, your financial symphony crescendos, reaching a peak of growth and stability that resonates with your aspirations.

Just as a symphony's crescendo evokes a powerful emotional response, your asset allocation strategy culminates in a tangible financial outcome. The crescendo represents the culmination of your efforts and decisions, leading to a harmonious blend of risk and reward that propels you closer to your financial objectives. And as a conductor guides the orchestra toward a climactic finale, you guide your asset allocation toward the crescendo of your financial success.

7.4.3 Risk Management

Orchestrating Resilience in Your Financial Composition

In the grand orchestra of investment, risk management assumes the role of a skilled conductor, harmonizing the elements of risk and reward to create a balanced and resilient financial composition.

The Conductor's Baton: Guiding Risk and Reward

Envision risk management as the conductor's baton that skillfully guides the orchestra of risk and reward within your investment portfolio. Just as a conductor shapes the tempo and dynamics of a musical composition, risk management directs the delicate balance between higher-risk and lower-risk investments, creating a harmonious financial performance.

In this orchestration of risk and reward, your role as the conductor is to ensure that each instrument – each investment – plays its part in perfect harmony. Just as a conductor controls the flow of a musical piece, you control the ebb and flow of risk within your portfolio, orchestrating a symphony of returns that resonates with your financial objectives.

The Dance of Risk and Reward: Choreographing Performance

Consider risk management as a masterful choreographer crafting a dance between risk and reward. Like dancers moving in mesmerizing synchrony, you choreograph the movements of higher-risk investments, such as stocks, and lower-risk ones, like bonds or cash. This choreography creates a captivating performance that entices potential returns while maintaining resilience.

Just as a choreographer creates a dance routine that captivates the audience, you design your risk management strategy to captivate your financial goals. The dance of risk and reward is a delicate yet powerful movement that guides your portfolio's performance with grace and precision.

Balancing Act: A Symphony of Stability

Envision risk management as a high-stakes balancing act on a tightrope. Just as a performer maintains equilibrium while walking the rope, you carefully maintain equilibrium in your portfolio by counterbalancing higher-risk elements with lower-risk ones. This symphony of balance creates a stable and harmonious financial performance that withstands the unpredictable winds of the market.

As you balance risk and reward, you ensure that the melody of your financial composition remains steady and soothing, even in the face of market turbulence. This delicate balancing act contributes to a financial performance that resonates with stability and inspires confidence.

Diversification Dance: Minimizing Portfolio Volatility

Imagine risk management as an intricate dance of diversification. Like a choreographer selecting diverse dance styles, you diversify your portfolio by incorporating different asset classes. This dance minimizes the impact of any single investment's volatility on your overall portfolio performance, ensuring a smoother and more harmonious journey.

Through the diversification dance, you create a symphony of investments that work together in harmony, each offsetting the movements of the other. This ensemble approach reduces the sharpness of market fluctuations and adds layers of protection to your financial composition.

Harmonizing with Objectives: Aligning Risk and Goals

Consider risk management as the guiding force that aligns your risk tolerance with your investment objectives. Just as a conductor ensures that the musicians' performances align with the composer's vision, risk management ensures that the level of risk in your portfolio resonates with your financial aspirations.

Your risk management strategy becomes the conduit through which your risk appetite meets your financial goals. It shapes the narrative of your financial symphony, ensuring that the balance between risk and reward harmonizes perfectly with your long-term vision.

Tuning the Orchestra: Adjusting Risk Levels

Visualize risk management as an ongoing process of tuning the orchestra of your investments. Just as a musician tunes an instrument to achieve the right pitch, you continually adjust your risk levels by adding or reducing higher-risk or lower-risk investments. This dynamic tuning process fine-tunes the harmony within your portfolio.

As you make these adjustments, you create a seamless flow within your financial composition, ensuring that each note – each investment – contributes to the overall harmony. Your skillful tuning maintains the integrity of your portfolio's performance, even as market conditions change.

Protecting the Melody: Preserving Capital

Envision risk management as a protective shield that envelops your financial composition. Like a guardian watching over a precious melody, risk management safeguards your capital from extreme market fluctuations. This protective layer ensures that your financial performance maintains its resonance and stability, allowing you to weather the storms and maintain your intended path.

As you protect the melody of your financial symphony, you preserve the core of your investment efforts. Your risk management strategy becomes the guardian of your capital, shielding it from the unpredictable crescendos and decrescendos of the market.

The Maestro's Baton: Guiding Long-Term Success

Consider yourself the maestro who guides your portfolio's journey toward long-term success. Just as a maestro leads an orchestra through various movements to create a symphony, you guide your portfolio through different market cycles by skillfully managing risk. Your expertise as the maestro ensures a harmonious and enduring financial composition that evolves over time.

In this role, you wield the baton of risk management to craft a captivating and resonant financial performance. Your decisions and actions guide the orchestra of risk and reward, shaping the overall sound and direction of your investment journey.

Harmonious Crescendo: Your Risk Management Symphony

Imagine your risk management strategy as a grand symphony building toward a harmonious crescendo that aligns with your financial goals. Like a musical piece that gradually intensifies, your risk management strategy gradually amplifies your portfolio's resilience. With each well-timed note of risk management, your financial symphony reaches a crescendo of stability, growth, and achievement.

As you conduct this risk management symphony, you orchestrate a sequence of actions that build upon each other, creating a powerful and resonant final movement. This crescendo represents the culmination of your risk management efforts, leading to a harmonious and triumphant financial performance that echoes your aspirations.

7.4.4 Rebalancing

Fine-Tuning Your Financial Composition

In the intricate composition of your investment portfolio, the act of rebalancing emerges as a conductor that harmonizes the symphony of asset allocation, ensuring that your portfolio's performance remains in tune with your risk tolerance and investment objectives.

Conducting a Harmonious Performance: The Essence of Rebalancing

Envision the practice of rebalancing as if you were the conductor of an investment orchestra, skillfully orchestrating a harmonious performance by readjusting the instruments of your portfolio. Just as a conductor fine-tunes the musicians to maintain coherence, rebalancing fine-tunes your investments to sustain the desired alignment and harmony.

Rebalancing is the art of maintaining equilibrium in your investment portfolio. Much like a conductor who ensures that each instrument contributes to the overall sound, rebalancing ensures that each asset class's contribution to your portfolio remains proportionate to your initial allocation strategy. Over time, market fluctuations can cause some assets to outperform while others underperform, altering the composition of your portfolio. Without rebalancing, your portfolio's risk profile could become skewed, potentially leading to unintended exposure. By periodically rebalancing, you gently guide your investments back to their intended positions, keeping your financial performance in tune with your objectives.

The Maestro's Baton: Guiding Asset Realignment

Picture rebalancing as the maestro's baton, elegantly guiding the elements of your portfolio in a synchronized dance. Similar to a maestro's role in directing each section of the orchestra to maintain harmony, you use rebalancing to realign your investments, ensuring that each asset class contributes to the overall balance and melodic composition.

In the financial realm, rebalancing is your tool for recalibrating risk and reward. When certain asset classes experience significant gains, they might dominate your portfolio's composition, potentially exposing you to higher levels of risk than you originally intended. Just as a conductor ensures that no single section overpowers the orchestra, rebalancing ensures that no single asset class exerts undue influence over your financial performance. By conducting periodic rebalancing acts, you ensure that the interplay between your investments remains harmonious, preventing the dominance of any one asset and allowing your portfolio to resonate with stability and the potential for sustained growth.

Harmonizing Asset Harmony: A Symphony of Realignment

Visualize the act of rebalancing as the conductor of a symphony, delicately orchestrating the harmony of asset allocation within your portfolio. Just as a composer ensures that each instrument contributes seamlessly to the overall musical experience, you take on the role of maintaining equilibrium among your investments. By skillfully adjusting the weights of different asset classes, you create a financial composition that sings with balance, preventing any single asset class from overpowering the melody.

The symphony of rebalancing is a thoughtful process that allows you to fine-tune your portfolio's allocation to align with your risk tolerance and long-term goals. Just as a conductor's careful guidance ensures that no single section of the orchestra drowns out the others, your periodic rebalancing efforts ensure that no single asset class dominates your investment landscape. This orchestration of balance can help to mitigate the impact of market volatility and maintain a harmonious performance over time, ultimately leading to a more stable and resilient portfolio.

Balancing Act: Restoring Equilibrium

Envision rebalancing as a deft performer on a seesaw, skillfully shifting your investment weights to restore equilibrium and alignment within your portfolio. Just as a performer adjusts their weight to regain balance, you make calculated adjustments to your investments to bring your portfolio back to its intended allocation. This careful equilibrium ensures that your portfolio maintains a steady and aligned performance, even in the face of market fluctuations.

The practice of rebalancing is a proactive approach to risk management, helping to control the potential for overexposure to certain asset classes that may have experienced significant gains. By periodically rebalancing, you ensure that no single asset class dominates your portfolio's composition, preventing it from becoming too heavily skewed towards high-risk or low-risk assets. In essence, rebalancing acts as a safeguard, maintaining the harmony of your financial composition and helping you stay on course to meet your investment objectives.

Timeless Choreography: Adjusting Over Time

Imagine rebalancing as a timeless choreography, elegantly adapting to the changing rhythm of the market. Similar to a choreographer who modifies dance routines to suit different stages of a performance, you adjust your portfolio over time to suit the evolving market conditions. This dynamic adjustment ensures that your portfolio's composition remains harmonious and well-suited to prevailing economic circumstances.

Just as a skilled choreographer considers the tempo, mood, and style of a performance, you consider various factors when rebalancing, including market trends, economic indicators, and your own risk tolerance. This ongoing adaptation allows your portfolio to dance gracefully through market ups and downs, maintaining its alignment with your investment objectives. By performing this timeless choreography of rebalancing, you ensure that your financial composition remains in step with your goals, resulting in a harmonious and enduring performance.

Preserving the Melody: Sustaining Long-Term Goals

Imagine rebalancing as the vigilant guardian of your investment melody, steadfastly protecting the harmonious tune of your long-term financial objectives. Much like a guardian cherishes and safeguards a cherished piece of music, you ensure that your portfolio's composition remains true to your original intentions. Through regular and disciplined rebalancing, you work to prevent the natural drift that can occur within your portfolio over time, keeping it aligned with your overarching financial goals.

Just as a guardian takes deliberate actions to shield a priceless artifact from deterioration, you take proactive steps to shield your investments from the erosive effects of market fluctuations. By consistently adjusting your portfolio's asset allocation back to its target, you preserve the essence of your investment strategy and the melodic rhythm of your financial aspirations. This steadfast dedication to preserving the melody of your long-term goals through rebalancing ensures that your financial composition remains harmonious and in tune, even in the face of changing market dynamics.

Harmonious Crescendo: The Rebalancing Symphony

Consider your rebalancing strategy as a symphony gradually building to a crescendo, infusing your financial performance with depth and intensity. Just as a musical composition intensifies, becoming more captivating and powerful, your rebalancing symphony gradually enhances the resonance of your investment portfolio. With each thoughtfully calculated adjustment, your financial composition achieves a harmonious crescendo characterized by stability, alignment, and sustained growth.

Similar to the way a musical crescendo adds layers of complexity and richness to a performance, your rebalancing symphony adds layers of stability and strength to your portfolio. As you periodically realign your investments to their intended proportions, you fine-tune the harmonious balance of risk and reward, optimizing your portfolio's potential for long-term success. This symphonic approach to rebalancing ensures that your financial composition reaches its highest point of performance, echoing a harmonious and enduring melody of financial well-being.

7.4.5 Consideration of Time Horizon

Harmonizing Your Investment Symphony

In the orchestration of your investment journey, the consideration of your time horizon serves as a key note, influencing the composition of your portfolio's asset allocation. Just as a composer tailors a piece to match the length of a performance, you craft your investment strategy to harmonize with your unique timeline.

Time as a Musical Score: Shaping Asset Allocation

Visualize your investment timeline as a musical score that intricately shapes the tempo and rhythm of your portfolio's performance. Just as a musical piece adapts its pace to suit the composition's mood, you tailor your asset allocation strategy based on your investment horizon. This intentional adjustment creates a harmonious blend of risk and potential return that resonates with your financial objectives.

Much like a skilled composer selects instruments and melodies to evoke specific emotions, you craft your asset allocation to align with your financial goals and the time you have available. Your investment score guides the ebb and flow of your allocation, ensuring that as your timeline progresses, your portfolio's melody becomes more refined and attuned to your desired outcomes. This symphonic approach to asset allocation transforms the passage of time into a strategic melody, producing a financial composition that harmonizes risk and reward with your overarching aspirations.

Conductor of Patience: Navigating Fluctuations

Envision yourself as the conductor of patience, leading your investment orchestra through the intricate movements of market fluctuations. Just as a conductor maintains a steady rhythm in the face of musical variations, you skillfully navigate short-term market ups and downs by adjusting your asset allocation according to your investment timeline. This conductor's role involves understanding that the journey towards financial success requires a steady hand and a long-term perspective.

Similar to how a musical performance requires adjustments in pacing to maintain a coherent piece, your role as the conductor of patience involves staying aligned with your investment horizon. As you fine-tune your asset allocation, you demonstrate the art of steadiness and composure, allowing your investments to withstand the turbulence of market volatility for the promise of creating a harmonious financial future. Your symphony of patience and strategic allocation ensures that your financial composition remains steadfast in its trajectory, ultimately reaching a crescendo of long-term stability and growth.

Symphony of Gradual Crescendo: Embracing the Long Run

Consider your investment timeline as a symphony gradually building to a crescendo, gaining momentum and intensity over time. Similar to the way a musical composition unfolds, your portfolio's asset allocation may evolve, embracing a strategic progression toward growth-oriented investments as your investment horizon extends. This symphonic transition aligns with the principle that longer timelines can tolerate a higher degree of risk, potentially leading to more significant rewards.

Much like a conductor guides the symphony through its various movements, you guide your portfolio through different phases of your financial journey. As you extend your investment timeline, you may increase your allocation to assets with greater growth potential, all while maintaining harmony between risk and reward. This symphony of gradual crescendo represents your evolving understanding of the power of time in shaping the potential of your investments. As your portfolio matures, it crescendos toward the realization of your financial goals, producing a harmonious and well-timed performance of long-term success.

Composing Harmony in Phases: A Multistage Approach

Imagine your investment journey as a multi-movement composition, akin to a symphony with distinct phases. Just as a musical piece flows seamlessly from one movement to another, your asset allocation may transition from a more conservative stance to a growth-oriented one as your investment timeline progresses. This orchestrated progression creates a harmonious symphony of risk and reward that aligns with your evolving financial goals.

Like a composer who carefully crafts each movement to evoke specific emotions, you tailor your asset allocation to resonate with the objectives of each phase. Your allocation acts as a well-arranged chord progression, reflecting your changing aspirations. This multistage approach ensures that your portfolio's composition harmonizes with the unique melody of each phase, ultimately producing a financial composition that resonates with your overarching financial symphony.

Resonating with Maturity: Tailoring to Objectives

Visualize your investment timeline as a resonating chord, with each phase representing a note that contributes to the overall harmony of your financial composition. Just as a chord progression in music develops over time, your asset allocation adjusts to reflect your changing financial objectives. Each note within the chord resonates with a specific phase, ensuring that your portfolio's composition remains in tune with your aspirations.

As your financial journey matures, your asset allocation adapts accordingly. This harmonic approach to allocation ensures that your investment strategy is finely tuned to each phase, creating a symphony of financial growth that echoes your evolving goals. Much like a skilled musician adjusts their playing style to suit different parts of a musical piece, you adjust your asset allocation to suit the distinctive needs of each stage, creating a balanced and harmonious financial performance.

Adapting the Melody: Flexibility Across Phases

Consider your investment timeline as a flexible and adaptable melody that can be played in various keys. Just as a melody can be transposed to suit different musical contexts, your asset allocation may shift to accommodate various market conditions and life stages. This dynamic flexibility ensures that your investment composition remains in harmony with your overarching financial objectives, regardless of the changing external circumstances.

Like a melody that weaves through different musical themes, your asset allocation weaves through the phases of your financial journey. By adjusting your allocation to match the rhythm of each stage, you ensure that your portfolio's performance remains consistent and aligned with your goals. This adaptable approach to asset allocation allows your financial composition to evolve gracefully, creating a symphony of stability and growth.

Harmony through Patience: A Long-Term Crescendo

Envision your investment timeline as a symphony of patience, where each note represents a distinct phase of your financial journey. Just as a symphony gradually builds in intensity, your asset allocation adjusts in harmony with your timeline. This patient and deliberate approach to allocation creates a crescendo of long-term growth and financial achievement.

Similar to how a conductor guides a symphony through its various movements, you guide your portfolio through different phases of your financial life. Each adjustment to your asset allocation is like a carefully orchestrated note, contributing to the overall harmony of your financial composition. As you patiently conduct your investment symphony, you create a crescendo that resonates with the achievement of your long-term financial goals.

7.4.6 Regular Monitoring

Conducting a Harmonious Financial Performance

In the grand orchestral arrangement of your investment journey, regular monitoring takes on the role of a vigilant conductor, ensuring that every note of your portfolio resonates in harmony with your financial goals. Just as a conductor ensures each instrument is in tune, you oversee your investments to ensure they remain aligned with your objectives.

The Maestro of Vigilance: Monitoring for Alignment

Picture yourself as the vigilant maestro, meticulously overseeing every section of your investment orchestra. Just as a conductor's attentive ear captures each instrument's note, you carefully monitor your portfolio's performance, ensuring it resonates in perfect alignment with your financial goals. This role of vigilant supervision ensures that your investment composition stays on track, producing a harmonious financial symphony.

Like a maestro who adjusts the orchestra's tempo and dynamics, you respond to changes in the financial landscape. Your keen watch over market trends, economic shifts, and your portfolio's performance enables you to make timely adjustments. By harmonizing your vigilance with your investment strategy, you create a financial composition that flows seamlessly through changing market conditions, much like a well-conducted musical piece.

Harmonizing with Economic Crescendos: Responding to Shifts

Visualize your investment journey as a musical score that adapts to the crescendos and decrescendos of the economy. Just as a musical composition responds to shifts in tempo and mood, your portfolio's asset allocation may require recalibration in response to changing economic conditions. This dynamic adjustment ensures that your investment composition remains harmonious and finely tuned to prevailing economic circumstances.

Much like a skilled composer who weaves different musical themes together, you harmonize your asset allocation with economic shifts. By responding to market highs and lows, you maintain the rhythm of your portfolio's performance. This proactive approach to aligning your investments with economic dynamics ensures that your financial composition produces a melodious and resonant investment experience.

A Symphony of Knowledge: Staying Informed

Consider yourself as the conductor of knowledge, constantly staying informed about industry trends, market developments, and financial insights. Just as a conductor meticulously studies the musical score, you immerse yourself in economic data and investment news. This commitment to continuous learning empowers you to make informed decisions, fine-tuning your financial performance.

Your role as the maestro of knowledge allows you to anticipate potential shifts in the financial landscape. By staying attuned to global events and economic indicators, you conduct your investment orchestra with precision. This symphony of knowledge ensures that your financial composition is not only harmonious but also strategically aligned with the ever-changing currents of the financial world.

Adapting the Score: Flexibility in Decision-Making

Imagine your investment journey as a dynamic musical score that evolves and adapts over time. Just as a composer tailors a musical piece to different performances, you flexibly adjust your investment strategy based on new information and changing circumstances, ensuring that your financial composition remains in perfect harmony with your objectives. This adaptive approach allows you to fine-tune your investment score to create the best possible outcome.

Much like a composer who alters a piece to suit different audiences, you make strategic decisions that align with your evolving financial goals. By remaining open to adjustments and being responsive to market shifts, you compose an investment symphony that maintains its resonance and relevance through various market conditions.

Fine-Tuning for Performance: Prudent Adjustments

Envision your investment portfolio as a finely tuned instrument, requiring regular adjustments to achieve optimal performance. Similar to a musician fine-tuning their instrument before a performance, you make prudent adjustments to your asset allocation. This careful recalibration ensures that your portfolio remains in tune with your risk tolerance and goals, producing a melodious financial performance.

Just as a musician listens attentively to the sound of their instrument, you pay close attention to your portfolio's performance. By conducting periodic reviews and assessments, you identify areas that require fine-tuning. This hands-on approach to decision-making guarantees that your financial composition plays harmoniously, generating the desired outcome and resonating with stability and growth.

A Conductor of Progress: Monitoring for Growth

Imagine yourself as the conductor of a grand orchestra, directing the continuous progress of your investment symphony. Just as a conductor guides skilled musicians through a musical piece, you steer your investments towards consistent growth and financial success. Your role involves maintaining a keen watch over your portfolio's performance and making necessary adjustments to the composition whenever needed.

Similar to how a conductor listens attentively to each instrument, you listen to the signals and cues that your investments provide. Through vigilant monitoring, you ensure that your financial composition remains on track to achieve your desired outcomes. By identifying areas that require fine-tuning or strategic shifts, you orchestrate a symphony of progress that resonates with growth and stability.

Symphony of Proactivity: Achieving Harmonious Results

Envision your monitoring efforts as a symphony of proactivity, harmoniously blending informed decision-making and strategic adjustments. Just as a symphony reaches its crescendo through well-sequenced transitions, your proactive monitoring ensures that your investment composition steadily ascends to its peak performance over time.

Much like a conductor who anticipates the needs of the orchestra, you anticipate the changing market dynamics and economic shifts that may impact your investments. By staying attuned to these changes, you make timely and informed decisions that propel your financial symphony towards achieving harmonious and rewarding results. Your role as the conductor of progress guarantees that your investment composition remains finely tuned, producing a melody of growth and prosperity.

7.4.7 Seek Professional Guidance

Conducting Your Financial Symphony with Expertise

In the grand symphony of investment management, seeking professional guidance is akin to inviting a virtuoso conductor to lead your orchestra. Just as a skilled conductor enhances the performance of a musical composition, a financial advisor elevates your investment journey to new heights of precision and expertise.

The Virtuoso's Baton: Navigating Complex Passages

Imagine a financial advisor as the virtuoso conductor of your investment orchestra, skillfully wielding a baton of knowledge and experience. Just as a conductor expertly navigates complex musical passages, a financial advisor guides you through the intricate landscape of asset allocation, risk assessment, and investment strategy.

In this collaborative symphony of financial management, your financial advisor's expertise becomes the guiding melody. Much like a conductor who interprets a musical score, your advisor interprets your financial goals and aspirations, orchestrating a composition that harmonizes with your unique circumstances.

Harmonizing with Tailored Advice: The Advisor's Expertise

Envision your relationship with a financial advisor as a harmonious dialogue, where each note of advice is finely tuned to create a cohesive financial composition. Just as a conductor tailors their guidance to accentuate the strengths of each musician, a skilled financial advisor tailors their recommendations to your specific financial situation. They carefully consider your risk appetite, investment timeline, and financial objectives, ensuring that the ensemble of your investments produces a harmonious and rewarding performance.

Much like a conductor who conducts the orchestra with precision, your financial advisor conducts your financial journey with expertise, guiding you towards a well-orchestrated and balanced portfolio that resonates with your long-term goals.

A Symphony of Evaluation: Assessing Risk Tolerance

Consider the financial advisor's role as that of an evaluator of risk tolerance, adeptly helping you navigate the delicate balance between risk and reward. Like a conductor who understands the capabilities and nuances of each instrument, a financial advisor comprehends your risk tolerance profile. They provide valuable insights into the level of risk that aligns with your comfort and goals, helping you select investments that create a harmonious blend of potential returns and risk mitigation.

By leveraging their experience and knowledge, your financial advisor ensures that your investment symphony maintains a balanced and resonant performance, adapting to changes and challenges while staying true to your financial aspirations.

Crafting Investment Crescendos: Designing Strategies

Visualize a financial advisor as a master composer, skillfully crafting investment strategies that crescendo towards your financial objectives. Just as a composer carefully weaves melodies together to create a symphony, a financial advisor artfully weaves together investment vehicles and asset allocation to compose a strategy that resonates harmoniously with your unique goals and aspirations.

In this intricate composition of wealth management, your financial advisor's role becomes that of a conductor, directing the various elements of your portfolio to create a cohesive and impactful financial performance. They take into account your risk appetite, investment horizon, and desired outcomes, orchestrating a strategy that builds towards a crescendo of financial success.

The Maestro of Diversification: Building Balanced Portfolios

Envision your financial advisor as the maestro of diversification, akin to a conductor who skillfully blends different instruments to create a harmonious and enchanting sound. In the realm of finance, your advisor blends various investments to build balanced portfolios that resonate with your risk tolerance and objectives.

Just as a conductor carefully balances the volume and presence of each instrument in an orchestra, your financial advisor balances the allocation of different asset classes – stocks, bonds, real estate, and more – to create a symphony of stability and growth. This skillful orchestration of diversification ensures that your portfolio performs harmoniously even in the face of market volatility.

An Overture of Confidence: Making Informed Decisions

Consider your collaboration with a financial advisor as an overture of confidence, setting the stage for informed decision-making and eventual financial triumph. Similar to an overture that introduces the main themes of a musical piece, a financial advisor introduces the themes of financial growth, stability, and wealth accumulation.

Guided by their expertise, you embark on a symphonic investment journey with a sense of assurance and clarity. The financial advisor's insights and strategic direction form the introductory notes of your financial overture, building anticipation for the harmonious melodies of wealth creation that follow. With their guidance, you navigate the complex financial landscape with confidence, ultimately achieving a grand crescendo of financial success.

The Conductor of Progress: Achieving Financial Crescendos

Visualize your financial advisor as the conductor of your investment progress, leading you towards crescendos of financial growth. Just as a conductor guides an orchestra through dynamic changes in tempo, a financial advisor guides you through changing market conditions, ensuring your investment composition remains in harmony with your goals. The Symphony of Collaboration: A Harmonious Financial Future Envision your partnership with a financial advisor as a symphony of collaboration, where your goals and aspirations blend with their expertise to create a harmonious financial future. Like a symphony that unites different musical elements into a seamless performance, your collaboration with a financial advisor unites your aspirations with their knowledge, leading to a harmonious and successful investment journey.

The Conductor of Progress: Achieving Financial Crescendos

Imagine your financial advisor as the conductor of your investment progress, skillfully leading you towards crescendos of financial growth. Just as a conductor navigates an orchestra through dynamic changes in tempo and intensity, a financial advisor guides you through the ever-changing landscape of market conditions, ensuring that your investment composition remains finely tuned and in harmony with your overarching goals.

Much like a conductor's precise cues bring out the best in each section of an orchestra, your financial advisor's timely advice and strategic adjustments bring out the best in your investment portfolio. They adeptly maneuver through market fluctuations, making nuanced decisions to optimize your portfolio's performance, and leading you towards a triumphant crescendo of financial success.

The Symphony of Collaboration: A Harmonious Financial Future

Envision your partnership with a financial advisor as a symphony of collaboration, a harmonious blend where your financial aspirations seamlessly combine with their expert knowledge to compose a prosperous future. Just as a symphony unites different musical elements into a seamless and captivating performance, your collaboration with a financial advisor unites your unique goals and dreams with their comprehensive expertise, resulting in a well-orchestrated and successful investment journey.

In this symphony of collaboration, your financial advisor acts as a conductor, skillfully guiding the various elements of your financial plan to produce a harmonious and impactful outcome. They listen to your financial needs, interpret your aspirations, and craft a customized strategy that resonates with your values. Together, you create a financial masterpiece, with your advisor's insights and guidance adding depth and richness to your composition, leading you towards a crescendo of financial well-being and accomplishment.

Remember, investing entails risk, and past performance isn't indicative of future outcomes. Thorough research, diversification, and ongoing portfolio evaluation are paramount to ensuring your investments align with your goals and risk tolerance.

Chapter 8: Risk Management and Insurance

8.1 Identifying Financial Risks

8.1.1 Property Risks: Safeguarding Your Haven

Consider the concept of identifying and addressing financial risks as a dedicated guardian standing watch over the haven of your property. This vigilant guardian is tasked with shielding your valuable assets from a range of potential threats that could disrupt the tranquility and security you've established. These property risks encompass an array of perils, each capable of causing significant damage or even complete loss if left unattended.

Fire: The Unrelenting Devourer The specter of fire looms as an indiscriminate force of destruction, capable of consuming your cherished property with a relentless and voracious blaze. It takes but a spark, a minor mishap in the hearth, or a more profound structural calamity to set in motion a cascade of catastrophic consequences. The aftermath of a fire is as merciless as its advance, leaving in its wake devastation that extends beyond the charred remains. The haven you've painstakingly nurtured over time, a culmination of your hard work and aspirations, could be reduced to desolate ashes within an astonishingly brief span. The absence of comprehensive safeguards casts a shadow over the sanctuary you've woven into the fabric of your life, making the presence of precautionary measures not just a choice, but a critical imperative. In this realm of uncertainty, vigilance and preparedness stand as the bulwark against fire's capricious whims, ensuring that the flames of destruction remain at bay, preserving the haven you've endeavored to create.

Theft: Stealthy Intruders Theft represents another lurking threat to your property's sanctuary. Unwanted intruders can bypass even the most well-fortified defenses, making away with your cherished belongings. From valuable heirlooms to essential equipment, the loss resulting from theft can extend far beyond mere material possessions, impacting your sense of security and stability.

The shadow of theft emerges as a stealthy and insidious intruder, a constant reminder of the vulnerability that can breach the sanctuary of your property. In a disconcerting display of cunning, even the most robust fortifications can be circumvented by unwanted visitors, leaving you defenseless against their nefarious intentions. They vanish into the night, escaping with your irreplaceable treasures, a collection of sentimental heirlooms and practical essentials alike. Yet, the loss from theft permeates far deeper than the absence of physical possessions. Its repercussions ripple through the fabric of your existence, gnawing at your sense of security and unsettling the foundations of stability you've meticulously built. In a world where trust is betrayed and boundaries are violated, countering this threat becomes an endeavor of paramount significance. By shoring up your defenses and embracing prudent safeguards, you forge a bulwark against these stealthy intruders, safeguarding not just your possessions, but the tranquility and equilibrium of your haven.

Natural Disasters: Unpredictable Fury Nature's fury knows no bounds, with earthquakes, floods, hurricanes, and other natural disasters capable of wreaking havoc on your property. These events can lead to extensive damage and financial strain, potentially leaving you grappling with the aftermath for years to come.

The wrath of natural disasters emerges as an unpredictable and unyielding force, transcending all confines. From the earth's trembling tremors to the surging torrents of floods and the tempestuous winds of hurricanes, these cataclysmic events bear the potential to unleash havoc upon your cherished property. Their indiscriminate fury spares no corner, leaving a trail of destruction in their wake. These upheavals carry the power to inflict extensive damage, both in terms of the physical and the fiscal. They strike not just at the structural integrity of your haven, but also at the very core of your financial stability. The aftermath of such calamities is a prolonged and arduous journey, marked by the painstaking process of recovery that can span years. The financial strain ensuing from these natural upheavals is not a fleeting matter, but a weight that lingers, challenging your resilience and testing your mettle. In the face of this unyielding force, proactive preparedness and strategic response hold the keys to resilience. By fortifying your haven against the unpredictable whims of nature, you stand a better chance of weathering the storm and emerging from its wake with your property and financial well-being intact.

Accidents: Unforeseen Misfortune Accidents, often arising from mundane daily activities, can also disrupt the haven of your property. From a slip and fall on your premises to a vehicular collision involving your assets, accidents have the potential to create unexpected financial burdens that may ripple through various aspects of your life.

Unforeseen misfortune can strike in the form of accidents, mundane occurrences that possess the power to disrupt the sanctuary of your property. These incidents, born from the routine activities of daily life, carry the potential to unravel the harmony you've meticulously cultivated. A simple slip and fall within the confines of your property or a sudden collision involving your valuable assets can set in motion a chain of events with far-reaching consequences. Accidents, often unexpected and disorienting, possess the capacity to inflict more than just physical harm. They carry the potential to trigger an unexpected financial burden, one that reverberates through the various dimensions of your existence. The haven you've sculpted with care becomes marred, overshadowed by the unforeseen repercussions of a singular, fleeting moment. In the face of such unpredictability, preparedness becomes a shield against these incalculable disruptions. By adopting precautionary measures and maintaining a vigilant stance, you empower yourself to mitigate the impact of accidents, safeguarding both your property and the delicate balance of your financial landscape.

Just as a skilled conductor meticulously orchestrates every note of a symphony to create a harmonious melody, recognizing and addressing these property risks is essential for preserving the integrity of your financial composition. By acknowledging these potential threats and proactively implementing protective measures, you ensure that the sanctuary you've built remains resilient and impervious to unforeseen events. In the chapters ahead, we will delve into strategies and insights to fortify your haven against these risks, allowing you to continue your financial journey with confidence and peace of mind.

8.1.2 Liability Risks: A Shield Against Discord

Guardians of Financial Equilibrium: Understanding Liability Risks

In the intricate realm of fortifying your cherished financial haven, the notion of liability risks stands as a steadfast and vigilant sentinel. It assumes a role akin to an unwavering shield, poised resolutely to intercept and deflect the turmoil that legal obligations and financial strains may unleash. These risks, often unassuming at their inception yet harboring the potential for monumental impact, find their roots in a diverse array of circumstances. They encompass scenarios ranging from bodily injury to property damage, and even extend to encompass potential legal claims directed towards either you or your business. These lurking perils symbolize the latent tremors capable of unsettling the very bedrock of your financial stability. Their potency to disrupt underscores the need for adept management and mitigation, lest they burgeon into forces that could undermine the haven you've so diligently erected.

The tranquility of your financial sanctuary hinges upon your ability to navigate and manage these nuanced risks.

In the interconnected tapestry of our modern world, the fallout from even seemingly trivial incidents can cascade into a symphony of financial and legal challenges. A slip and fall, a mishap during your business operations, or an inadvertent instance of property damage can all act as the catalyst for a sequence of events that threaten to cast disarray into your haven.

However, this potential turmoil need not be feared if met with strategic preparedness and prudent action. By cultivating a nuanced understanding of liability risks, you empower yourself to anticipate, address, and mitigate these potential upheavals. You are granted the ability to proactively engage in measures that fortify your financial defenses and uphold the integrity of your haven. Liability risks, once comprehended, can indeed be tamed and transformed into opportunities for vigilance and growth.

Thus, as you tread the landscape of financial management, bear in mind the sentinels that liability risks embody. Acknowledge their presence, respect their potential, and respond with a resolve to remain unwavering in your pursuit of fortification. Through this commitment, you weave a narrative of financial strength and resilience, where the guardians of equilibrium stand watchful, ensuring that your haven remains an oasis of stability and prosperity amidst the ebbs and flows of the financial world.

The Varied Forms of Liability Risks

- *Bodily Injury Liabilities:* A slight misstep, an unfortunate accident – such occurrences can quickly escalate into liabilities stemming from bodily injury. These risks manifest when individuals sustain harm within your premises or due to your actions, necessitating medical attention and potential legal action.

- *Property Damage Liabilities:* Your haven, as well as your actions, can inadvertently cause harm to the property of others. Property damage liabilities come into play when your activities lead to damages to someone else's belongings, requiring you to bear the financial consequences.
- *Legal Claims and Lawsuits:* In an intricate dance between individuals and businesses, legal claims and lawsuits can cast a long shadow over your financial haven. These liabilities can arise from disputes, contractual disagreements, or allegations of negligence, demanding your attention, time, and financial resources.

The Harmonious Blend: Liability Insurance

Much like the harmonious fusion of diverse musical notes that coalesce into an enchanting melody, liability insurance orchestrates a symphony of legal protection and financial security. In this composition, the individual elements harmonize to create a harmonious whole, acting as a robust shield against the potential discord that legal entanglements and financial strains may usher in. This elegant amalgamation is purposefully designed to safeguard your haven, preserving its serenity in the face of turbulent legal proceedings and onerous financial obligations.

Liability insurance serves as a masterful conductor, orchestrating a composition that resonates with resilience and stability. It steps forward as an unwavering buffer, shouldering the weight of legal claims and deflecting the impact of unforeseen damages. This protective barrier extends beyond a mere defense, encompassing the covering of legal expenses and the potential compensation for losses incurred. In this role, liability insurance upholds the intricate cadence of your financial equilibrium, ensuring that your haven remains impervious to the dissonance that external challenges may introduce.

Much as a conductor guides a symphony to its crescendo, liability insurance navigates the complexities of legal intricacies and financial uncertainties, guiding you through potential tumult. By embracing this blend of legal and financial safeguard, you fortify the foundations of your haven, allowing its serene melody to persist unblemished. This harmonious blend of liability insurance weaves itself into the very fabric of your financial strategy, crafting a narrative of security and preparedness that resounds with the promise of stability and prosperity.

Weaving a Resilient Shield: The Importance of Preparedness

When confronted with the looming specter of liability risks, the art of proactive preparedness emerges as the foundational cornerstone upon which your shield against potential discord is meticulously crafted. This shield, intangible yet potent, is forged through a blend of foresight and strategic action. It is a powerful countermeasure, standing resolute against the disarray that legal complexities and financial uncertainties may attempt to sow.

Within the tapestry of this preparedness lies a collection of meticulous safety measures, each woven with the threads of prudence and careful consideration. These measures stand as sentinels, guardians that stand watch over your financial haven, ready to intercept and repel any potential disruption. Adhering to industry best practices further reinforces this shield, infusing it with the wisdom of collective experience and tried-and-tested methodologies.

Yet, the true strength of this shield lies in the realm of conscious action. It's in the everyday choices, the calculated steps, and the measured decisions that you breathe life into your preparedness. By exercising prudence in your actions, you cultivate an environment where risks are identified, assessed, and mitigated even before they take root.

This holistic approach extends beyond the mere alleviation of potential liabilities. It transcends the confines of legal safeguards and financial protections, weaving itself into the very fabric of your financial landscape. By embracing this comprehensive mindset, you not only fortify your defenses but also create an atmosphere where harmony is paramount.

This is a realm where the dissonance of financial upheaval finds no fertile ground to flourish. Instead, harmony prevails, as the symphony of your financial haven plays out without the jarring interruptions that liability risks may attempt to introduce. By weaving this resilient shield of preparedness, you stand poised to navigate the complex interplay of legal obligations and financial uncertainties, ensuring that your haven remains a steadfast bastion of stability and prosperity.

Preserving the Melody: Navigating the Financial Landscape

Much like a skilled orchestra conductor seamlessly blends and harmonizes various instruments to create a symphonic masterpiece, the task of addressing liability risks involves a similar art of harmonization. In this case, the instruments at play are legal safeguards and financial stability, and the resulting composition is a safeguarded haven of equilibrium.

Embracing liability insurance serves as a pivotal note in this symphony. It's the resonating chord that unites legal protection with financial security, adding depth and resonance to your financial composition. This insurance, like the conductor's baton, guides and directs, ensuring that you're shielded from the jarring dissonance that can emerge from unexpected legal proceedings and financial turbulences.

Yet, the symphony of preparedness goes beyond insurance alone. It extends to the cultivation of a mindful culture, one steeped in attentiveness and responsibility. This culture acts as the underlying rhythm, grounding your actions and decisions in a manner that seeks to prevent rather than react.

Just as a conductor meticulously prepares each musician for their part, you, as the steward of your financial haven, meticulously ready yourself. You become attuned to potential risks, ready to navigate the crescendos and decrescendos that the financial landscape presents.

With liability risks acknowledged, and their management ingrained within your financial score, you traverse this landscape with a remarkable blend of confidence and grace. The intricate melody of your haven remains intact, a harmonious interplay of legal resilience and fiscal stability.

As you progress through the financial opus of life, this melody persists, carried by the harmonious rhythm of preparedness, insurance, and mindfulness. Just as a symphony leaves an indelible impression, your journey through the financial landscape is marked by the enduring legacy of a preserved melody - one that echoes with the promise of security, poise, and enduring prosperity.

8.1.3 Health and Medical Risks: Nurturing Well-being

Harmonizing Well-being: Exploring Health and Medical Risks

Within the symphony of safeguarding your financial sanctuary, the concept of health and medical risks emerges as a nurturing melody, dedicated to the preservation of your overall well-being. These notes of caution resonate with a profound purpose, ensuring that your health remains shielded against potential adversities that could jeopardize your financial equilibrium.

Composing the Tune: The Spectrum of Health and Medical Risks

- *Medical Expenses:* In the delicate composition of life, unexpected medical expenses can be an unwelcome dissonance. From routine check-ups to unforeseen emergencies, the strains of medical costs have the potential to disrupt the rhythm of your financial haven.

- *Disability and Loss of Income:* Like an unexpected tempo change, disability or loss of income due to illness or injury can send ripples through your financial composition. The inability to work can result in not only medical expenses but also a loss of the steady cadence of income.

Harboring Resonance: The Role of Health Insurance

Health insurance, much like a comforting lullaby, cradles your well-being within a protective cocoon. It cushions the impact of medical expenses, creating a buffer against the dissonance of healthcare costs. Just as a melody soothes and reassures, health insurance offers you the peace of mind that your financial harmony remains undisturbed, even in the face of health-related uncertainties.

Crafting a Harmonious Future: Nurturing Your Financial Well-being

In the grand symphony of life, your health plays a pivotal role in maintaining the melody of your financial well-being. By nurturing a lifestyle that values wellness and prioritizes self-care, you contribute to the harmonious tapestry of your financial composition. Just as a conductor guides the musicians towards a harmonious crescendo, you guide your own journey towards a future where health and financial harmony are in perfect sync.

As you navigate the passages of life, remember that the notes of health and medical risks are integral to the composition. Embrace the assurance of health insurance, cultivate mindful health practices, and let the resonance of well-being reverberate through the entirety of your financial symphony.

8.1.4 Life Risks: Ensuring Melodic Continuity

Harmonizing Through Loss: Unveiling Life Risks

Within the grand orchestration of your financial symphony, the concept of life risks takes center stage as a weaving thread, ensuring an unbroken melodic continuity even amid the most poignant moments of loss. These threads of risk are intrinsically linked to the potential financial repercussions that follow an individual's passing, particularly if they are the cornerstone breadwinner for their dependents.

Composing the Verse: The Tune of Life Risks

- *Financial Consequences of Death:* In the intricate score of life, the unexpected absence of a primary earner can strike a dissonant chord. The financial consequences of such loss can reverberate deeply, affecting the melody of livelihood for those left behind.

Embracing the Chorus: The Role of Life Insurance

Much like a poignant refrain that echoes through a composition, life insurance steps forward as a powerful chorus. It imbues your symphony with an unwavering safety net, designed to catch those who may stumble in the wake of a loved one's passing. Just as a refrain lingers in memory, life insurance ensures that the financial melody you've painstakingly composed endures, providing support and stability to those you hold dear.

Crafting a Legacy: Orchestrating Financial Security

In the grand opus of your life, the threads of life risks are pivotal in sustaining the harmonious continuity of your financial symphony. Through the inclusion of life insurance, you orchestrate a legacy that stretches beyond your time, embracing the future well-being of your dependents. Like a conductor directing a timeless piece, you chart a course where the composition remains intact, unbroken even by the passage of time or the challenges that it may bring.

As you navigate the delicate cadence of existence, remember that life risks are a profound part of your financial composition. Embrace the power of life insurance, intertwine it with the broader melody of your financial strategy, and ensure that the harmonious resonance of support and continuity echoes through the chapters of your life's symphony.

8.1.5 Financial and Investment Risks: Navigating Economic Harmonies

Conducting Economic Variations: Unveiling Financial and Investment Risks

As your financial symphony unfolds, envision financial and investment risks as the nuanced tempo changes that guide your navigation through the ebbs and flows of markets and economies. These dynamic shifts introduce the possibility of market volatility, economic downturns, or underperformance in investments that hold the potential to influence the realization of your financial aspirations.

Composing the Score: The Melody of Financial and Investment Risks

- *Market Volatility:* In the intricate score of your financial journey, market volatility emerges as a distinct note. It signifies sudden shifts in market sentiment that can either uplift or cast shadows over your financial melodies.
- *Economic Downturns:* Like a sudden shift in key, economic downturns create a different timbre within your financial composition. These periods of economic contraction can ripple through your financial landscape, affecting income, investments, and stability.
- *Poor Investment Performance:* Within the symphony of investments, the occasional discordant note of poor performance may emerge. It echoes the reality that not every investment will yield the expected returns, introducing variability into your financial rhythm.

Harmonizing the Variations: The Role of Adaptation

Just as a skilled conductor adjusts the tempo and orchestrates transitions in a musical piece, your financial strategy learns to dance with these economic variations. It embraces the role of adaptation, aiming not only to weather the storm but to harmonize these fluctuations into the broader melody of your financial objectives.

Crafting Financial Resilience: Achieving Harmonious Growth

In the grand composition of your financial symphony, the nuances of financial and investment risks are integral parts. By weaving them into your financial strategy, you craft a narrative of resilience. This narrative revolves around an understanding that while economic harmonies may shift and melodies may change, the overarching symphony continues to progress, guided by your informed decisions and a steadfast commitment to your financial goals.

As you navigate the diverse cadences of the financial landscape, remember that financial and investment risks are not disruptive dissonances, but rather dynamic variations within your symphony. Embrace the role of conductor, adjusting your strategy to the rhythm of the markets, mitigating risks, and striving for harmonious growth that remains unwavering even in the face of economic variations.

8.1.6 Legal and Regulatory Risks: Complying with Regulatory Score

Harmonizing with Legal Measures: Unfolding Legal and Regulatory Risks

Picture the notion of legal and regulatory risks as an intricately crafted compliance score within your financial symphony, orchestrating a harmonious alignment with the legal landscape. These subtle yet impactful risks encompass an array of potential challenges, including compliance breaches, legal disputes, or shifts in laws and regulations that have the capacity to influence the cadence of your financial situation.

Crafting the Melody: The Composition of Legal and Regulatory Risks

- *Compliance Breaches:* Much like an off-key note disrupts a melody, compliance breaches can introduce discord within your financial composition. These risks emerge when your actions inadvertently deviate from legal and regulatory requirements.
- *Legal Disputes:* In the intricate rhythm of financial management, legal disputes act as unexpected crescendos. They arise from disagreements, contractual conflicts, or other legal intricacies that demand your attention and resources.
- *Dynamic Regulatory Changes:* Just as musical interpretations evolve over time, laws and regulations can shift unexpectedly. These fluctuations introduce a layer of complexity, potentially altering the very tempo of your financial strategy.

Conducting the Ensemble: The Role of Adaptation

Similar to a meticulous conductor adhering to musical guidelines, your financial strategy navigates the nuanced complexities of legal and regulatory risks. It embraces a role of adaptation, ensuring that every financial decision and action remains in harmonious compliance with the legal score.

Fostering Legal Harmony: Navigating the Regulatory Landscape

In the grand opus of your financial journey, legal and regulatory risks form an essential component. By weaving these risks into the fabric of your financial strategy, you craft a narrative of legal harmony. It's a narrative that recognizes the dynamic interplay between legal constraints and financial aspirations, one that aims to create a seamless resonance between the two.

As you traverse the intricate score of your financial landscape, remember that legal and regulatory risks are not disruptive dissonances, but rather elements of the regulatory score that guides your financial symphony. Embrace the conductor's role, adapting your strategy to the evolving legal landscape, harmonizing legal and financial considerations, and thus ensuring that your financial composition resonates in perfect legal harmony.

8.2 Types of Insurance Coverage

8.2.1 Property Insurance: Safeguarding Your Melodic Haven

Harmonizing Protection: The Role of Property Insurance

Imagine property insurance as a masterful conductor, skillfully orchestrating a protective shield around the melodic haven of your tangible assets. This vital coverage emerges as a sentinel, standing guard against the potential discord that damage or loss of property could introduce into your financial composition. From the sanctuary of your home to the mobility of your vehicle and the foundation of your business premises, property insurance casts a comprehensive net of security.

Composing the Score: The Coverage of Property Insurance

- *Protection Against Covered Perils:* Much like a crescendo punctuates a musical piece, covered perils punctuate the landscape of property risks. Property insurance extends its embrace to shield your assets from these perils, encompassing scenarios such as fire, theft, natural disasters, and accidents.

Orchestrating Restoration: The Symphony of Repairs and Replacements

Similar to a conductor guiding each musician to their note, property insurance steps forward to guide the process of restoration. In the face of unforeseen events, it directs the delicate dance of repairs and replacements, ensuring that the harmony of your financial symphony remains unbroken. The damages suffered become mere pauses in your composition, seamlessly addressed by the attentive conductor that is property insurance.

Preserving Financial Serenity: The Melody of Assurance

In the grand opus of your financial endeavors, property insurance is not just a safeguard but a crucial component of your composition. It is the assurance that unexpected disruptions do not crescendo into financial turmoil. It reinforces the notion that while the melody of life may occasionally encounter dissonance, your symphony remains steadfast and undisturbed.

As you navigate the diverse movements of your financial journey, remember that property insurance plays a vital role in preserving the resonant haven you've curated. Just as a conductor ensures the unity of the orchestra, property insurance ensures that the melodic haven of your tangible assets remains unblemished, allowing your financial composition to flourish with confidence and grace.

8.2.2 Liability Insurance: Harmonizing Legal Protection

The Melody of Legal Harmony: Unveiling Liability Insurance

Visualize liability insurance as the key harmonizing note within your financial symphony, resonating with a powerful purpose. This note embodies a shield against the potential dissonance that legal conflicts can introduce. This coverage acts as a guardian, a buffer that stands watch against legal claims and financial responsibilities stemming from bodily injury or property damage inflicted upon others.

Composing the Composition: The Scope of Liability Insurance

- *Guardianship Against Claims:* Just as a melodic phrase seamlessly blends into a musical piece, liability insurance seamlessly integrates into your financial strategy. It provides a guard against legal claims, shouldering the weight of potential disputes and legal intricacies.
- *Protection from Financial Liabilities:* Like a seamless transition between musical movements,

liability insurance ensures a fluid transition from legal claims to financial resolution. It offers financial security, covering the costs that may arise from legal actions.

A Symphony of Defense and Security: The Role of Liability Insurance

Much like a skilled composer harmonizes various instruments, liability insurance orchestrates a blend of legal defense and financial security. It creates a symphony of protection, allowing your financial melody to play smoothly even in the face of potential legal challenges. By harmonizing these elements, liability insurance ensures that your financial composition remains in tune, undisturbed by the legal discord that may otherwise disrupt its rhythm.

Preserving the Musicality of Finances: Legal Resonance in Harmony

In the grand arrangement of your financial opus, liability insurance is more than a mere instrument; it's a conductor that guides the harmonious progression of legal and financial elements. As you journey through the diverse movements of life, remember that this harmonizing note is essential to preserving the melodic nature of your financial symphony. Just as a well-composed piece flows effortlessly, liability insurance enables your financial composition to resonate with legal harmony, allowing you to navigate the complexities of the modern world with grace and assurance.

8.2.3 Health Insurance: A Melodic Cushion

Harmonious Support: The Role of Health Insurance

Envision health insurance as a gentle melodic cushion woven into the fabric of your financial symphony. This vital coverage emerges as a soothing resonance, bolstering your well-being and ensuring that your financial composition plays on seamlessly, unaffected by the potential discord of unexpected health challenges.

Composing the Tune: The Scope of Health Insurance

- *Coverage for Medical Expenses:* Just as a melodic note brings depth to a musical piece, health insurance extends its embrace to encompass a spectrum of medical expenses. It acts as a guardian against the financial strains that can accompany healthcare costs, offering a cushion against the unexpected.
- *Mitigating Health-Related Burdens:* Similar to a harmonizing chord that creates a sense of unity, health insurance mitigates the financial burden of health-related adversities. It cushions the impact of hospitalization, treatments, and other healthcare necessities, allowing your financial composition to remain harmonious.

A Melody of Assurance: Navigating Health Challenges

In the grand symphony of your financial journey, health insurance assumes a fundamental note. It's the assurance that your well-being is supported, allowing your financial melody to resonate unhindered. Just as a comforting melody brings solace, health insurance ensures that unexpected medical expenses don't create dissonance within your financial composition.

Crafting a Resonant Future: Well-being and Financial Serenity

As you move through the movements of life, remember that health insurance is more than a safety net; it's a key player in your financial composition. Like a skilled conductor guiding an orchestra, health insurance orchestrates a harmonious blend of well-being and financial stability. With this melodic cushion in place, you navigate health challenges with grace, allowing your financial symphony to play on smoothly, undisturbed by the potential strains of unforeseen medical costs.

8.2.4 Life Insurance: Sustaining Melodic Legacies

Harmonizing Continuity: The Role of Life Insurance

Imagine life insurance as an enduring note that reverberates through the entirety of your financial symphony, carrying it forward even in moments of absence. This profound coverage assumes the mantle of a guardian, extending its reach to safeguard your loved ones in the event of your passing. It's a note that resonates with the promise of financial protection, ensuring that your composition remains harmonious and uninterrupted.

Composing the Melody: The Scope of Life Insurance

- *Financial Support Beyond Life:* Just as a melodic passage lingers in memory, life insurance extends its support beyond your lifetime. It offers a financial safety net, shouldering the weight of living expenses, debts, and future financial needs that your loved ones may face in your absence.

- *Preserving Legacies:* Similar to the preservation of a timeless melody through generations, life insurance safeguards the legacies you've crafted. It ensures that your aspirations and financial contributions continue to resonate, even when you are no longer present.

Harboring Resonance: The Assurance of Life Insurance

In the grand symphony of your financial narrative, life insurance is not just a note but a pivotal chord. It is the embodiment of assurance, a promise that your financial composition will remain on course, sustaining the melodic flow you've orchestrated. Just as a timeless melody holds its sway, life insurance ensures that your financial legacy endures, providing a harmonious continuity that echoes through the lives of your loved ones.

Crafting a Lasting Overture: Financial Harmony Across Time

As you journey through the movements of life, remember that life insurance plays a profound role in shaping your financial opus. It's not merely a contract; it's a testament to your thoughtful planning and consideration for those you care about. Like a conductor leading an enduring overture, life insurance ensures that your financial symphony carries forward, creating a legacy of harmony and stability that transcends time and circumstance.

8.2.5 Disability Insurance: Preserving Financial Harmony

Sustaining the Melody: The Role of Disability Insurance

Envision disability insurance as the unwavering bassline that preserves the rhythm of your financial symphony, even when the lead notes falter. This coverage stands as a steadfast guardian, ready to step in during periods of income loss due to disability. It's a bassline that echoes with the promise of vital financial support, ensuring that your standard of living remains uninterrupted, and the tempo of your life endures.

Composing the Cadence: The Scope of Disability Insurance

- *Replacing Income Loss:* Much like a reliable rhythm grounds a musical composition, disability insurance provides a solid foundation in times of need. It steps in to replace a portion of your income if disability prevents you from working, acting as a buffer against the potential discord of financial strain.

Maintaining the Tempo: The Assurance of Disability Insurance

In the grand arrangement of your financial orchestration, disability insurance is not just a note but a critical underpinning. It symbolizes the assurance that your financial composition will continue to flow, even if the lead instruments falter. Just as a dependable rhythm guides a musical piece, disability insurance guides your financial rhythm, allowing you to sustain the tempo of your life and maintain your financial harmony.

Crafting Resilience: A Melodic Journey Through Adversity

As you traverse the diverse movements of life, remember that disability insurance plays a pivotal role in crafting resilience. It's not merely a safeguard against the unexpected; it's a testament to your foresight and dedication to upholding your financial harmony. Like a skilled bassist supporting the ensemble, disability insurance ensures that your financial symphony remains grounded and undisturbed, allowing you to navigate the fluctuations of life's melody with confidence and grace.

8.2.6 Long-Term Care Insurance: A Verse of Care

Harmonizing Compassion: The Role of Long-Term Care Insurance

Imagine long-term care insurance as a tender verse woven into the tapestry of your financial symphony, offering a compassionate layer of protection for the chapters of life that may require extended care. This coverage, akin to a heartfelt lyric, encompasses the potential costs of long-term care services, whether in nursing homes or through home healthcare. Like a reassuring tune, long-term care insurance provides not only financial support but also the promise that your melody remains harmonious even amidst the strains of health challenges.

Composing the Lyric: The Scope of Long-Term Care Insurance

- *Embracing Extended Care:* Just as a lyric encapsulates emotions, long-term care insurance encapsulates the possibility of extended care needs. It encompasses the costs associated with nursing homes, assisted living, or home healthcare services, ensuring that your financial composition remains soothing even during health challenges.

A Melody of Reassurance: Navigating Health Transitions

In the grand composition of your financial journey, long-term care insurance assumes a deeply nurturing role. It's the embodiment of reassurance, a promise that the potential strains of extended care won't disrupt your financial composition. Just as a heartfelt lyric brings solace, long-term care insurance ensures that your melody of financial stability continues, offering support and tranquility as you navigate the transitions that health challenges may bring.

Crafting Comfort: A Song of Care Across Time

As you traverse the diverse verses of life, remember that long-term care insurance isn't merely an optional note; it's a profound expression of care and consideration. Like a cherished lyric that remains etched in memory, long-term care insurance becomes an enduring part of your financial narrative. It's a testament to your thoughtfulness, ensuring that the strains of extended care won't create discord within your financial symphony. With this verse of care in place, you journey through health challenges with a sense of comfort, allowing your financial composition to resonate with enduring harmony and peace.

8.2.7 Auto Insurance: Safeguarding Your Journey

Guardian of the Road: The Role of Auto Insurance

Envision auto insurance as the steadfast guardian of your journey, watching over both your vehicle and the intricate financial melody you've orchestrated. This coverage takes on the role of a vigilant protector, embracing damages, liability, and theft that may arise while you're on the road. Much like a reliable navigator, auto insurance ensures that unexpected roadblocks don't interfere with the harmonious rhythm of your financial composition.

Composing the Path: The Scope of Auto Insurance

- *Comprehensive Protection:* Just as a path is lined with various features, auto insurance provides comprehensive protection. It encompasses coverage for damages to your vehicle, liabilities arising from accidents, and even safeguards against the potential loss through theft.

Navigating Smoothly: The Assurance of Auto Insurance

In the grand arrangement of your financial journey, auto insurance is more than a mere accessory; it's an integral guide. It signifies the assurance that your financial symphony can continue playing undisturbed, even on the bustling highways of life. Similar to a navigator ensuring a smooth course, auto insurance charts a path of financial security, safeguarding your vehicle and preserving the seamless rhythm of your composition.

Crafting a Smooth Passage: Harmony on the Road

As you traverse the intricate paths of life, remember that auto insurance isn't just about protection; it's about ensuring your journey remains in tune. Like a skilled driver maneuvering through twists and turns, auto insurance guides you through potential bumps in the road, allowing your financial symphony to continue with grace. With auto insurance as your vigilant guardian, you travel confidently, secure in the knowledge that unexpected roadblocks won't disrupt the harmonious flow of your financial composition.

8.2.8 Business Insurance: Shielding Entrepreneurial Melodies

Guardian of Entrepreneurial Harmony: The Role of Business Insurance

Imagine business insurance as a robust shield that envelops the entrepreneurial melodies you compose. This coverage stands as a vigilant protector, safeguarding your business against the unpredictable storms that may arise. Like a conductor guiding a business symphony, business insurance ensures that your ventures continue to play harmoniously, even amidst the complex dynamics of risks and uncertainties.

Composing the Overture: The Scope of Business Insurance

- *Comprehensive Safeguarding:* Just as a composition weaves together diverse musical elements, business insurance provides comprehensive safeguarding. It extends its reach to cover property damage, liability claims, business interruption, and the intricacies of employee-related risks.

Conducting Resilience: The Assurance of Business Insurance

In the grand symphony of your entrepreneurial journey, business insurance plays a pivotal role. It's not just a safety net; it's a conductor orchestrating the seamless continuation of your business melody. Like a steady hand guiding an orchestra, business insurance ensures that your entrepreneurial pursuits persist, undeterred by the unpredictable challenges that may arise.

Crafting a Prosperous Sonata: Entrepreneurial Harmony Amid Uncertainties

As you steer your entrepreneurial ship through the ever-changing tides of business, remember that business insurance isn't just a precaution; it's an essential note in your composition. Like a conductor's expertise enhancing a musical performance, business insurance enhances your ventures, allowing them to flourish with a sense of security. With business insurance as your shield, you compose a prosperous sonata, guiding your entrepreneurial melodies through the complexities of the business landscape, and ensuring that your symphony of success remains unwavering and harmonious.

8.3 Selecting the Right Insurance Policies

8.3.1 Assess Your Risks: A Prelude to Protection

Harmonizing Preparedness: The Role of Risk Assessment

Imagine risk assessment as the skillful tuning of instruments before a musical performance, setting the stage for harmonious protection in your financial symphony. This step serves as a preliminary note, a prelude that establishes the foundation for your insurance coverage. It involves a comprehensive evaluation of your financial situation, assets, and potential vulnerabilities.

Setting the Tone: The Process of Risk Assessment

- *Evaluating Vulnerabilities:* Just as a composer listens keenly to each instrument, risk assessment listens to the nuances of your financial landscape. It identifies potential vulnerabilities, whether they're related to your health, property, liabilities, or business ventures.
- *Aligning with Needs:* Similar to tuning each instrument to the right pitch, risk assessment ensures that your insurance coverage aligns precisely with your unique needs. It tailors your protection, making certain that every note in your financial composition is in tune.

Crafting a Harmonious Composition: The Assurance of Risk Assessment

In the grand composition of your financial journey, risk assessment is the foundation upon which protection is built. It signifies preparedness, a thoughtful acknowledgement of potential dissonance and a proactive step to mitigate it. Like a conductor orchestrating the ensemble, risk assessment ensures that your insurance coverage harmonizes seamlessly with the intricacies of your financial needs.

Navigating the Symphony of Protection: A Prelude to Harmony

As you prepare for the various movements of life, remember that risk assessment isn't just a preliminary task; it's a conductor's baton that guides the symphony of your financial protection. Like a seasoned conductor leading a performance, risk assessment leads the way to a harmonious financial composition. By assessing your risks diligently, you ensure that your insurance coverage is finely tuned, allowing your financial symphony to play on smoothly and confidently, undisturbed by potential dissonances.

8.3.2 Determine Coverage Needs: Crafting Your Melodic Shield

Harmonizing Protection: The Role of Coverage Determination

Envision the determination of coverage needs as the intricate crafting of a bespoke shield for your financial symphony. This process involves the careful calibration of appropriate coverage limits for each type of insurance, drawing from the canvas of your assets, liabilities, income, and potential financial responsibilities. Much like a skilled artisan tailors each element, determining coverage needs ensures that your protection resonates harmoniously with your unique circumstances.

Crafting the Melodic Shield: The Process of Coverage Determination

- *Balancing the Notes of Protection:* Just as a skilled composer balances notes within a musical composition, coverage determination finds the equilibrium between your various insurance needs.

It ensures that each type of coverage—be it health, life, property, or liability—is aligned with the dimensions of your financial score.

- *Tailoring to Unique Circumstances:* Similar to a tailor measuring and stitching fabric to fit perfectly, determining coverage needs customizes your protection. It takes into account the intricacies of your financial situation, crafting a shield that fits snugly against potential risks.

Ensuring Melodic Resonance: The Assurance of Coverage Determination

In the grand symphony of your financial journey, coverage determination assumes the role of a masterful craftsman. It's not just about choosing insurance; it's about sculpting a shield that preserves the melodic nature of your financial composition. Like a skilled artisan adding finishing touches, coverage determination ensures that your protection is finely tailored, allowing your financial symphony to play on, undisturbed by the dissonance of under-coverage or excess.

Crafting Protection in Tune: A Tailored Shield of Harmony

As you navigate the various movements of your financial opus, remember that determining coverage needs isn't a mere calculation; it's an art form. Like a master conductor guiding an orchestra, coverage determination orchestrates a symphony of protection, ensuring that each note is in tune. By crafting your melodic shield meticulously, you empower your financial composition to play on confidently and gracefully, its harmonious rhythm safeguarded by a shield that resonates perfectly with your unique circumstances.

8.3.3 Research Insurance Providers: The Quest for Melodic Guardians

Harmonizing Protection: The Role of Provider Research

Envision researching insurance providers as embarking on a noble quest to find the perfect guardians for your financial composition. This step involves the diligent exploration of reputable insurance companies that offer the coverage your symphony requires. Similar to a vigilant seeker on a quest, researching insurance providers is a journey that ensures your protection is entrusted to reliable and steadfast guardians.

Embarking on the Quest: The Process of Provider Research

- *Exploring Reputable Guardians:* Just as an explorer seeks trustworthy guides, provider research involves exploring reputable insurance companies. It delves into their backgrounds, histories, and industry standings to ensure they possess the qualities of a reliable guardian for your financial melody.
- *Comparing Qualities:* Similar to weighing the merits of different paths, researching insurance providers compares their policies, coverage options, and customer reviews. It also examines their financial strength ratings, determining their

ability to stand as resilient protectors.

Discovering Melodic Sentinels: The Assurance of Provider Research

In the grand composition of your financial journey, provider research is the quest for melodic sentinels who will safeguard your symphony. It's not just about selecting an insurance provider; it's about entrusting your financial harmony to steadfast guardians. Like an astute observer seeking harmony, provider research ensures that your protection is placed in the capable hands of those who can uphold the melody of your financial composition.

Crafting a Resonant Ensemble: Guardians of Financial Melody

As you set forth on the path of financial protection, remember that researching insurance providers isn't a mere task; it's a quest for harmony. Like a determined seeker on a noble quest, provider research uncovers the guardians who will watch over your financial opus. By selecting your protectors with care and diligence, you assemble an ensemble of reliable and capable guardians, each playing their part to ensure that your financial symphony remains undisturbed and resonant.

8.3.4 Understand Policy Terms and Exclusions: Decoding the Harmonic Contract

Harmonizing Understanding: The Role of Policy Decoding

Envision the process of understanding policy terms and exclusions as akin to decoding the intricate musical notation of your insurance contract. It's a meticulous endeavor that involves delving into the fine details of the policy, thoroughly reading and comprehending its terms and conditions. Just as a discerning musicologist deciphers musical nuances, understanding policy terms ensures that you grasp the subtleties and intricacies of your insurance protection.

Decoding the Harmonic Contract: The Process of Understanding Policy Terms

- *Reading the Musical Notation:* Just as a musicologist studies musical scores, understanding policy terms involves studying the written document. It includes analyzing coverage limits, deductibles, exclusions, and the conditions under which claims can be filed.
- *Grasping Nuances:* Similar to identifying the nuanced expressions within a musical piece, understanding policy terms enables you to discern the fine print. It helps you recognize what is covered and what falls outside the scope of protection.

Harmonizing Assurance: The Benefit of Understanding Policy Terms

In the grand symphony of your financial protection, understanding policy terms and exclusions is more than a cursory glance; it's a masterclass in interpretation. It assures that you're not only aware of the melody but also the underlying notes and pauses that compose your insurance coverage. Like a seasoned conductor guiding a performance, understanding policy terms ensures that you're fully aware of the nuances that shape your financial protection.

Crafting Resonance: The Melody of Insurance Understanding

As you navigate the complexities of insurance contracts, remember that understanding policy terms isn't just a chore; it's a harmonizing practice. Like a dedicated musicologist unraveling the intricacies of a composition, policy understanding allows you to navigate the symphony of your insurance coverage with confidence. By delving into the details and nuances, you ensure that your financial composition is played with precision and assurance, with each note and rest contributing to the harmonious melody of your protection.

8.3.5 Seek Professional Advice: The Maestros of Insurance Guidance

Harmonizing Expertise: The Role of Professional Advice

Envision seeking professional advice as the act of consulting with maestros who possess the expertise to guide you through the intricate symphony of insurance options. These experts, whether insurance agents or brokers, step into the role of seasoned conductors, providing knowledgeable guidance that resonates with your unique needs. Like a conductor leading an orchestra to harmonious performance, seeking professional advice ensures that your insurance ensemble plays with precision and harmony.

Conducting the Symphony: The Process of Seeking Professional Advice

- *Expert Guiding Baton:* Just as a conductor leads an orchestra, insurance professionals hold the baton of expert guidance. They help you decipher the musical score of insurance options, tailoring their advice to match your financial composition.
- *Navigating Complexity:* Similar to a conductor's understanding of musical intricacies, insurance experts navigate the complexities of policies. They assist in deciphering policy terms, coverage details, and exclusions, ensuring that you make informed decisions.

Harmonizing Assurance: The Benefit of Seeking Professional Advice

In the grand arrangement of your financial symphony, seeking professional advice is more than a consultation; it's a collaboration with seasoned musicians. It assures that your insurance choices are orchestrated with finesse, and your coverage ensemble performs flawlessly. Like a maestro guiding an orchestra to perfection, seeking professional advice ensures that your insurance protection is aligned precisely with the harmonious rhythm of your needs.

Crafting a Melodic Ensemble: The Art of Expert Guidance

As you navigate the complexities of insurance options, remember that seeking professional advice isn't just a choice; it's an investment in harmony. Like a conductor fine-tuning every section of an orchestra, insurance experts fine-tune your coverage, ensuring each note is in tune. By collaborating with these maestros, you create a melodic ensemble of insurance protection that plays with confidence and assurance, crafting a symphony of financial security that resonates harmoniously throughout the movements of your life.

8.4 Mitigating Risk through Insurance

8.4.1 Financial Security: A Harmonious Safety Net

Consider insurance as the harmonious safety net that cushions you from the impact of potential losses. By transferring the financial burden to an insurance company, you ensure that you aren't solely responsible for shouldering the full weight of unexpected events. Like a protective barrier, insurance maintains the rhythm of your financial symphony even when faced with discordant notes.

Harmonizing Protection: The Role of Insurance

Envision insurance as the harmonious safety net that gracefully cushions you from the impact of potential losses. This safety net is a bridge connecting you to the supportive realm of an insurance company, relieving you from the burden of shouldering the full weight of unexpected events alone. Like a steadfast barrier, insurance ensures that the rhythm of your financial symphony remains steady even when confronted with discordant notes.

The Symphony of Financial Security: The Assurance of Insurance

- *Transferring the Melodic Burden:* Just as a symphony conductor guides the orchestra, insurance transfers the burden of potential financial strain to a reliable source. It ensures that you don't stand alone in facing the challenges that life's unpredictable twists can bring.

- *Maintaining Harmonious Rhythm:* Similar to a protective embrace during tumultuous times, insurance maintains the harmonious rhythm of your financial composition. It allows you to navigate uncertainties without losing the flow of your financial symphony.

Crafting a Resilient Melody: The Melodic Safety Net

In the grand composition of your financial journey, insurance isn't just a contractual agreement; it's a resonant safety net woven into your symphony. It assures that you can navigate the ebbs and flows of life's narrative with confidence. Like a masterful conductor leading an orchestra through challenging sections, insurance ensures that your financial composition maintains its melodious stride, even when faced with unexpected dissonance.

Ensuring Financial Harmony: The Protective Song of Insurance

As you journey through life's stages, remember that insurance isn't merely a transaction; it's a protective song that harmonizes your financial landscape. Like a guardian watching over a performance, insurance stands as a vigilant protector, allowing your symphony to flourish even in the face of unexpected turns. By embracing this harmonious safety net, you weave a resilient melody of financial security that plays on, undisturbed by the occasional dissonant notes that life may bring.

8.4.2 Asset Protection: Preserving Melodic Treasures

Imagine insurance as the guardian of your melodic treasures, safeguarding your assets from unforeseen risks. Whether it's your home, vehicle, or business, insurance coverage steps in to repair or replace damaged or lost assets in the event of an insured incident. Like a vigilant sentry, insurance ensures that your financial composition retains its harmonious melody.

Harmonizing Preservation: The Role of Insurance

Envision insurance as the vigilant guardian of your melodic treasures, standing watch over your assets and shielding them from the uncertainties of unforeseen risks. Whether it's the haven of your home, the journey of your vehicle, or the symphony of your business, insurance coverage steps in like a valiant defender, ready to repair or replace damaged or lost assets in the event of an insured incident. Much like a vigilant sentry, insurance ensures that your financial composition retains its harmonious melody.

Symphony of Asset Preservation: The Assurance of Insurance

- *Safekeeping Melodic Treasures:* Just as a curator safeguards priceless artifacts, insurance safeguards your assets. It steps in to protect your home, your vehicle, your business premises, and other valuable assets from the unexpected storms that life may unleash.

- *Maintaining Harmonious Composition:* Similar to a skillful conductor maintaining the rhythm of a performance, insurance ensures that your financial symphony remains undisturbed. It allows you to navigate unexpected disruptions without missing a beat.

Crafting a Resonant Legacy: The Melodic Guardian

In the grand composition of your financial journey, insurance transcends being a mere safeguard; it's a melodic guardian of your valuable assets. It assures that your life's treasures remain protected and preserved, allowing you to carry on your financial opus with confidence. Like a vigilant guardian watching over a cherished performance, insurance stands as a steadfast protector, ensuring that your financial melody resonates harmoniously, even in the face of unforeseen challenges.

Preserving the Melody: The Protective Overture of Insurance

As you traverse the stages of your financial narrative, remember that insurance is more than a transaction; it's a protective overture for your assets. Like a sentinel guarding a masterpiece, insurance shields your assets, enabling your financial composition to continue playing its harmonious tune. By embracing this protective harmony, you weave a resilient legacy of asset preservation, ensuring that the treasures you've gathered along your journey remain integral parts of your harmonious financial symphony.

8.4.3 Liability Coverage: A Legal Sonata

Think of liability coverage as a legal sonata that shields you from potential legal dissonance. This aspect of insurance safeguards you against legal and financial consequences in case of accidents, injuries, or property damage for which you may be held accountable. Like a skilled composer, liability coverage orchestrates legal defense and financial resolution, harmonizing your protection.

Harmonizing Legal Protection: The Role of Liability Coverage

Envision liability coverage as a meticulously composed legal sonata, skillfully shielding you from the potential dissonance of legal challenges. This facet of insurance acts as a harmonious conductor, safeguarding you against the legal and financial consequences that may arise from accidents, injuries, or property damage for which you might be held accountable. Much like a seasoned composer, liability coverage orchestrates the intricate notes of legal defense and financial resolution, ensuring a symphony of protection.

Legal Sonata of Protection: The Assurance of Liability Coverage

- *Safeguarding from Legal Dissonance:* Just as a sonata weaves musical notes into a harmonious arrangement, liability coverage weaves legal protection into your financial symphony. It shields you from potential legal disruptions and ensures that the rhythm of your life isn't disrupted by unexpected legal challenges.

- *Harmonizing Legal and Financial Aspects:* Similar to a conductor merging different musical elements, liability coverage seamlessly merges legal defense and financial resolution. It steps in to navigate legal intricacies and provide financial restitution, allowing you to continue your life's composition without discord.

Crafting a Legal Melody: The Symphonic Shield of Liability Coverage

In the grand composition of your financial journey, liability coverage isn't just a shield; it's a legal melody that resonates with protection. It assures that you can navigate the complex legal landscape without missing a beat. Like a virtuoso composer harmonizing different instruments, liability coverage harmonizes legal protection and financial stability, allowing you to pursue your life's symphony confidently and gracefully.

Harmonious Resonance: The Legal Symphony of Liability Coverage

As you traverse life's stages, remember that liability coverage is more than a policy; it's a legal symphony that safeguards your harmony. Like a conductor leading a symphony through intricate passages, liability coverage guides you through legal challenges, ensuring that your financial composition maintains its melodious flow. By embracing this legal sonata, you create a resonant melody of legal protection that plays on, undisturbed by the potential legal dissonance that life may bring.

8.4.4 Business Continuity: Sustaining Entrepreneurial Symphony

Consider business insurance as the sustaining rhythm that maintains the entrepreneurial symphony you've composed. It offers protection against risks that could disrupt the continuity of your business, such as property damage, liability claims, or business interruption. Like a conductor guiding a business ensemble, business insurance ensures that your entrepreneurial melody persists through challenges.

Harmonizing Business Protection: The Role of Business Insurance

Envision business insurance as the unwavering rhythm that sustains the entrepreneurial symphony you've carefully composed. This insurance genre provides a protective backdrop against risks that could disrupt the continuity of your business, including perils like property damage, liability claims, or unforeseen interruptions. Much like a conductor guiding an orchestra through complex movements, business insurance orchestrates a harmonious blend of protection, ensuring that your entrepreneurial melody endures even amidst challenges.

Symphony of Entrepreneurial Continuity: The Assurance of Business Insurance

- *Sustaining the Entrepreneurial Melody:* Just as a reliable rhythm holds together a musical ensemble, business insurance holds together your entrepreneurial venture. It safeguards your business from potential threats and ensures that your symphony of entrepreneurship continues to play on, undisturbed.

- *Guiding Through Challenges:* Similar to a conductor leading an orchestra through intricate passages, business insurance guides you through the complex world of business risks. It steps in to mitigate disruptions, allowing you to focus on composing your business's success story.

Crafting Resilient Entrepreneurship: The Melodic Sustainment

In the grand composition of your entrepreneurial journey, business insurance isn't just a policy; it's a sustaining force that harmonizes with your entrepreneurial aspirations. It assures that your business's melody continues to resonate, even in the face of uncertainties. Like a guiding conductor preserving the essence of a musical performance, business insurance preserves the core of your entrepreneurial symphony, allowing it to flourish and thrive.

Sustaining the Melody: The Business Symphony of Insurance

As you navigate the dynamic stages of entrepreneurship, remember that business insurance is more than a financial transaction; it's a symphony of protection for your venture. Like a steadfast conductor leading a business ensemble, business insurance directs you through the complexities of risk management. By embracing this sustaining rhythm, you weave a resilient melody of entrepreneurial continuity, ensuring that your business's symphony plays on, undeterred by the occasional discordant notes that the business world may introduce.

8.4.5 Peace of Mind: The Harmonic Serenity

Imagine insurance as the source of harmonic serenity that allows you to pursue personal and professional endeavors without constant worry. Having the right coverage in place provides the peace of mind that comes from knowing you're financially protected. Like a soothing melody, insurance assures that potential risks don't disrupt the harmony of your life.

Harmonizing Peace: The Role of Insurance

Envision insurance as the wellspring of harmonic serenity that liberates you to chase personal and professional aspirations without the weight of perpetual concern. The presence of appropriate coverage offers a calming peace of mind, akin to a soothing melody that assures you're shielded financially. Much like a tranquil refrain, insurance ensures that potential risks remain harmoniously managed, preserving the rhythm of your life.

Symphony of Assurance: The Comfort of Insurance

- *Unburdening Daily Worries:* Just as a gentle melody washes away daily worries, insurance alleviates the burden of constant apprehension. It empowers you to engage in life's pursuits without the shadow of potential financial setbacks looming overhead.
- *Harmonious Protection:* Similar to a melodic tune bringing tranquility, insurance provides a sense of safety. It creates an environment where you can explore, innovate, and live fully, knowing that your financial landscape is secure.

Crafting a Melodic Serenade: The Assurance of Insurance

In the grand composition of your life's narrative, insurance transcends being a mere contract; it's a harmonizing serenade that plays in the background, allowing you to revel in life's symphony. It ensures that your pursuits are not stifled by constant worry but are instead buoyed by the confidence of protection. Like a reassuring melody accompanying your every step, insurance crafts a melodic serenade that resonates with harmonious tranquility.

Embracing Serenity: The Melody of Insurance Comfort

As you navigate the vibrant cadence of life, remember that insurance is more than just a practicality; it's a symphony of comfort that weaves through your existence. Like a calming balm on a restless day, insurance provides a backdrop of assurance. By embracing this harmonic serenity, you infuse your life's composition with a soothing melody of protection, allowing you to dance through the symphony of your days without fear of dissonance from unforeseen risks.

8.4.6 Risk Transfer: The Melodic Exchange

Think of insurance as the melodic exchange that transfers the burden of financial risks to an insurance provider. By paying premiums, you shift the responsibility of potential losses to the company, which has the resources to manage and mitigate such risks. Like a collaborative duet, insurance partners with you to ensure your financial composition plays smoothly.

Harmonizing Risk Management: The Role of Insurance

Envision insurance as a harmonious exchange that elegantly transfers the weight of financial risks to an expert partner. Just as a collaborative duet blends different musical voices, insurance joins forces with you to shift the responsibility of potential losses to an insurance provider. Through the payment of premiums, you create a melodic exchange where the company assumes the role of a skilled performer, equipped with the resources to manage and mitigate risks that could disrupt your financial composition.

Symphony of Collaborative Protection: The Assurance of Risk Transfer

- *Melodic Burden Transfer:* Just as a skilled musician takes over a challenging passage in a duet, insurance assumes the burden of financial risks. Your premiums serve as the notes that facilitate this exchange, creating a harmonious partnership.
- *Managing and Mitigating Risks:* Similar to a collaborative performance that blends different instruments into a seamless composition, insurance leverages its expertise and resources to manage and mitigate the risks you've transferred. It ensures that your financial symphony plays smoothly, even in the face of potential disruptions.

Crafting Resonant Protection: The Melodic Symphony of Insurance

In the grand composition of financial protection, insurance surpasses being a mere contract; it's a melodic exchange that harmonizes with your risk management efforts. It assures that potential dissonances in the form of financial setbacks are met with expert skill. Like a seamless blend of musical voices creating a harmonious piece, insurance crafts a symphony of collaborative protection, allowing you to navigate the rhythms of life confidently.

Transcending Risks: The Collaborative Symphony of Insurance

As you journey through life's movements, remember that insurance is more than a transaction; it's a symphony of collaborative risk management. Like a well-coordinated duet, insurance complements your efforts, ensuring that your financial composition maintains its fluidity. By embracing this melodic exchange, you compose a resilient protection that resonates through the chapters of your life, creating a harmonious arrangement where potential risks are transformed into confident melodies.

8.4.7 Legal Compliance: The Harmonious Accord

Consider insurance as the harmonious accord that aligns with legal requirements. In certain situations, insurance coverage is mandated by law, such as auto insurance in many jurisdictions. Complying with these requirements ensures you meet legal obligations while protecting yourself and others. Like a well-composed refrain, insurance harmonizes legal compliance with financial safeguarding.

Harmonizing Legal Alignment: The Role of Insurance

Envision insurance as the harmonious accord that gracefully synchronizes with legal mandates. In certain contexts, insurance coverage is a harmonizing force that resonates with legal requirements. For instance, auto insurance is often mandated by law in many jurisdictions. By adhering to these obligations, insurance ensures that you meet legal requirements while simultaneously safeguarding your interests and the well-being of others. Much like a well-composed refrain, insurance blends legal compliance with the melody of financial protection.

Symphony of Legal Harmony: The Assurance of Compliance

- *Alignment with Legal Requirements:* Just as a well-executed accord creates a sense of unity in a musical piece, insurance aligns with legal mandates, ensuring that you are in compliance with necessary regulations. It transforms legal obligations into a harmonious part of your financial composition.
- *Protection and Adherence:* Similar to a skillful performer staying true to the score of a musical piece, insurance safeguards your interests while adhering to legal requirements. It orchestrates a balanced harmony where legal compliance doesn't disrupt the rhythm of your financial symphony.

Crafting a Melodic Accord: The Legal and Financial Composition

In the grand arrangement of your financial journey, insurance transcends being a mere necessity; it's a melodic accord that seamlessly integrates with legal obligations. It assures that you can navigate the intricate notes of the legal landscape without missing a beat in your financial composition. Like a beautifully orchestrated passage that adds depth to a musical piece, insurance crafts a symphony of legal compliance and financial safeguarding, ensuring a harmonious blend.

Harmonious Compliance: The Legal Symphony of Insurance

As you navigate the intricacies of life's score, remember that insurance is more than a legal requirement; it's a symphony of legal harmony. Like a well-coordinated ensemble playing in unison, insurance ensures that your financial composition remains aligned with legal mandates while preserving its melodic flow. By embracing this harmonious accord, you craft a resilient protection that resonates with the cadence of compliance, weaving a harmonious tapestry where legal adherence and financial safeguarding harmonize in perfect unity.

8.4.8 Recovery Support: The Melodic Healing

Imagine insurance as the melodic healing that supports you in the aftermath of an insured event. Insurance companies provide guidance and assistance throughout the claims process, facilitating repairs, replacements, and financial compensation as stipulated in your policy. Like a comforting melody, insurance aids in the recovery process, helping you restore your financial composition.

Harmonizing Post-Event Recovery: The Role of Insurance

Envision insurance as the gentle melody of healing that embraces you in the aftermath of an insured event. Just as a soothing melody provides solace, insurance companies offer support and guidance throughout the claims process, orchestrating repairs, replacements, and financial compensation as outlined in your policy. Like a comforting and reassuring tune, insurance becomes a partner in your recovery journey, aiding in the restoration of your financial composition.

Symphony of Post-Event Healing: The Assurance of Support

- *Guided Recovery:* Much like a nurturing melody guiding you through difficult times, insurance steps in to guide your recovery after an insured event. It ensures that you're not navigating the aftermath alone but are supported by professionals who understand the intricacies of the process.
- *Restoration and Assistance:* Similar to a soothing melody easing discomfort, insurance aids in restoring normalcy. It facilitates the necessary steps, whether it's repairing property, replacing assets, or providing financial compensation, so you can rebuild and move forward.

Crafting a Melodic Healing: The Journey to Restoration

In the grand composition of your life's narrative, insurance extends beyond being a mere policy; it's a melodic healing that resonates with empathy and support. It assures that you're not left to navigate the aftermath on your own, but are embraced by the melody of assistance. Like a caring tune that provides solace, insurance crafts a symphony of recovery support, helping you mend and rebuild the notes of your financial composition.

Recovering Harmony: The Healing Symphony of Insurance

As you progress through the chapters of life, remember that insurance is more than a contractual agreement; it's a symphony of healing that envelopes you after adversity. Like a harmonious choir offering comfort, insurance ensures that your recovery is guided and supported. By embracing this melodic healing, you weave a resilient tapestry of restoration, where the aftermath of an insured event becomes a chapter in your life's symphony, marked by the soothing strains of recovery and renewal.

Chapter 9: Tax Planning and Optimization

9.1 Understanding the Essentials of Tax Planning

In the intricate composition of your financial journey, tax planning emerges as a vital orchestrator, conducting the harmonious interplay of income, deductions, and regulations. This segment introduces you to the foundational principles that guide this symphony of optimization, empowering you to navigate the complexities of tax laws with finesse and strategic acumen.

9.1.1 The Melody of Taxable Income: Sources and Strategies

Much like a symphonic arrangement, your income streams resonate with unique tones, each subject to specific tax treatments. Wages, investment gains, self-employment earnings, and rental proceeds create a harmonious ensemble of taxable income sources. Understanding the nuances of how these sources are taxed grants you the ability to craft a melodic financial composition, orchestrating your financial decisions to resonate with tax efficiency.

The Wage Waltz: Your earned wages take the lead in this financial symphony, forming the foundation of your taxable income. Just as a waltz's graceful steps are meticulously choreographed, understanding how your wages are taxed allows you to choreograph your financial moves, optimizing deductions and credits to create a harmonious tax outcome.

Investment Crescendo: Investment gains play a compelling role, akin to a crescendo building within a musical piece. Whether it's capital gains from stocks or interest from bonds, the tax treatment varies. Much like a composer building anticipation, strategic investment decisions can help you manage the tax impact of your gains, ensuring that your financial melody reaches a harmonious climax.

The Solo Act of Self-Employment: Self-employment earnings bring forth a unique solo performance in your tax orchestration. Like a virtuoso showcasing their skills, understanding self-employment taxes empowers you to navigate estimated tax payments, deductions for business expenses, and the complexities of being your own conductor in the financial realm.

Rental Rhapsody: Rental income creates a harmonious rhapsody in your taxable income composition. Like composing a symphony, managing rental income involves understanding allowable deductions, depreciation, and potential tax benefits. By mastering the art of rental property taxation, you ensure that your financial composition resonates with optimal tax efficiency.

Harmonizing Strategies: Just as a skilled composer blends different instruments to create a harmonious composition, employing strategies for each income source enhances your tax efficiency. From deferring income to strategic timing of investments, each strategy contributes to the orchestration of your financial melody, resulting in a tax-efficient symphony.

Creating Your Tax Sonata: In the grand performance of tax planning, each income source plays a distinct role, contributing its unique notes to the symphony of taxable income. This section equips you with the knowledge to compose your own tax sonata, allowing you to play the keys of taxation with precision and finesse, ensuring that your financial composition is a masterpiece of harmonious tax efficiency.

9.1.2 Tax Brackets: Crafting Harmonic Income Management

Tax brackets introduce dynamic shifts in your financial composition, akin to the changing tempo in a musical piece. Just as a skilled conductor navigates various rhythms in a symphony, understanding tax brackets empowers you to craft a harmonious score for income management. By artfully conducting your financial choices within these brackets, you can strike a melodic balance between income and taxation, orchestrating a composition that optimizes your financial melody.

The Prelude to Taxation: Like the opening notes of a musical prelude, tax brackets set the stage for the financial performance ahead. Understanding where your income falls within these brackets allows you to gauge the overall tax impact and strategically adjust your financial decisions for maximum benefit.

Composing with Marginal Rates: Much like a composer modulates between keys for emotional impact, tax brackets introduce shifts in marginal tax rates. This knowledge empowers you to decide when to increase or decrease your income, akin to changing the emotional tone in a musical piece, all in pursuit of a harmonious tax outcome.

The Crescendo of Tax Savings: Just as a musical crescendo builds intensity, navigating tax brackets can lead to a crescendo of tax savings. Shifting income to lower tax brackets through strategies such as deferring income or maximizing deductions orchestrates a powerful crescendo, reducing the overall tax burden and allowing your financial melody to reach its peak performance.

Striking a Chord with Efficiency: Just as chords create depth in music, efficiently managing your income within tax brackets creates depth in your financial composition. Understanding the optimal threshold for each tax bracket enables you to make informed financial decisions that strike a harmonious chord between income and taxation.

Harmonizing Financial Decisions: Similar to orchestrating different instruments to create a harmonious musical piece, navigating tax brackets involves harmonizing various financial decisions. From investment timing to retirement withdrawals, each decision plays a distinct note in your financial symphony, contributing to a composition that resonates with tax efficiency.

The Art of Financial Symphony: Tax brackets offer you the conductor's baton, allowing you to shape the tempo and rhythm of your financial composition. This section provides you with the tools to create a symphony of income management, where each note of income is precisely tuned to strike a harmonious balance with taxation. By mastering the art of conducting within tax brackets, you can compose a financial melody that resonates with optimal tax efficiency, ensuring that your composition reaches its full melodic potential.

9.1.3 Filing Status: Your Taxation Ensemble

Much like the various roles in an orchestra, choosing your filing status influences the collaborative nature of your tax composition. Just as different instruments contribute distinct tones to a musical ensemble, your filing status determines the harmonious interaction of deductions and tax treatment. Whether performing as a soloist, harmonizing with a partner, or leading the ensemble as head of household, your filing status significantly shapes the orchestration of your tax liability. The decision you make in this regard resonates throughout your financial opus, dictating the overarching tune of your tax liability.

Soloist's Serenade: Opting for the "Single" filing status allows your financial composition to take center stage. Like a soloist commanding attention, this status simplifies your tax journey by focusing solely on your individual income and deductions, allowing you to play a clear and distinct tax melody.

Harmony in Unison: Choosing "Married Filing Jointly" harmonizes your financial notes with a partner. Like a duet creating a rich blend of melodies, this status combines your incomes and deductions, often resulting in favorable tax rates and a coordinated financial arrangement that resonates in unison.

Duet of Independence: If you and your spouse choose "Married Filing Separately," it's akin to performing a duet while maintaining individuality. Like two instrumentalists playing in harmony yet maintaining distinct notes, this status can offer specific advantages in certain financial situations, while requiring careful coordination to ensure the melody remains balanced.

Leading the Ensemble: Heading the household comes with its own distinct rhythm. Like a conductor guiding an orchestra, the "Head of Household" status is reserved for those providing a home for dependents. This status orchestrates deductions and tax rates to support your role as the financial leader of your household's ensemble.

The Solo and Symphony of Taxes: Just as a soloist contributes unique melodies to a symphony, your chosen filing status contributes its own notes to the symphony of your taxes. Understanding the role each status plays allows you to compose your financial composition with finesse, whether as a soloist, part of a harmonious duo, or leading a household ensemble. Each filing status forms a part of your financial melody, shaping the overall tune of your tax liability in this intricate symphony of taxation.

9.1.4 Prelude to Tax Optimization: Conductor's Insights

As the curtain rises on the stage of tax planning, this preliminary section sets the tone for your journey toward tax optimization. Much like a musical prelude introduces motifs that later form the heart of a symphonic masterpiece, these foundational understandings of taxable income, tax brackets, and filing status lay the groundwork for your comprehensive tax strategy.

A Composer's Palette of Income: Just as a composer selects instruments for a palette of sounds, understanding taxable income sources provides the palette for your tax strategy. Wages, investments, self-employment, and rentals each form a unique hue, ready to be orchestrated in your financial symphony.

Crafting Tax Harmonies with Brackets: Like the subtle shifts in mood brought by key changes, tax brackets introduce varying levels of taxation. Your understanding of these brackets empowers you to compose harmonies of income management, conducting the tempo of your financial decisions.

The Filing Status Sonata: Much like a musical sonata, your chosen filing status carries distinct melodies. The soloist's clarity, the duet's harmony, the independence of the married filing separately, and the leadership of the head of household—all contribute to your financial composition.

Conductor of Tax Optimization: With these insights in hand, you ascend to the conductor's podium of your financial symphony. Just as a conductor shapes the orchestra's performance, you orchestrate your financial choices for tax efficiency. The instruments of taxable income, the harmonies of tax brackets, and the melodies of filing status—all under your guidance—blend to create an arrangement that's both harmonious and tax-optimized.

Setting the Stage for Tax Symphony: Much like a prelude primes the audience for the main performance, this section readies you for the intricate symphony of tax optimization. Armed with these foundational insights, you stand as the conductor, ready to lead your financial instruments in a composition that resonates with harmony and fiscal efficiency. With each subsequent movement of tax planning, you'll weave these principles into a symphonic masterpiece of financial wisdom and tax advantage.

9.2 Composing the Overture: Tax Deductions and Credits

In the grand symphony of tax planning, deductions and credits play a resounding overture, introducing opportunities to harmonize your financial composition with potential tax benefits. This section unveils the intricate melodies of deductions and credits, allowing you to blend them seamlessly into your score of financial well-being.

9.2.1 Deductions Unveiled: Crafting Your Melodic Reductions

As the curtain rises on the stage of tax planning, this preliminary section sets the tone for your journey toward tax optimization. Much like a musical prelude introduces motifs that later form the heart of a symphonic masterpiece, these foundational understandings of taxable income, tax brackets, and filing status lay the groundwork for your comprehensive tax strategy.

A Composer's Palette of Income: Just as a composer selects instruments for a palette of sounds, understanding taxable income sources provides the palette for your tax strategy. Wages, investments, self-employment, and rentals each form a unique hue, ready to be orchestrated in your financial symphony.

Crafting Tax Harmonies with Brackets: Like the subtle shifts in mood brought by key changes, tax brackets introduce varying levels of taxation. Your understanding of these brackets empowers you to compose harmonies of income management, conducting the tempo of your financial decisions.

The Filing Status Sonata: Much like a musical sonata, your chosen filing status carries distinct melodies. The soloist's clarity, the duet's harmony, the independence of the married filing separately, and the leadership of the head of household—all contribute to your financial composition.

Conductor of Tax Optimization: With these insights in hand, you ascend to the conductor's podium of your financial symphony. Just as a conductor shapes the orchestra's performance, you orchestrate your financial choices for tax efficiency. The instruments of taxable income, the harmonies of tax brackets, and the melodies of filing status—all under your guidance—blend to create an arrangement that's both harmonious and tax-optimized.

Setting the Stage for Tax Symphony: Much like a prelude primes the audience for the main performance, this section readies you for the intricate symphony of tax optimization. Armed with these foundational insights, you stand as the conductor, ready to lead your financial instruments in a composition that resonates with harmony and fiscal efficiency. With each subsequent movement of tax planning, you'll weave these principles into a symphonic masterpiece of financial wisdom and tax advantage.

Standard Deduction: The Fundamental Note

Much like a foundational note in music, the standard deduction is a fundamental component of your tax score. This fixed deduction amount reduces your taxable income, simplifying the complexity of your financial composition. Like a steady beat, the standard deduction ensures that every financial note remains in rhythm, offering a straightforward reduction option for many taxpayers.

Itemized Deductions: The Intricate Harmonies

Choosing itemized deductions is akin to weaving intricate harmonies within your financial composition. Like a composer selecting distinct instruments for varied tones, you meticulously select deductions that reflect your unique financial scenario. Mortgage interest, property taxes, medical expenses, and charitable contributions are among the instruments in your deduction orchestra. Just as a conductor balances different instruments, you balance these deductions to create a tax reduction symphony tailored to your circumstances.

The Composition of Deduction Strategy

Crafting your melodic reductions involves a careful composition of deduction elements. Similar to how musical layers build to a crescendo, your deductions combine to create a harmonious reduction strategy. The decision to opt for standard or itemized deductions becomes a conductor's choice, determining the overall resonance of your tax composition. Your mastery in this realm enables you to play the tax reduction melody that aligns perfectly with your financial goals.

A Symphony of Reductions

In this intricate dance of deductions, you act as both composer and conductor. The standard deduction provides a solid foundation, akin to the grounding notes of a melody. Itemized deductions add depth and variation, like harmonies and counterpoints enriching a musical arrangement. The interplay between these deduction elements becomes the symphony of your tax strategy, echoing the careful orchestration of a maestro crafting a masterpiece.

Harmonizing Deductions with Goals

As you unveil the art of deductions, remember that each choice harmonizes with your financial goals. Just as a composer tailors a piece to evoke a specific emotion, your deduction strategy should reflect your financial aspirations. By skillfully weaving the threads of deductions—standard and itemized—into your financial fabric, you create a reduction composition that resonates harmoniously with your unique financial symphony.

9.2.2 Homeownership Harmonies: Deductions in Your Abode

As your financial symphony unfolds, homeownership emerges as a distinctive and melodious theme, complete with a range of deductions that compose a harmonious score of financial advantages. Much like a skilled composer carefully selects instruments to create a balanced piece, your role as a homeowner involves orchestrating deductions that harmonize with your tax planning strategy.

Mortgage Interest Deduction: A Fundamental Note

The mortgage interest deduction stands as a fundamental note within the homeownership harmonies. Like a recurring motif in music, this deduction allows you to subtract the interest paid on your mortgage from your taxable income. The result is a reduction that echoes throughout your financial composition, creating a rhythm of tax savings that resonates with the benefits of owning a home.

Property Tax Deduction: A Resonant Chord

The property tax deduction adds a resonant chord to your homeownership melody. Just as different chords evoke distinct emotions in music, property taxes shape the financial atmosphere of your abode. This deduction enables you to subtract your paid property taxes from your taxable income, creating a harmonious reduction that contributes to your overall tax strategy.

The Home Office Sonata: Self-Employed Advantage

For those conducting their financial symphony as self-employed individuals, the home office deduction becomes a symphonic note of advantage. Similar to a soloist taking center stage, this deduction allows you to claim a portion of your home-related expenses when used for business purposes. By skillfully integrating this deduction, you create a unique harmony that intertwines your workspace with your tax planning efforts.

Crafting Your Homeownership Composition

Within the grand arrangement of your homeownership, these deductions form the heart of your composition. Like a composer weaving different melodies to create a tapestry of sound, you weave the mortgage interest, property tax, and home office deductions together. The resulting composition resonates with the benefits of owning a home, while at the same time harmonizing with your tax planning strategy.

The Harmonic Convergence

Just as a symphony crescendos to a powerful climax, your homeownership harmonies converge to create a harmonious financial result. The mortgage interest, property tax, and home office deductions interweave, creating a symphonic arrangement that underscores the advantages of homeownership while complementing your overall tax planning goals. As you conduct this section of your financial composition, you blend the unique melodies of homeownership into a harmonious tax strategy that resounds with financial wisdom.

9.2.3 Educational Crescendo: Credits for Learning

In the intricate composition of your financial symphony, an educational crescendo emerges as a vibrant and dynamic theme, elevating the richness of your melody through a range of education-related deductions and credits. Much like the crescendo in a musical piece, these elements add layers of depth and complexity to your financial arrangement, harmonizing the pursuit of knowledge with the art of tax optimization.

The American Opportunity Credit: A Resounding High Note

The American Opportunity Credit takes center stage as a resounding high note in your educational crescendo. Like a powerful crescendo building to its peak, this credit provides a substantial reduction in your tax liability for eligible education expenses. Whether you're pursuing an undergraduate degree or other qualifying educational pursuits, this credit adds a vibrant layer of financial advantage to your composition.

The Lifetime Learning Credit: A Melodic Variation

In the ensemble of education-related credits, the Lifetime Learning Credit introduces a melodic variation. Just as different musical variations breathe new life into a theme, this credit offers financial support for a broader spectrum of educational endeavors. Whether you're expanding your knowledge through courses, workshops, or skill development, the Lifetime Learning Credit contributes a unique and harmonious element to your financial arrangement.

The Sonorous Student Loan Interest Deduction: A Subtle Harmony

Amid the crescendo of education-related benefits, the student loan interest deduction provides a subtle yet crucial harmony. Like an underlying harmony enriching the musical texture, this deduction allows you to subtract the interest paid on qualifying student loans from your taxable income. This financial layer contributes depth to your composition, resonating with the effort you've invested in your education.

Education-Related Savings Accounts: The Cadence of Future Learning

The cadence of education-related savings accounts adds a distinctive rhythm to your educational crescendo. Accounts such as 529 plans and Coverdell Education Savings Accounts create a financial space for future learning endeavors. Similar to the anticipation of a cadence in music, these accounts allow you to set aside funds for educational expenses, providing a harmonious bridge between financial planning and educational aspirations.

Crafting Your Educational Composition

In the grand symphony of your financial journey, these educational credits, deductions, and savings accounts intertwine to create a harmonious composition. Just as a composer weaves different musical motifs to create a masterpiece, you skillfully integrate the American Opportunity Credit, Lifetime Learning Credit, student loan interest deduction, and education-related savings accounts. The result is a composition that harmonizes the pursuit of knowledge with astute tax optimization, resonating with the virtuosity of both your intellectual and financial endeavors.

The Harmonic Confluence

As your educational crescendo reaches its culmination, the harmonious confluence of these elements enriches your financial melody. The American Opportunity Credit, Lifetime Learning Credit, student loan interest deduction, and education-related savings accounts blend seamlessly, creating a symphonic arrangement that underscores the value of education while complementing your overarching tax planning goals. In this section of your financial composition, you cultivate a harmonious balance between learning and financial wisdom, infusing your melody with the richness of both intellectual and fiscal achievement.

9.2.4 The Retirement Symphony: Contributions and Deductions

In the grand orchestration of your tax planning ensemble, the retirement symphony emerges as a powerful and resonant theme. Like a collection of diverse instruments playing distinct melodies, contributions to retirement accounts such as 401(k) plans and Individual Retirement Accounts (IRAs) add depth and richness to your financial composition. This symphony weaves together tax-deductible contributions and the potential for tax-deferred growth, resulting in a harmonious melody of financial security that resonates with both retirement preparation and strategic tax optimization.

401(k) Plans: The Majestic Prelude

Within the vibrant spectrum of the retirement symphony, 401(k) plans take center stage as a majestic prelude. These employer-sponsored retirement accounts offer a dual benefit: your contributions are made on a pre-tax basis, reducing your current taxable income, and they benefit from tax-deferred growth over time. Much like a resounding prelude setting the tone for a grand performance, 401(k) plans lay the foundation for a harmonious interplay of contributions and fiscal growth.

Individual Retirement Accounts (IRAs): A Harmonic Counterpoint

Amid the retirement symphony, Individual Retirement Accounts (IRAs) contribute a harmonious counterpoint. Just as a skilled musician adds depth to a melody, IRAs provide you with a personal avenue for tax-advantaged retirement savings. Traditional IRAs allow for tax-deductible contributions, offering immediate benefits by reducing your taxable income. Additionally, the potential for tax-deferred growth creates a compelling harmony that resonates throughout your financial arrangement.

Conducting Your Retirement Composition

Much like a conductor skillfully guides an orchestra through a symphony, you have the opportunity to orchestrate your retirement composition with finesse. By strategically choosing between 401(k) plans and IRAs, you craft a harmonious blend of contributions and deductions that align with your retirement goals and tax optimization aspirations. The interplay of tax-deductible contributions and tax-deferred growth creates a dynamic and melodic arrangement that underscores your commitment to securing your financial future.

Harmony Between Preparation and Optimization

As the retirement symphony reaches its crescendo, the harmonious interweaving of contributions and deductions emerges as a defining motif. Your orchestration of 401(k) plans and IRAs harmonizes the act of retirement preparation with astute tax optimization. This harmonious fusion not only ensures the steady crescendo of your retirement savings but also resonates with the overarching theme of creating a financial composition that is both secure and strategically aligned. In this section of your financial opus, you embrace the responsibility of conductor, shaping a symphony that echoes with the melodies of both financial readiness and tax efficiency.

9.3 Conductor's Techniques: Strategies to

Tune Your Tax Composition

Just as a conductor shapes a musical performance, tax planning involves strategic techniques that mold your financial composition. This section introduces a suite of tactics designed to harmonize your tax liabilities and financial goals, transforming your fiscal arrangement into a masterful orchestration of financial well-being.

9.3.1 Tax-Efficient Investments: The Harmonic Portfolio

Within the grand arrangement of your financial orchestra, investments are the instruments that produce distinct tones, each contributing to the overall composition. Tax-efficient investments, akin to skilled musicians, play a pivotal role in orchestrating the symphony of your tax strategy. Much like a conductor carefully selecting instruments that blend seamlessly, the choice of tax-efficient investment vehicles, such as index funds and tax-managed funds, creates a harmonious melody that resonates with minimized tax implications and optimized returns.

Index Funds: The Unifying Melody

In the intricate score of your tax-efficient portfolio, index funds take on the role of a unifying melody. These investment vehicles aim to replicate the performance of a specific market index, such as the S&P 500. Their structure inherently reduces the need for frequent buying and selling of individual securities, leading to fewer taxable events. Similar to a resonating musical theme that runs through an entire composition, index funds provide consistency and harmony to your investment strategy while minimizing the tax impact.

Tax-Managed Funds: The Skillful Arrangement

Tax-managed funds, like a skillful arrangement of musical instruments, showcase deliberate planning and execution. These funds are meticulously designed to minimize capital gains distributions, often through strategies like tax-loss harvesting. This careful curation ensures that your investments not only flourish but also avoid unnecessary tax burdens. Like an artful conductor crafting an intricate arrangement, tax-managed funds fine-tune your portfolio to produce a harmonious balance between growth and tax efficiency.

Crafting Your Tax-Efficient Symphony

Just as a composer selects instruments with precision to create a balanced musical composition, you have the opportunity to craft your tax-efficient symphony through thoughtful investment choices. By including tax-efficient investments like index funds and tax-managed funds, you strike a harmonious chord between financial growth and prudent tax management. This composition resonates with the principles of tax optimization, orchestrating a melody where reduced tax liabilities harmonize with enhanced investment performance.

The Resonance of Tax Efficiency

As the tax-efficient investments section of your financial opus unfolds, the resonance of tax efficiency becomes a dominant motif. The symphony you create, with index funds and tax-managed funds as integral players, produces a resonant and balanced melody. This melody echoes through the entire composition, representing your commitment to not only nurturing your investments but also conducting them with a keen awareness of tax implications. In embracing tax-efficient investments, you empower your financial composition with a harmonious blend of growth, stability, and strategic tax planning.

9.3.2 The Tempo of Timing: Income and Expenses

In the intricate score of your financial composition, the timing of income and expenses serves as a dynamic tempo change, much like the shifts in rhythm that infuse music with depth and emotion. Just as a skilled conductor modulates the tempo to evoke different moods, strategically orchestrating when income is received and expenses are paid can create harmonious fluctuations in your tax landscape. This technique, akin to adjusting the tempo of a musical piece, allows you to fine-tune your financial symphony for optimal tax efficiency.

Deferring Income: The Crescendo of Tax Savings

Deferring income, much like building up to a crescendo in music, involves postponing the receipt of certain earnings to a future tax year. By doing so, you create a gradual rise in your taxable income, potentially placing you in a lower tax bracket. This deliberate modulation of income not only reduces your immediate tax liability but also harmonizes with a strategy of long-term financial growth.

Accelerating Deductible Expenses: A Swift Allegro

In the realm of tax planning, accelerating deductible expenses resembles the brisk tempo of an allegro movement.

This technique involves bringing forward deductible expenditures, such as charitable contributions or business expenses, into the current tax year. By doing so, you create a rapid succession of deductions that can offset your taxable income, producing a harmonious diminuendo in your tax bill.

Crafting Your Tax Rhythm

Much like a composer crafting a captivating melody, you have the power to shape the rhythm of your tax planning composition. By strategically timing your income and expenses, you manipulate the ebb and flow of your tax liability, creating a symphony that resonates with both financial prudence and tax efficiency. Just as a conductor molds a musical piece to convey specific emotions, your orchestration of timing can evoke the nuanced harmony of reduced taxes and optimized financial well-being.

The Harmonic Blend of Timing

As the tempo of your financial composition is influenced by the timing of income and expenses, a harmonic blend emerges between financial choices and tax optimization. The ebb and flow you create, carefully choreographed with the precision of a conductor, forms a symphony where income and expenses harmonize seamlessly. This harmonious blend not only enhances your financial melody but also amplifies the resonance of tax efficiency, ensuring that your composition resounds with both fiscal wisdom and a rhythmic cadence of smart financial decisions.

9.3.3 Tax Loss Harmony: Minimizing Capital

Gains

Within the intricate orchestration of investment, the interplay between capital gains and losses forms a dynamic and nuanced melody. In this symphony of financial growth, tax loss harvesting emerges as a virtuoso conductor, orchestrating a harmonious balance between gains and losses. This technique, akin to blending diverse musical notes, involves strategically selling investments that have incurred losses to offset capital gains. By deftly harmonizing these financial elements, you craft a composition that not only optimizes your investment portfolio but also conducts a symphony of minimized tax liability.

The Art of Tax Loss Harvesting

Just as a composer weaves contrasting musical themes into a cohesive masterpiece, tax loss harvesting artfully combines the rise and fall of investment values to create a seamless financial composition. When the market yields losses on certain investments, this technique allows you to "harvest" those losses by selling them. These losses can then be strategically used to offset the taxable gains from other investments, leading to a harmonious reduction in your overall taxable income.

Balancing the Melody of Gains and Losses

Much like a conductor striking a balance between different sections of an orchestra, tax loss harvesting enables you to harmonize the melody of gains and losses within your investment portfolio. By thoughtfully offsetting capital gains with losses, you create a symphony where the crescendos of profits are counterbalanced by the diminuendos of losses. This harmonious equilibrium not only optimizes your investment returns but also orchestrates a cadence of minimized tax burden.

Fine-Tuning Your Tax Composition

Just as a composer fine-tunes each note to perfection, you have the power to fine-tune your investment strategy through tax loss harvesting. By skillfully selecting investments to sell at opportune times, you create a financial melody that resonates with both sound investment choices and tax efficiency. This composition not only produces a harmonious rhythm within your investment portfolio but also ensures that your tax liability remains in tune with your broader financial goals.

The Symphony of Tax Efficiency

In the grand symphony of financial planning, tax loss harvesting emerges as a conductor guiding your investments towards harmonious tax efficiency. The delicate balance achieved through this technique results in a composition where gains and losses meld into a unified financial melody. Just as a maestro elicits nuanced emotions through music, your mastery of tax loss harvesting crafts a composition that harmonizes both financial growth and minimized tax impact, allowing your investment symphony to resonate with both fiscal wisdom and strategic acumen.

9.3.4 Charitable Contribution Crescendo: Giving Back, Gaining Benefits

Within the symphony of financial planning, charitable contributions resonate as a powerful crescendo, blending the harmonies of benevolence and tax optimization. Just as a musical piece reaches its climactic peak, your act of contributing to qualified charitable organizations orchestrates a resounding chorus of generosity while harmonizing with significant tax benefits. With each donation, you craft a composition that not only enriches society but also conducts a symphony of financial advantages, demonstrating that the act of giving back can indeed be harmonious with your tax strategy.

The Harmony of Generosity and Tax Optimization

Similar to a composer skillfully weaving multiple instruments into a crescendo, your charitable contributions merge the virtuous notes of giving with the harmonics of tax efficiency. When you donate to qualified charitable organizations, you create a harmonious interplay between your philanthropic intentions and your financial goals. This virtuoso performance aligns with the legal framework that rewards your generosity with tax deductions, enhancing the overall harmony of your financial composition.

Meticulous Records: The Sheet Music of Giving

Much like a meticulous musician follows detailed sheet music, your approach to charitable contributions involves keeping meticulous records. These records serve as the musical notation of your charitable journey, ensuring that every note of your giving is documented for tax purposes. By maintaining a clear record of your donations, you create an organized and harmonious composition that substantiates your philanthropic endeavors while maximizing the tax benefits you receive.

Composing a Meaningful Tax Strategy

Just as a composer carefully selects notes to convey a specific emotion, you have the opportunity to select charitable causes that resonate with your values. By contributing to organizations that align with your beliefs and passions, you compose a meaningful tax strategy that echoes the authenticity of your giving. This thoughtful composition not only enriches the lives of those you support but also orchestrates a harmonious arrangement that optimizes your tax situation.

Harmonizing for the Greater Good

In the grand symphony of financial planning, the charitable contribution crescendo stands as a poignant movement. Your generous contributions create a harmonious resonance that extends beyond your individual financial score, enriching the lives of those in need. As the crescendo builds, it harmonizes with the virtuoso performance of your tax strategy, showcasing that the act of giving back can create a symphony of benefits that echo throughout both your financial composition and the broader community.

9.4 Expert Collaborations: Working with Tax Professionals

In the symphony of tax planning, collaborating with experts is akin to inviting skilled musicians to enhance your composition. This section delves into the invaluable role of tax professionals, who bring their expertise to your financial ensemble, ensuring that every note is in harmony with tax laws and regulations.

9.4.1 Certified Public Accountants (CPAs): The

Maestros of Tax

In the grand symphony of financial management, Certified Public Accountants (CPAs) step onto the stage as the maestros of tax, wielding a baton of expertise to conduct intricate and harmonious tax arrangements. Much like a conductor guides an orchestra to create a seamless musical masterpiece, CPAs orchestrate the complexities of tax laws and regulations to compose a financial composition that resonates with precision and strategic finesse.

Conducting Complex Tax Arrangements

Just as a maestro skillfully navigates complex musical scores, CPAs excel in deciphering intricate tax scenarios. Their deep understanding of tax codes and regulations allows them to harmonize various financial elements, ensuring that your tax arrangement is composed with accuracy and attention to detail. Whether you're an individual or a business owner, CPAs possess the knowledge to create a symphony of financial strategies that align with your goals.

A Symphony of Comprehensive Services

Similar to how a maestro coordinates every instrument in an orchestra, CPAs offer a symphony of services that encompass every aspect of your tax journey. From meticulous tax return preparation to strategic tax planning, CPAs guide you through a harmonious process that optimizes your financial composition. Their expertise extends beyond mere number-crunching, as they conduct an ensemble of services that encompass tax minimization, compliance, and financial growth.

Striking the Chords of Financial Goals

Just as a maestro interprets musical notes to evoke emotions, CPAs interpret your financial data to help you achieve your financial goals. With their guidance, you can fine-tune your financial composition to strike the chords of wealth accumulation, tax reduction, and long-term financial success. By harmonizing your aspirations with their expert insights, CPAs create a financial symphony that resonates with your unique melody of goals.

Navigating the Tax Symphony

Much like a maestro steers an orchestra through different movements, CPAs navigate the complex and ever-changing landscape of tax laws. They ensure that your financial composition adheres to legal guidelines while exploring innovative strategies to optimize your tax situation. By entrusting your tax arrangements to the maestros of tax, you gain the assurance that your financial symphony will be conducted with precision, expertise, and an unwavering commitment to your financial harmony.

9.4.2 Enrolled Agents (EAs): The Tax Virtuosos

In the intricate composition of tax planning and optimization, Enrolled Agents (EAs) emerge as the virtuosos, wielding a profound understanding of tax matters akin to a master musician's command over their instrument. Authorized by the IRS, EAs offer a symphony of expertise in tax planning, preparation, and representation. Their role parallels that of a virtuoso musician, ensuring that your financial melody resonates harmoniously while adhering to the nuanced intricacies of tax regulations.

Mastery in Tax Matters

Just as a virtuoso musician displays unmatched mastery over their instrument, EAs exhibit an exceptional command of tax matters. Their rigorous training and in-depth knowledge of tax codes and regulations equip them to navigate the complex symphony of tax laws. Whether you're an individual taxpayer or a business owner, EAs bring their virtuosity to the forefront, harmonizing your financial decisions with the legal nuances of taxation.

Guiding Your Tax Composition

Similar to how a virtuoso musician guides their instrument to create captivating melodies, EAs guide your tax composition with precision and finesse. They provide comprehensive support in tax planning, helping you craft a symphony of strategies that optimize your tax situation. EAs offer their expertise not only in minimizing tax liabilities but also in ensuring compliance, enabling you to conduct your financial affairs with confidence.

A Performance of Representation

Just as a virtuoso musician's performance captivates an audience, EAs represent you before the IRS with poise and professionalism. If you encounter tax disputes, audits, or inquiries, EAs step onto the stage as your advocates, showcasing their virtuosity in resolving tax matters. Their ability to navigate the intricate tax landscape ensures that your financial melody remains harmonious even in the face of challenges.

Harmonizing with Tax Regulations

Much like a virtuoso musician harmonizes with a musical score, EAs harmonize your financial decisions with the symphony of tax regulations. They ensure that your tax composition adheres to the legal guidelines set by the IRS, allowing you to create a financial arrangement that is both compliant and strategically optimized. By enlisting the services of EAs, you invite tax virtuosos to collaborate on your financial composition, producing a symphony that resonates with accuracy, expertise, and the artistry of tax optimization.

9.4.3 Tax Attorneys: The Legal Composers

In the grand orchestration of tax planning and optimization, tax attorneys assume the role of adept composers, crafting intricate tax solutions for the most complex scenarios. Much like a skilled composer intricately weaves musical notes to create a harmonious composition, tax attorneys navigate the intricate notes of tax laws to harmonize legal aspects within your financial arrangement. Their expertise spans from offering seasoned advice on intricate tax matters to conducting the legal symphony of representing you in disputes and audits.

Crafting Legal Symphonies

Just as a composer meticulously arranges musical elements to form a symphony, tax attorneys meticulously arrange legal strategies to form a tax-efficient composition. Their deep understanding of tax laws allows them to compose solutions that are both compliant and strategically advantageous. Whether you're an individual taxpayer or a business entity, tax attorneys wield their legal expertise to orchestrate intricate tax harmonies that resonate within the boundaries of the law.

Expertise in Complex Tax Matters

Similar to how a composer's expertise allows them to handle complex musical compositions, tax attorneys possess the expertise to navigate the complexities of tax matters. They are well-versed in nuanced tax regulations, making them the virtuosos of legal tax advice. From international taxation to intricate business structures, tax attorneys interpret the legal notes of tax laws, ensuring that your financial melody is composed with precision.

Conducting Legal Representation

Just as a composer conducts an orchestra to create a symphonic masterpiece, tax attorneys conduct legal representation to ensure your tax composition is well-structured. If you find yourself in the midst of tax disputes, audits, or legal proceedings, tax attorneys step onto the podium as your legal conductors. Their role extends beyond providing advice; they artfully guide your legal interactions, harmonizing your actions with the legal intricacies of tax regulations.

Harmonizing Legal Compliance

Much like a composer ensures that musical compositions adhere to musical rules, tax attorneys harmonize your financial arrangements with legal compliance. They skillfully integrate the legal notes of tax laws into your financial symphony, allowing you to create a composition that is both legally sound and optimized for your financial goals. Engaging tax attorneys is akin to inviting legal composers to collaborate on your financial masterpiece, ensuring that every legal note is precisely orchestrated within the symphony of tax planning.

It's important to note that while tax planning can help reduce your tax liability, it should always be done within the boundaries of the law. Engage the services of qualified tax professionals who can provide personalized advice based on your specific circumstances. By being proactive in your tax planning efforts, you can make informed financial decisions, maximize your after-tax income, and achieve your long-term financial goals.

Chapter 10: Monitoring and Adjusting Financial Control

In the captivating symphony of your financial journey, the art of monitoring and adjusting takes center stage. This chapter unravels the intricacies of maintaining effective financial control, ensuring that your composition plays in perfect harmony and evolves with the changing rhythms of your life. Just as a conductor fine-tunes an orchestra, you'll learn how to fine-tune your financial strategies to achieve long-lasting success.

10.1 Regularly Reviewing Financial Progress

Monitoring Your Financial Symphony

Imagine yourself as the maestro of your financial orchestra, standing before a stage adorned with income, expenses, and investments. In this symphonic performance of wealth management, the act of regularly reviewing your financial progress takes on the role of your meticulously composed musical score, guiding you through the ebbs and flows of your financial journey.

Much like a conductor scrutinizes every note and melody, you, too, examine the intricate components of your financial symphony. The process of monitoring your financial progress becomes a harmonious blend of art and strategy, allowing you to navigate the evolving composition of your financial life.

Visualize your financial progress as a melodic crescendo. Each review session is a chance to witness your financial opus gradually reaching its peak, guided by your decisions and conduct. Regular reviews empower you to recognize the rhythmic patterns of your income, discern the harmonious balance of your expenses, and perceive the intricate harmonies of your investments.

As you stand on the conductor's podium of your financial journey, these reviews provide vital cues. They signal whether you're following the intended tempo or if adjustments are needed to maintain the desired harmony. Much like a conductor guides musicians, you guide your financial decisions, ensuring they resonate with your overarching financial score.

These review sessions also enable you to identify any off-key notes or dissonances. Should unexpected variations arise – perhaps an expense that crescendos unexpectedly – your vigilant oversight allows you to immediately address them, ensuring the rhythm of your financial composition remains smooth and unbroken.

Just as a conductor brings out the best in each musician, these reviews bring out the best in your financial performance. They provide the opportunity to fine-tune your financial instruments, making sure they produce the desired tones. With each review, you become more attuned to the intricacies of your financial masterpiece, allowing you to orchestrate your wealth with precision and finesse.

In this symphony of financial management, the act of regularly reviewing your financial progress is your baton, your compass, and your guiding light. It ensures that every note, every expense, and every investment is in harmony with your financial goals. So, step onto the conductor's podium, pick up your baton, and let the mesmerizing rhythm of your financial symphony lead you to the crescendo of your financial success.

10.1.1 Financial Statements: Insights in Melodic Metrics

Imagine your financial journey as a gallery adorned with intricate artworks – your balance sheets, income statements, and cash flow statements. These documents, akin to masterpieces, hold the essence of your financial performance. Engaging in regular analysis of these financial canvases unveils the dynamic ebb and flow of your monetary symphony.

Much like a discerning art connoisseur, you, too, dissect these statements to reveal the nuances of your financial composition. As you carefully examine each brushstroke of financial data, a melodic story begins to emerge – a story of income, expenses, and the rhythm of your financial decisions.

Your balance sheet, resembling a grand canvas, showcases the snapshot of your financial position. Each asset and liability is like a note in a melody, contributing to the overall harmony. Regular analysis illuminates the changes in your financial landscape – whether the crescendo of increasing assets or the decrescendo of diminishing liabilities.

The income statement, a lyrical arrangement of revenue and expenses, paints a vivid picture of your financial performance over time. Just as a melody unfolds in musical notation, your income and expenses create a harmonious interplay. By scrutinizing this composition, you can uncover the patterns of your financial melody – are expenses rising like a fortissimo, or is revenue a delicate pianissimo?

The cash flow statement, a rhythmic cadence of cash inflows and outflows, encapsulates the movement of your financial resources. It's like the rhythm section of your financial orchestra, keeping the beat of your monetary transactions. Regular analysis allows you to understand the fluidity of your cash movement – is it a steady rhythm or a syncopated pattern?

As you delve into these financial masterpieces, you decipher the symphony of your financial decisions. You recognize the crescendos of robust financial months and the diminuendos of leaner periods. You identify the harmonious balance between income and expenses, much like the interplay of instruments in a symphony orchestra.

With each analysis, you gain valuable insights – insights that guide your financial decisions. Just as a conductor listens intently to every note, you listen to the story your financial statements tell. You adjust your financial score, ensuring that it resonates with your overarching goals.

In the gallery of financial management, your balance sheets, income statements, and cash flow statements are your masterpieces – painted with numbers, composed with data, and performed through analysis. Regular review offers you the lens to view your financial symphony's intricate details, enabling you to conduct with precision and finesse. So, step into the gallery, analyze with purpose, and let the harmonious dance of your financial composition unfold before you.

10.1.2 Budget vs. Actual Analysis: Orchestrating Balance

Imagine yourself as the conductor of a grand orchestra, guiding each instrument to play in perfect harmony. In the realm of financial management, comparing your actual income and expenses to your meticulously crafted budget serves as your baton, ensuring that every financial element resonates in equilibrium. This practice, akin to conducting a symphony, orchestrates a melodious balance in your fiscal performance.

Just as a vigilant conductor listens for any discordant note, you, too, scrutinize your financial performance through the lens of budget versus actual analysis. This analytical scorecard reveals the intricate interplay between your planned financial movements and the actual steps taken. By noting significant deviations, you tune your ears to the nuances of your financial composition.

Consider a crescendo in your expenses – a sudden surge that catches your attention. Like a conductor investigating a section playing too loudly, you delve into the underlying causes. Was it an unforeseen expense, a shift in priorities, or perhaps a momentary lapse in financial discipline? By tracing the notes back to their origin, you gain a clearer understanding of the harmonious balance you strive to achieve.

Similarly, a pianissimo in your income might raise concerns. Just as a conductor seeks to amplify a softer section, you explore the factors contributing to this gentle financial movement. Did a planned income source fall short, or is it indicative of broader economic shifts? With this insight, you can make informed decisions, adjusting your financial composition to bring it back to a harmonious equilibrium.

This process of budget versus actual analysis is your conductor's wand, capable of orchestrating adjustments that fine-tune your financial performance. It empowers you to make proactive decisions, preventing disharmony from gaining a foothold in your financial symphony.

As a conductor weaves together the various sections of an orchestra, you weave together your income and expenses. By continually comparing your financial movements to your budgeted plan, you ensure that each note is played in alignment with the grand composition of your financial goals. Deviations become opportunities for adjustment, discord transforms into harmony, and your financial symphony gains depth and resonance.

So, take up your conductor's baton – your budget – and lead your financial orchestra with precision. Embrace the art of budget versus actual analysis, and let the harmonious equilibrium you create resonate throughout your financial journey. Just as a skilled conductor shapes a memorable performance, you shape your financial success through the delicate balance of orchestration and adjustment.

10.1.3 Financial Ratios: The Harmony of Insight

Imagine your financial landscape as a majestic symphony, each note representing a unique aspect of your fiscal health.

In this composition, financial ratios are the harmonious chords that resonate through the score, offering profound insights into the intricate melody of your financial control. Just as a skilled composer blends different musical notes to create a harmonious melody, calculating liquidity ratios, profitability ratios, and debt ratios reveals the harmonious interplay of your financial well-being.

Liquidity ratios, akin to the rhythm section in an orchestra, provide the heartbeat of your financial composition. They measure your ability to meet short-term obligations, much like a drummer maintains the rhythm of a musical piece. As you calculate and interpret these ratios, you gain a clear sense of your financial pulse. Are you in tune with your immediate financial commitments, or is there a need to adjust the tempo of your spending?

In the brass section of profitability ratios, you find the uplifting melodies that showcase your financial performance. These ratios illuminate your ability to generate profit from your operations – the triumphant fanfare of your financial success. Like a skilled trumpeter hitting the high notes, a healthy profitability ratio signals a well-tuned financial performance. Should you find these notes off-key, it's a cue to explore ways to fine-tune your revenue streams and orchestrate cost-efficient operations.

Debt ratios, resembling the strings section, create the harmonious foundation upon which your financial composition is built. They reveal the proportion of debt in relation to your assets and equity – the deep resonance of your financial structure. Just as a string section provides the rich undertones in music, a well-calculated debt ratio establishes the stability and balance of your financial harmony. Adjusting these ratios is like tuning the strings of your financial instrument, ensuring they produce the desired harmonies.

Much like a skilled conductor fine-tunes the performance of an orchestra, analyzing financial ratios empowers you to fine-tune your financial composition. These ratios are your guideposts, illuminating areas where your financial symphony may need adjustment. By heeding their melodies, you gain the insight needed to make informed financial decisions, harmonizing your financial actions with your goals.

So, embrace the harmony of financial ratios – the musical notes of insight in your financial symphony. Let them guide your understanding, helping you strike the perfect balance between liquidity, profitability, and debt. As a conductor shapes a musical performance, you shape your financial destiny by composing a symphony of financial control, with ratios as your ever-present musical score.

10.2 Key Performance Indicators (KPIs) for Financial Control

Measuring the Symphonic Pulse

Every conductor relies on key indicators to gauge the heartbeat of their orchestra. Similarly, financial KPIs provide a rhythmic pulse of your financial control efforts, allowing you to assess your progress with clarity and precision.

10.2.1 Revenue Growth Rate: The Dynamic

Crescendo

Imagine your financial journey as a musical composition, with different elements weaving together to create a harmonious melody. Just as a crescendo in music signifies an increase in volume and intensity, the revenue growth rate serves as the dynamic crescendo in your financial symphony. This Key Performance Indicator (KPI) captures the exhilarating rise of your income over a specific period, revealing the powerful impact of your sales and marketing efforts.

In the world of business, revenue is the driving force, much like the melody in a musical piece. The revenue growth rate, then, becomes the crescendo that showcases the amplified intensity of your income generation. Just as a crescendo adds dimension and excitement to a musical performance, a healthy growth rate infuses vitality into your financial composition.

Calculating the revenue growth rate is akin to measuring the volume of your financial progress. By comparing your current revenue to that of a previous period, you determine the magnitude of your growth. This KPI functions as the conductor's baton, guiding you in understanding how your business strategies are resonating with your target audience.

Is your revenue growth rate a gentle swell, akin to a soft crescendo that builds anticipation? Or is it a grand crescendo that signifies a surge of success and impact? The answer lies in the rate itself, painting a vivid picture of your business's performance. This KPI isn't just a number; it's a narrative that tells the story of your business's journey.

As a conductor shapes the intensity of a musical piece, the revenue growth rate guides you in fine-tuning your strategies. A slower growth rate might prompt a review of your marketing tactics, while a soaring growth rate could signify that your efforts are striking the right chords with your audience. Just as a crescendo adds excitement to a musical arrangement, a healthy revenue growth rate adds vigor to your financial journey.

So, embrace the dynamic crescendo of the revenue growth rate. Let it be your guide as you orchestrate your business's trajectory. Use it to adjust your strategies, amplify your successes, and navigate any dips. Like a skilled composer building anticipation before the grand finale, the revenue growth rate sets the stage for your business's triumphant success.

10.2.2 Gross Profit Margin: The Sound of Efficiency

Visualize your financial landscape as a grand symphony, with each instrument playing its unique part to create a harmonious whole. Just as an orchestra's resonance is shaped by the interplay of various sounds, your business's financial health is reflected in the Gross Profit Margin – a key metric that resonates with the sound of efficiency.

In the orchestra of business operations, revenue represents the melody, while the Gross Profit Margin provides the underlying rhythm. This powerful Key Performance Indicator (KPI) reveals the percentage of revenue that remains after subtracting the cost of goods sold (COGS). It's a measure of your ability to orchestrate your resources and control costs while producing a beautiful financial melody.

As a conductor expertly balances the instruments to create a harmonious sound, you, too, manage the delicate interplay between revenue and costs. The Gross Profit Margin paints a vivid picture of this balance. A higher margin signifies a more efficient use of resources, like a symphony where each note is played with precision, contributing to the overall brilliance of the performance.

Much like a well-conducted orchestra resonates with an audience, a healthy Gross Profit Margin resonates with the financial world. It demonstrates your mastery in optimizing the production process, controlling expenses, and ensuring that the core of your business – its operations – generates profits that resonate far and wide.

Calculating the Gross Profit Margin is akin to fine-tuning the sound of each instrument. By subtracting the cost of bringing your product or service to market from your revenue and then expressing it as a percentage, you create a clear and resonant note that echoes through your financial composition.

Just as a symphony's resonance is a result of meticulous rehearsal and skilled conducting, your Gross Profit Margin is a reflection of your strategic decision-making and operational efficiency. It's the sound of a well-tuned business orchestra playing in harmony, creating a financial composition that captivates stakeholders and investors alike.

So, listen closely to the sound of your Gross Profit Margin. Let it guide your financial decisions, fine-tune your operations, and elevate the efficiency of your business's performance. As you master this powerful KPI, your financial symphony will fill the air with the enchanting melody of efficiency and success.

10.2.3 Net Profit Margin: A Melody of Profitability

Just as a melody captures the essence of a musical piece, the net profit margin captures the essence of your financial performance. Calculate the percentage of revenue remaining as net profit after all expenses, including taxes, are deducted. This KPI reveals your overall profitability and efficiency in managing costs.

10.2.4 Cash Conversion Cycle: The Rhythm of Cash Flow

In the symphony of financial control, cash flow is the heartbeat. Similar to a rhythmic pulse guiding a musical composition, the cash conversion cycle measures the time taken for cash to flow from your business through the operating cycle. This KPI assesses the efficiency of your cash management and working capital, ensuring your financial composition remains melodiously balanced.

10.2.5 Debt-to-Equity Ratio: The Balance of Leverage

Like a well-conducted orchestra maintains a balance between various instrument sections, your financial leverage is a delicate balance that requires careful management. The debt-to-equity ratio quantifies this equilibrium, reflecting the proportion of total debt to total equity. This KPI serves as a barometer of financial risk, helping you orchestrate a harmonious capital structure.

10.3 Adjusting Strategies and Goals as Needed

Adapting the Melody

Just as a composer adjusts musical arrangements to suit the changing mood of a performance, you must adapt your financial strategies and goals to harmonize with shifting circumstances. Flexibility and nimbleness ensure that your financial composition remains in tune with your aspirations.

10.3.1 Goal Evaluation: The Melodic Evolution

Picture your financial journey as a captivating symphony, where each movement is guided by a distinct melody. Just as a composer fine-tunes their composition, you too must regularly evaluate your financial goals to ensure they harmonize with the evolving rhythm of your life.

In the grand orchestra of your financial existence, goals serve as the guiding notes that shape each movement. Much like a conductor adjusting the tempo to match the mood, you must assess whether your goals still align with your current circumstances and aspirations. Just as a melody can evolve over time, your financial objectives may need refining to create a harmonious and impactful composition.

Life's cadence is ever-changing, and as you navigate its twists and turns, your financial goals may need to shift as well. Perhaps you've achieved a milestone that warrants a new set of objectives, or maybe external circumstances have altered the landscape. By regularly evaluating your goals, you ensure that your financial symphony remains in tune with the present moment.

Consider this evaluation process as the conductor's pause between movements – a moment of reflection and adjustment. Are your goals still in harmony with your desires and the reality you face? Are there new instruments (opportunities) you wish to introduce to your composition? Or do certain notes (goals) need to be fine-tuned to create a more melodious arrangement?

Just as a symphony's evolution is guided by the conductor's expert ear, your financial journey's evolution is guided by your astute assessment. This assessment involves not only your personal aspirations but also the larger economic and societal rhythms that surround you.

As you evaluate and adapt your financial goals, you ensure that your symphony remains relevant, engaging, and inspiring. By making adjustments where needed, you craft a financial composition that resonates deeply with the current phase of your life's journey. Just as a timeless symphony continues to captivate audiences through the ages, your ever-evolving financial goals will lead to a legacy of harmony and achievement.

10.3.2 Strategy Review: The Dynamic Ensemble

10.3.2 Strategy Review: The Dynamic Ensemble

Imagine your financial strategies as the skilled musicians of an ever-evolving ensemble. Just as a symphony adapts to new compositions and artistic directions, your financial strategies must undergo periodic reviews to ensure they remain in harmony with your evolving goals.

In the grand performance of your financial life, strategies serve as the instrumentalists that contribute to the overall melody. Much like a conductor fine-tunes each musician's contribution, you must assess whether your strategies are producing the desired outcomes. Just as a symphony's instrumentation may change to create a more captivating sound, your financial strategies may need adjustment to create a more resonant financial composition.

The nature of the financial landscape, much like the music world, is constantly changing. New instruments (investment opportunities) emerge, and different techniques (financial control practices) come to the forefront. By regularly reviewing your strategies, you can identify areas for enhancement and innovation. Just as a conductor may introduce new elements to create a dynamic performance, you can introduce new strategies to enhance your financial arrangement.

Consider this review process as the conductor's attentive ear during rehearsals – listening carefully to each instrument's contribution and making adjustments to achieve perfect harmony. Are your strategies still producing the desired results, or have new developments called for a change in tune? Is there an innovative approach that could elevate your financial composition to new heights?

Much like a symphony's ensemble can be enriched by new talents and perspectives, your financial strategies can benefit from fresh ideas and insights. By conducting a thorough strategy review, you ensure that your financial composition remains captivating, relevant, and effective. Your willingness to adapt and innovate ensures that your financial symphony continues to evolve and captivate, leading to a masterpiece that reflects your ever-evolving.

10.3.3 Risk Assessment: Navigating Harmonious Waters

Imagine your financial journey as a voyage across the vast ocean of possibilities. In this dynamic expanse, risk emerges as the ever-present undertow, capable of shaping the course of your journey. Just as a skilled sailor adjusts the sails to catch the changing winds, continuous risk assessment becomes your compass, guiding you through unpredictable waters.

Much like a sailor reads the signs of the sea to anticipate rough waters, you must be vigilant in assessing potential financial risks. This vigilance is your key to maintaining the harmonious flow of your financial composition. Consider risk assessment as a tune played softly in the background – a steady rhythm that keeps your financial symphony on track.

Just as the sea's conditions can change unexpectedly, the financial landscape is subject to sudden shifts. Economic fluctuations, market volatility, and unforeseen events can disrupt your carefully orchestrated financial arrangement. By adjusting your risk management strategies, you ensure that your financial ship remains steady, even in choppy waters.

Think of this risk assessment as the conductor's role during a live performance. Just as a conductor must adapt to unexpected changes during a concert, you must be prepared to adjust your strategies when faced with unexpected financial challenges. Your ability to navigate these challenges with grace and poise ensures that your financial composition remains in harmony.

Remember that risk is an integral part of any journey, just as changing tempos and dynamics are essential to a musical masterpiece. By acknowledging and addressing potential risks, you take a proactive approach to safeguarding your financial symphony. The result is a composition that flows smoothly, even in the face of uncertainty, and a financial journey that resonates with confidence and resilience.

10.3.4 Continuous Learning: The Symphony of Knowledge

Imagine your financial journey as a symphony, with each note representing a piece of valuable knowledge. In this ever-changing world of finance, continuous learning is the conductor that guides your mastery of this intricate composition. Just as a musician dedicates countless hours to refining their technique, you too must immerse yourself in the art of financial knowledge.

Consider continuous learning as the foundation upon which your financial symphony is built. Just as a symphony evolves with each practice session, your understanding of industry trends, regulatory shifts, and financial best practices deepens with every learning opportunity. This symphony of knowledge becomes the driving force behind your financial decisions.

Much like a musician studies the classics and explores new genres, you too must explore a diverse range of financial topics. From investment strategies to tax optimization, each area of expertise adds a new instrument to your financial orchestra. Your commitment to learning ensures that your symphony remains rich and vibrant, full of innovative harmonies.

Think of professional development as a series of rehearsals for your financial performance. Each workshop, seminar, or course hones your skills, refines your techniques, and prepares you to conduct your financial symphony with precision. Just as a conductor guides a symphony to perfection, your continuous learning guides your financial decisions towards optimal outcomes.

Remember that the world of finance is a dynamic stage, with new instruments, melodies, and players constantly entering the scene. By staying attuned to these changes through continuous learning, you ensure that your financial symphony remains relevant and resonant. The result is a composition that is not only masterful but also adaptable, capable of creating beautiful harmonies even in the face of new challenges.

So, embrace the symphony of knowledge, and let it be your guiding melody. With each new piece of information, you add depth and complexity to your financial composition. Just as a symphony captures the essence of human emotion, your continuous learning captures the essence of financial wisdom, enabling you to create a masterpiece of financial control and success.

10.4 Seeking Professional Assistance when Necessary

Collaborating with Masters

In the grand symphony of financial management, there are moments when the expertise of professionals becomes instrumental. Just as a composer collaborates with virtuoso performers, seeking professional assistance harmonizes your financial composition with expert insights and guidance.

10.4.1 Financial Advisors: Maestros of Insight

In the grand symphony of your financial journey, a financial advisor plays the role of a skilled maestro, conducting your financial decisions with precision and expertise. Just as a conductor interprets the nuances of a musical score, a financial advisor interprets the intricate landscape of your finances, guiding you towards harmonious financial outcomes.

Think of a financial advisor as the conductor of your financial orchestra. They bring years of experience and extensive knowledge to the stage, orchestrating your financial instruments in a way that creates a melodious composition. Their expertise allows them to navigate the complexities of investment strategies, retirement planning, tax optimization, and overall financial management, ensuring that every note of your financial melody is in tune.

Engaging a financial advisor is like having a seasoned conductor at your side during a performance. They have a deep understanding of various financial instruments and how they interact, enabling them to create a symphony that aligns with your unique goals and aspirations. With their guidance, you can navigate the shifting tempo of the financial world and make decisions that resonate with long-term success.

Just as a conductor enhances the performance of each individual musician, a financial advisor enhances your financial performance. They provide personalized recommendations, fine-tuning your financial strategy to achieve optimal results. Whether you're planning for retirement, navigating investments, or optimizing your tax situation, a financial advisor's insights can help you compose a financial masterpiece.

Consider your financial advisor as a collaborator in your symphony of wealth. They listen to your financial goals, understand your risk tolerance, and help you create a harmonious arrangement that encompasses both your short-term needs and long-term dreams. Their guidance empowers you to make informed decisions, ensuring that every decision you make contributes to the beautiful composition of your financial future.

In the intricate composition of your financial journey, a financial advisor is the maestro who brings your financial symphony to life. With their guidance, you can navigate the complex chords of financial decisions and create a masterpiece that echoes with success, stability, and lasting prosperity. Just as a conductor guides an orchestra to a flawless performance, a financial advisor guides you towards a future filled with financial harmony.

10.4.2 Accountants: Harmonizing Precision

In the symphony of your financial endeavors, accountants play the crucial role of harmonizing the intricate sections of your financial composition. Just as a skilled conductor blends different sections of an orchestra into a harmonious melody, accountants blend and analyze financial data and statements to create a cohesive and accurate financial picture.

Imagine your financial journey as a complex musical score, with various instruments playing their parts. Accountants step in as the conductor, ensuring that each note is played at the right time and in the right tone. They meticulously analyze your financial statements, balance sheets, and income reports, deciphering the musical patterns within the numbers to provide valuable insights.

Like a conductor fine-tuning the performance of each musician, accountants fine-tune your financial data. They meticulously examine the details, making sure that every aspect of your financial symphony is in alignment. Through their expertise, they reveal the underlying melodies of your finances, helping you understand the highs and lows, the crescendos, and the harmonies within your financial composition.

Just as a conductor's expertise brings out the best in every instrument, an accountant's expertise brings out the precision in your financial data. They have a deep understanding of tax regulations, compliance requirements, and financial best practices. They help you navigate the intricate choreography of tax planning, ensuring that your financial performance is in tune with legal standards.

Accountants are not only historians of your financial performance but also composers of strategies for financial control. They assist in crafting budgets, advising on expense management, and identifying areas for potential improvement. Their insights allow you to fine-tune your financial symphony, ensuring that every note contributes to the overall harmony of your financial goals.

Just as a conductor guides an orchestra to perfection, accountants guide your financial performance with meticulous precision. They bring clarity to complex financial compositions, ensuring that your financial journey follows the right tempo and stays on key. By harmonizing financial data, offering tax guidance, and enhancing your financial control, accountants play a vital role in orchestrating your path to financial success.

In the grand performance of your financial symphony, accountants are the harmonious force that ensures your financial composition resonates with accuracy, compliance, and strategic insights. Their expertise enhances your financial performance, allowing you to create a masterpiece of financial control and success.

10.4.3 Business Consultants: Orchestrators of Growth

In the intricate ensemble of business management, a business consultant takes on the role of a skilled orchestrator, guiding your financial composition toward harmonious growth. Just as a conductor brings together the various sections of an orchestra to create a seamless symphony, a business consultant assesses, refines, and enhances your financial strategies to create a melody of success.

Imagine your business as a symphony, with different departments and functions playing their unique melodies. A business consultant steps in as the conductor, carefully listening to each section, identifying areas that need fine-tuning, and harmonizing the overall performance. They possess a keen ear for understanding the nuances of your business's financial structure, operations, and goals.

Like a conductor who interprets the composer's intentions, a business consultant interprets the intricate details of your business's financial landscape. They delve deep into your financial statements, analyze revenue streams, scrutinize expenses, and decipher market trends. With this comprehensive understanding, they craft a strategy that resonates with your business's objectives, leading to a harmonious and synchronized financial composition.

Just as a conductor ensures that each instrument plays its part at the right moment, a business consultant ensures that every aspect of your financial strategy is aligned and coordinated. They identify potential inefficiencies, offer innovative solutions, and guide you in implementing changes that enhance your business's financial performance.

In the realm of business, change is constant, much like the evolving dynamics of a musical performance. A business consultant acts as a conductor who adapts to changing tempos and rhythms. They stay attuned to market shifts, emerging trends, and regulatory changes, adjusting your financial strategies accordingly. This adaptability ensures that your business's financial composition remains relevant and resonant in the ever-changing business landscape.

Collaborating with a business consultant is akin to having a conductor who helps your business orchestra achieve a flawless performance. Their expertise enhances your financial control practices, optimizes your operational efficiency, and guides you in making strategic decisions. By fine-tuning your financial composition, business consultants help you orchestrate a symphony of growth and success in the competitive business arena.

10.4.4 Legal Counsel: The Guardians of Compliance

In the grand symphony of financial management, legal counsel assumes the role of steadfast guardians of compliance, much like a conductor meticulously ensuring that each note adheres to the musical score. In the intricate choreography of complex financial matters, such as mergers and acquisitions, legal counsel serves as the guiding force, harmonizing legal expertise with financial decisions.

Just as a conductor interprets the composer's intentions to bring out the best in the orchestra, legal counsel interprets and navigates the intricate web of legal requirements and regulations. They possess an intricate understanding of the legal landscape, ensuring that every move your business makes is in perfect alignment with the legal score.

Imagine a financial arrangement as a symphony of contracts, agreements, and regulatory stipulations. Legal counsel steps in as the conductor, orchestrating a seamless performance where each legal aspect harmonizes with the financial composition. They scrutinize contracts, negotiate terms, and ensure that your financial strategies are conducted within the boundaries of the law.

Like a conductor who maintains the tempo and rhythm of a musical piece, legal counsel ensures that your financial decisions maintain the right pace of legal compliance. They offer expert advice on structuring transactions, mitigating legal risks, and ensuring that your financial symphony plays harmoniously within the realm of legality.

Just as a conductor's expertise enhances the musicians' performance, legal counsel's guidance enhances your financial decisions. They offer a comprehensive perspective on the legal implications of your financial strategies, helping you navigate potential pitfalls and challenges. Their presence safeguards your financial interests and ensures that your financial composition is in tune with the symphony of legal requirements.

In the dynamic world of finance, regulatory landscapes and legal requirements can change, much like the shifting dynamics of a musical piece. Legal counsel stays attuned to these changes, providing you with updated guidance to ensure ongoing compliance. Their vigilance helps you maintain the harmonious balance between legal adherence and financial success.

Collaborating with legal counsel is akin to having a conductor who ensures that every instrument in your financial orchestra plays in harmony with the legal score. Their expertise safeguards your financial arrangements, guiding your decisions with the wisdom of legal compliance. By seeking their advice, you integrate legal knowledge into your financial symphony, creating a masterpiece that resonates not only with financial success but also with adherence to legal standards.

In the grand composition of financial control, monitoring and adjusting is the overture to long-term success. Regular reviews, measured KPIs, strategic adaptations, and professional collaborations are the instruments that compose your financial symphony. Remember, just as a conductor fine-tunes a performance, your proactive approach to financial control ensures that your melody remains harmonious, vibrant, and in perfect rhythm with your aspirations.

Chapter 11: Long-Term Wealth Creation

11.1 Building a Sustainable Financial Future

Imagine your financial journey as the crafting of a timeless masterpiece. Just as an artist envisions their creation, building long-term wealth requires a strategic and sustainable approach to financial management. Consider these practices as the palette with which you paint your financial canvas.

11.1.1 Goal Setting: The Blueprint of Wealth

Every great masterpiece starts with a vision – a clear and vivid image of what is to be created. In the realm of wealth creation, this vision is cast through goal setting. Just as a composer envisions a symphony before it's played, you must define your long-term financial aspirations.

Imagine the canvas of your financial future. What do you see? Is it the picture of financial independence, a life free from monetary worries? Or perhaps it's the image of funding your children's education, ensuring their path to success? Maybe your vision is entrepreneurial, seeing yourself at the helm of a thriving business empire.

Much like a painter meticulously sketches the outlines of a masterpiece, set the parameters of your financial goals. Define them with clarity, specificity, and a sense of purpose. These goals will serve as the guiding stars, directing your financial decisions and actions towards a harmonious symphony of success.

Consider this process as laying the foundation for your own financial blueprint. Just as architects create detailed plans for buildings, you're crafting a roadmap that leads you towards your dreams. This blueprint is not static; it's a living document that evolves as you progress on your journey.

Within this blueprint, prioritize your actions wisely. Just as a conductor arranges the sequence of musical notes, prioritize steps that contribute directly to your goals. Each action you take is like a brushstroke on your canvas, gradually shaping your financial masterpiece.

As you embark on this creative journey, remember that goals are not just destinations; they're the path itself. Each milestone achieved is a brush of color on your canvas, bringing your dreams to life. So, take a moment to envision your financial symphony – the soaring crescendos of achievement, the steady rhythm of progress, and the harmonious melody of a life well-lived.

In the grand symphony of life, you are both the composer and the conductor. Define your goals, create your blueprint, and let the music of your financial success echo through time. As you take each step, remember that every note counts, and every decision contributes to the grandeur of your financial masterpiece.

11.1.2 Saving and Investing: The Brushstrokes of Growth

In the realm of art, a masterpiece emerges stroke by stroke, layer by layer. So too does your financial masterpiece take shape through the deliberate and consistent actions of saving and investing.

Imagine your financial canvas as a blank space, waiting for the vibrant colors of growth to be applied. Just as an artist adds brushstrokes to create depth and dimension, you can cultivate a habit of saving and investing, adding layer upon layer of financial security and potential.

Much like an artist dedicates time to each brushstroke, allocate a portion of your income to savings. This act is akin to carefully selecting the right hue or tone to match the vision in your mind. These savings are the foundation upon which your financial composition will be built.

Just as an artist uses a diverse palette to create a rich and captivating scene, explore a range of investment vehicles. Each investment opportunity is a brushstroke, contributing to the evolving masterpiece of your wealth. Consider stocks, bonds, mutual funds, real estate, and other options, each adding its unique shade to your financial canvas.

As an artist skillfully blends colors to achieve the desired effect, similarly, mix and match your investments to create a balanced and diversified portfolio. This blend of assets is what gives your financial composition depth and resilience. It allows you to weather market fluctuations and pursue opportunities for growth.

Remember, every brushstroke matters. Consistent saving and investing are the brushstrokes that gradually transform your financial canvas. Over time, your efforts compound, and your financial masterpiece evolves into a symphony of prosperity.

Just as an artist envisions the final image before starting, picture your financial future as you add each brushstroke of saving and investing. Envision the scenes of financial security, the landscapes of opportunity, and the portraits of a well-crafted retirement.

So, as you approach your financial canvas, remember that each act of saving and every investment decision contributes to the grandeur of your financial masterpiece. With each brushstroke, you're creating a composition that resonates with growth, potential, and the promise of a brighter tomorrow.

11.1.3 Diversification: The Harmony of Protection

In the world of art, a masterpiece is often created by harmoniously blending different elements. Just as a skilled artist combines various colors, textures, and techniques to craft a captivating artwork, you too can create a financial masterpiece through the art of diversification.

Imagine your investment portfolio as a canvas, awaiting the application of different shades and tones. Just as a painter strategically selects multiple hues to add depth and dimension, consider diversifying your investments across various asset classes. This practice is akin to selecting a diverse range of colors to create a visually captivating scene.

Diversification serves as a protective layer for your financial composition. Just as an artist might layer materials to create texture, spreading your investments across different asset classes can help mitigate risk. By allocating your resources to stocks, bonds, real estate, and other assets, you are creating a well-rounded composition that can weather market fluctuations.

Much like a painter's use of various techniques to enhance the visual experience, diversification enhances the potential returns of your portfolio. Just as a variety of brushstrokes contribute to the richness of a painting, a diversified portfolio has the potential to yield greater overall returns while reducing the impact of poor performance in any single investment.

Just as a skilled artist balances elements to create a harmonious composition, strive for balance in your investment allocation. This balance helps ensure that your financial masterpiece remains resilient and well-rounded, even in the face of economic challenges.

Remember, the art of diversification is not about avoiding risk altogether; rather, it is about managing and reducing risk while maximizing the potential for growth. By blending different asset classes, you're orchestrating a symphony of protection and opportunity.

As you approach your investment canvas, consider each asset class as a unique color on your palette. Blend them together thoughtfully to create a masterpiece that resonates with both security and growth. Just as an artist's careful selection and combination of colors create a captivating visual experience, your strategic diversification creates a financial composition that speaks of harmony and stability.

11.1.4 Risk Management: Safeguarding the Canvas

In the realm of art, protecting a valuable masterpiece is a top priority. Just as a masterpiece requires a sturdy frame and careful preservation, your financial composition demands robust risk management to ensure its enduring beauty.

Consider your risk management strategy as the frame that envelops your financial canvas. This frame not only enhances the artwork's visual appeal but also provides essential protection against external elements. Similarly, through comprehensive risk management, you can shield your financial masterpiece from potential hazards and uncertainties.

Insurance serves as a vital brushstroke in your risk management canvas. Just as an artist might use a protective varnish to shield their creation, insurance coverage safeguards your wealth and assets. Whether it's health, life, home, or business insurance, each policy adds a layer of protection, ensuring that unexpected events do not disrupt the harmony of your financial composition.

An emergency fund acts as a safety net beneath your financial canvas. Just as an artist places a cushioning layer between the canvas and the frame, an emergency fund cushions your financial stability. This fund provides a buffer against unforeseen expenses or sudden income disruptions, allowing your masterpiece to remain unblemished by unexpected financial shocks.

Thoughtful estate planning completes the protective frame around your financial artwork. Just as a skilled conservator ensures the longevity of a masterpiece through careful preservation, estate planning ensures the seamless transfer of your wealth to future generations. Wills, trusts, and power of attorney documents secure your legacy, ensuring that your financial composition remains intact and impactful for years to come.

The process of risk management is not merely about shielding your financial masterpiece from harm; it's about ensuring its endurance and resilience. Just as a well-preserved painting maintains its value over time, a comprehensive risk management strategy ensures that your financial legacy continues to benefit you and your loved ones.

As you navigate the intricate brushstrokes of risk management, remember that each layer of protection contributes to the overall integrity of your financial composition. By carefully framing your financial canvas with insurance, an emergency fund, and prudent estate planning, you're securing your masterpiece against the uncertainties of the future. Your financial artwork, like a cherished painting, becomes a lasting testament to your foresight and care.

11.2 Retirement Planning and Investment Vehicles

11.2.1 Retirement Goals: Picturing Your Golden Years

In the grand gallery of life, retirement is the masterpiece that awaits your final brushstrokes. Just as an artist envisions the focal point of their creation, you must imagine your retirement as the pinnacle of your financial masterpiece. It's a time when your canvas is complete, and you can step back to admire the grandeur of your life's work.

Envisioning your retirement is akin to an artist picturing the final composition before picking up the brush. Consider it a process of designing your own masterpiece, one that reflects your aspirations, desires, and the legacy you wish to leave behind. Just as an artist decides on the central theme of their artwork, you must define your retirement lifestyle – the heart of your financial opus.

As an artist considers the interplay of colors and shapes, you should contemplate the intricate details that make up your retirement dreams. Estimate the funds required to sustain your envisioned lifestyle. This financial foundation is essential to ensure that your retirement masterpiece stands strong, just as a painting needs a stable canvas.

Just as a painter accounts for different lighting conditions to evoke a specific mood, you must also consider various factors that influence your retirement canvas. Healthcare costs, for instance, are the shades of reality that must be incorporated into your vision. Like shadows and highlights, inflation and potential longevity must also be blended into your retirement goals to create a balanced and realistic image.

Remember, your retirement is not just a single stroke on the canvas of life. It's a culmination of every financial decision you make, every brushstroke of investment, and every layer of protection you lay down. It's the realization of your financial masterpiece, a symphony of security, comfort, and fulfillment.

As you ponder your retirement goals, imagine the final strokes of your financial masterpiece. Just as an artist draws their viewers into the world they've created, your retirement vision will inspire you to shape your financial decisions. By defining your retirement lifestyle and estimating the funds required, you're setting the stage for the most cherished part of your life's composition.

11.2.2 Retirement Accounts: The Palette of Savings

In the studio of financial planning, retirement accounts are the vibrant palette from which you draw the hues of your future. Much like an artist selects colors to bring their canvas to life, you have the power to choose from a range of retirement accounts, each contributing its unique shade to your financial masterpiece.

Think of these accounts as the pigments that infuse vitality into your retirement composition. Among the array of options, 401(k)s, IRAs, and pension plans stand out as the primary colors – essential elements that you can blend and mix to create a harmonious spectrum of financial security.

Maximizing contributions to these accounts is akin to an artist layering color upon color to achieve depth and richness. Just as an artist seeks to capture the essence of a scene, you aim to capture the essence of a comfortable retirement through diligent contributions.

But it's not just about the strokes; it's about understanding the intricate details of each hue. Just as an artist comprehends how colors interact on the canvas, you should grasp the tax benefits and withdrawal rules associated with each retirement account. These rules dictate the brushstrokes of your retirement journey, influencing when and how you can access the colors you've carefully placed on your palette.

Consider the tax benefits as the shading that adds dimension to your retirement landscape. Contributions to some accounts may offer immediate tax advantages, providing a light touch to your current financial situation. Other accounts may provide tax benefits upon withdrawal, casting a deeper hue on your retirement years.

Withdrawal rules, like the play of light and shadow, determine how your retirement masterpiece is unveiled. Some pigments may need time to fully develop, while others can be used more freely. Understanding these rules allows you to orchestrate the timing of your withdrawals, creating a balanced composition that suits your financial needs.

As you apply the brushstrokes of contributions and navigate the tax and withdrawal nuances, your retirement canvas begins to take shape. With each stroke, you're adding depth and vibrancy to your financial future. Just as an artist uses colors to evoke emotions, you're using retirement accounts to craft a future that's both vivid and meaningful.

So, as you stand before the palette of retirement accounts, remember that each contribution, each choice you make, is a stroke that contributes to the masterpiece of your retirement. With a clear understanding of the tax benefits, withdrawal rules, and the vibrant potential each account holds, you're well-equipped to infuse your financial canvas with the brilliance of a secure and fulfilling retirement.

11.2.3 Investment Strategies: Crafting Your Retirement Palette

In the studio of retirement planning, investment strategies are the skilled hand that wields the brushes, bringing depth and dimension to your financial canvas. Just as an artist selects brushes of various sizes and textures to create a masterpiece, you have the opportunity to craft an investment strategy that perfectly suits your unique retirement vision.

Think of this strategy as the palette from which you draw the colors of your financial future. Each investment vehicle – whether stocks, bonds, real estate, or other assets – represents a distinct hue that, when skillfully combined, creates a vibrant and compelling portrait of your retirement years.

Just as an artist considers their canvas's dimensions, you should consider your risk tolerance and time horizon. These elements shape the strokes you'll use to paint your retirement picture. A bolder approach might involve more vibrant colors and dynamic brushwork, while a more conservative style may employ softer, subtler shades.

Diversification is your blending technique, ensuring that no single color overwhelms the composition. Just as an artist weaves colors together to form a cohesive whole, you should spread your retirement investments across a range of assets. This diversification not only adds richness and complexity to your financial landscape but also mitigates risk, much like an artist balances light and shadow.

But it's not just about the individual brushstrokes; it's about the overall composition. Just as an artist steps back to view their work from a distance, you should regularly assess and adjust your investment strategy. Market fluctuations and life changes are like shifts in lighting, altering the way colors interact on your canvas. By periodically stepping back and fine-tuning your strategy, you ensure that your retirement portrait remains vivid and true to your vision.

As you apply your investment brushstrokes to your retirement canvas, remember that each decision you make contributes to the final masterpiece. Much like a skilled artist layers colors to create texture and depth, you're layering investments to create a financial landscape that is both secure and rewarding.

So, as you craft your investment strategy, approach it with the care and precision of a master artist. Consider your risk tolerance, time horizon, and the diverse hues of assets available to you. Blend and diversify these elements to create a retirement palette that captures the essence of your dreams and aspirations. With each stroke, you're adding depth and vitality to your financial canvas, ensuring that your retirement years are a work of art that brings joy and fulfillment.

11.2.4 Regular Review: The Ongoing Composition

Just as a master artist returns to their canvas, refining and adding final touches, so too must you revisit your retirement plan – your financial opus – and make necessary adjustments. The journey towards retirement is an ongoing composition, and much like a painter adds meticulous details to their work, your regular reviews ensure that your masterpiece maintains its brilliance.

As the years pass and retirement draws near, consider how an artist might transition from bold, sweeping strokes to precise, deliberate ones. Similarly, you might shift your retirement investments towards a more conservative stance. This is like adding those last meticulous brushstrokes that ensure your creation remains true to your original vision.

Your investment choices are the colors that define your retirement landscape. Just as an artist carefully selects the pigments to evoke the desired emotion, you have chosen assets to secure your financial future. As you approach retirement, consider blending these colors with care. Just as an artist softens edges and refines details, you can reduce risk by favoring investments that are less susceptible to market volatility.

Much like an artist's final review before unveiling their masterpiece, your regular reviews ensure that your retirement composition is aligned with your evolving vision. As life's circumstances change and the financial world shifts, these reviews allow you to make the necessary adjustments.

These reviews aren't just about monitoring your brushstrokes; they're about stepping back to appreciate the entire canvas. Just as an artist considers composition, balance, and harmony, you'll assess the balance of your retirement investments and how they align with your retirement goals. If needed, you'll introduce subtle shifts to maintain that delicate equilibrium.

So, in the ongoing composition of your retirement plan, remember to be both artist and conductor. Approach your regular reviews with the discerning eye of a master artist, ensuring that every element is in its rightful place. As you fine-tune your investment palette and make delicate adjustments, you'll realize that retirement, much like a well-painted canvas, is a work of art that is built layer by layer, stroke by stroke, and review by review.

11.3 Estate Planning and Wealth Transfer

11.3.1 Will and Trusts: The Legacy Blueprint

In the grand design of your financial life, estate planning serves as the intricate blueprint for the legacy you will leave behind. Just as an architect meticulously plans a structure, you too must carefully craft a will – the cornerstone of your legacy – to ensure that your wishes for asset distribution are precisely outlined.

Think of your will as the master plan, the guiding framework that dictates how your accumulated wealth will be allocated among your loved ones and causes dear to your heart. Just as an architect ensures that every beam and brick serves a purpose, your will allocates your resources in a way that reflects your values and intentions.

However, a comprehensive legacy involves more than a simple blueprint. Just as a grand building might have supporting pillars, consider the establishment of trusts to provide robust support for your legacy. Trusts can be the protective pillars that manage and safeguard assets for future generations. These structures, like architectural elements, provide a solid foundation that ensures your legacy stands strong, enduring through the passage of time.

Imagine your will and trusts as the guiding architecture of your legacy. They provide the structural framework that ensures your hard-earned assets are distributed according to your wishes. Just as an architect considers every detail in their design, you must consider every facet of your legacy – from financial assets to sentimental heirlooms – ensuring that your blueprint accurately reflects the life you've lived and the impact you wish to have.

As you embark on the process of crafting your legacy blueprint, approach it with the same attention to detail and foresight as an architect designing a masterpiece. Every clause in your will, every provision in your trusts, becomes a crucial element in the composition of your legacy. By thoughtfully and meticulously creating this blueprint, you are shaping the foundation upon which your impact will endure, much like a building that stands the test of time.

11.3.2 Power of Attorney and Healthcare Directives: Guiding Your Legacy

In the constellation of your legacy, consider the role of power of attorney and healthcare directives as guiding stars, lighting the way even in the darkest of times. Just as a guiding star provides direction, these legal documents designate trusted individuals to make critical financial and healthcare decisions on your behalf, should you become incapacitated.

Think of your chosen agents as navigators, steering the ship of your legacy when you are unable to do so. Much like a guiding star leads sailors through uncharted waters, your designated agents guide your legacy through the complexities of financial matters and healthcare choices.

They hold the compass that ensures your wishes are followed, even when you are unable to express them yourself.

Just as a star's brilliance can fade with time, it's important to regularly update and maintain these documents. Just as celestial navigation requires precise instruments, your power of attorney and healthcare directives must be clear and up-to-date to effectively guide your legacy. Regular review and updates ensure that your chosen path remains illuminated and your legacy remains on course.

Envision these documents as the luminous beacons of your legacy, illuminating the path for a seamless transition of responsibilities. Your designated agents, armed with the authority you've entrusted to them, become the custodians of your values and intentions, ensuring that your financial matters and healthcare choices are aligned with your wishes.

As you shape your enduring legacy, consider the power of attorney and healthcare directives as indispensable constellations in your cosmic plan. Just as a guiding star provides unwavering direction, these documents provide unwavering guidance, ensuring that your legacy continues to shine brightly and that your impact remains steadfast, even when you are no longer able to actively steer the course.

11.3.3 Tax Efficiency: Crafting a Tax-Optimized Legacy

In the sculpture of your legacy, tax efficiency serves as the chisel that carves intricate details, adding depth and dimension to your enduring masterpiece. Just as a skilled artist employs light and shadow to create visual richness, collaborating with estate planning professionals allows you to craft a legacy that is not only visually striking but also financially harmonious.

Think of tax efficiency as the masterful technique that sculpts your legacy, ensuring that every contour and curve is shaped with precision. Estate planning professionals, akin to expert sculptors, help you optimize your plan for tax efficiency, ensuring that your legacy retains its beauty while minimizing tax liabilities.

Similar to how an artist selects the finest materials, you strategize with professionals to make the most of tax-saving opportunities. Gifting, like delicate brushstrokes, allows you to pass on your wealth while reducing potential tax burdens. Exploring charitable donations adds vibrant hues to your legacy, not only benefiting causes you care about but also enhancing your tax efficiency.

Leveraging exemptions, much like an artist's meticulous attention to detail, ensures that your legacy remains a true reflection of your intentions. These techniques create layers of complexity and sophistication in your legacy, enhancing its overall impact and resonance.

Just as a sculptor envisions the final form, you collaborate with experts to shape a legacy that stands as a testament to your values and vision. Tax efficiency becomes the artistic touch that elevates your legacy, ensuring that it radiates financial harmony and echoes your impact for generations to come.

As you sculpt your tax-optimized legacy, remember that each strategic decision contributes to the intricate design of your financial sculpture. Every tax-saving technique is a stroke of the chisel, carving out a legacy that not only tells your story but also serves as a beacon of financial wisdom and foresight. By harnessing the power of tax efficiency, you sculpt a legacy that not only withstands the test of time but shines brighter with each passing year.

11.3.4 Beneficiary Designations: Aligning Your Legacy

In the gallery of your financial legacy, beneficiary designations serve as your signature – a clear and decisive mark that ensures your intentions are etched into the very fabric of your masterpiece. Just as an artist signs their creation, taking the time to review and update beneficiary designations on key assets is the final touch that aligns your legacy with your true wishes.

Consider beneficiary designations as the final brushstroke on your canvas – they bring the entire composition together, adding a sense of completion and coherence. By carefully aligning these designations with your current desires, you ensure that your legacy harmonizes seamlessly with your intentions.

Similar to how an artist chooses the perfect hue for the finishing touch, you select beneficiaries who reflect your values and priorities. Whether it's retirement accounts, life insurance policies, or other valuable assets, the chosen beneficiaries become the custodians of your legacy, entrusted with the responsibility of carrying your financial vision forward.

By updating beneficiary designations, you ensure that your legacy narrative remains consistent and vibrant. Just as an artist's signature endures, your legacy – as represented by these designations – will endure, standing as a testament to your foresight and meticulous planning.

As you consider the final strokes of your financial masterpiece, remember that beneficiary designations are the final stroke of your legacy's signature. By aligning them with your current wishes, you affirm that your legacy will continue to resonate with your values, long after the final note of your symphony has been played. Your legacy will stand as a true reflection of your life's composition – a work of art that inspires, empowers, and enriches the lives it touches.

11.4 Leaving a Lasting Financial Legacy

11.4.1 Philanthropy: The Stroke of Giving

In the grand gallery of your financial legacy, philanthropy emerges as a brushstroke of unparalleled impact. Just as a skilled artist adds layers of depth and emotion to their masterpiece, incorporating philanthropy into your legacy enriches it with a profound sense of purpose and resonance.

Imagine each act of philanthropy as a deliberate brushstroke, adding vibrant colors to the canvas of your financial journey. Whether supporting education, healthcare, the arts, or any cause that holds meaning to you, these brushstrokes of giving create a tapestry that extends far beyond the frame of your lifetime.

Consider the creation of charitable foundations or donor-advised funds as your masterful strokes, carefully placed to amplify your impact. These structures become the palette from which your generosity is painted, allowing you to shape and direct your contributions in a way that reflects your values and vision.

Just as an artist's brushstroke can evoke emotions and inspire contemplation, your acts of philanthropy will touch lives, inspire change, and leave a lasting impression. Your legacy, much like a work of art, will continue to breathe life into the world, making a positive difference that ripples through time.

As you approach the final strokes of your financial composition, remember that philanthropy is the stroke of giving that elevates your legacy to greatness. With each stroke, you infuse your legacy with compassion, empathy, and a commitment to making the world a better place. Your financial masterpiece, adorned with the brushstrokes of philanthropy, becomes a true testament to the impact one individual can have on the lives of many.

11.4.2 Education and Mentorship: Nurturing Future Creators

In the tapestry of your enduring legacy, education and mentorship emerge as brushstrokes that nurture and cultivate the creators of tomorrow. Just as a skilled artist imparts their expertise to guide a protégé's journey, your investment in education and mentorship leaves an indelible mark on the canvas of the future.

Picture each act of educational support as a deliberate brushstroke, adding layers of knowledge and opportunity to the evolving masterpiece of human potential. By offering financial assistance for educational pursuits, you provide the essential colors that enrich the lives of aspiring minds, enabling them to paint their dreams with confidence and purpose.

Mentorship, too, is a brushstroke that weaves threads of guidance and inspiration into the fabric of tomorrow's creators. Just as an artist imparts techniques and insights to a burgeoning talent, your mentorship imparts wisdom and empowers the next generation to navigate their own creative journeys.

As each brushstroke of educational support and mentorship finds its place, your legacy blossoms into a vivid tapestry of learning and growth. The artists, scientists, leaders, and innovators who benefit from your investment become the vibrant hues that illuminate the world with their brilliance.

Incorporate these brushstrokes into your legacy, and watch as they ripple through time, shaping a future where potential knows no bounds. Just as a masterpiece draws admirers into its world, your legacy of education and mentorship beckons future generations to step into the spotlight of their own creation. Your canvas becomes a beacon, guiding and inspiring those who follow in your footsteps.

11.4.3 Family Communication: Sharing Your Creative Vision

In the grand gallery of your financial legacy, family communication stands as a profound narrative thread, weaving the story of your creative vision. Just as an artist imparts the meaning and inspiration behind their masterpiece, fostering open and transparent communication with your loved ones ensures that your financial legacy is not only preserved but also cherished and carried forward.

Imagine each conversation about your financial plans as a stroke of the brush, adding depth and clarity to the portrait of your legacy. By sharing your values, intentions, and insights, you invite your family into the rich tapestry of your financial journey. Your narrative provides context to the colors and patterns that make up your legacy, enabling your loved ones to understand the significance of each stroke and shade.

Educating your family about responsible financial management is another layer of this narrative. Just as an artist imparts the techniques of their craft, you impart the wisdom of financial prudence. This knowledge equips your loved ones with the tools to not only honor your legacy but also contribute to its continued vibrancy.

As your narrative unfolds, it becomes a bridge connecting generations, ensuring that your creative vision remains vivid and relevant. Your financial decisions and intentions take on a deeper resonance, transforming from mere numbers on a balance sheet to a living, breathing testament to your values.

Incorporate family communication into your legacy, and watch as your narrative reverberates through time, guiding and inspiring generations to come. Your story becomes an integral part of your legacy, ensuring that your masterpiece is not only admired but also understood, cherished, and celebrated by those who follow in your footsteps.

11.4.4 Succession Planning: Passing the Torch

In the gallery of your financial legacy, business owners hold a distinct canvas, painted with the vibrant hues of entrepreneurship. Just as an artist's legacy is perpetuated through apprentices and proteges, succession planning becomes the brushstroke that ensures your creative vision endures, even as the curtain falls on your role as the lead artist.

Succession planning is akin to selecting a capable artist to continue your masterpiece. This strategic process involves grooming the next generation within your business or identifying worthy successors who can skillfully wield the brush you've laid down. Just as an artist imparts techniques and nuances to their apprentice, you share your insights, strategies, and values with those who will carry forward your entrepreneurial legacy.

Consider this process as the transition of the artist's palette. Your successors inherit the colors you've meticulously chosen, but they bring their own unique strokes, breathing new life into the canvas. By aligning their artistic talents with your vision, they contribute to a seamless transition, where your legacy becomes an evolving masterpiece rather than a static artifact.

Succession planning also ensures the continuity of your business's impact. The brushstroke of a well-executed plan safeguards jobs, sustains community engagement, and upholds the brand identity you've carefully crafted. Just as a master artist imparts a distinct style to their work, your business's essence remains intact under the guidance of capable hands.

As the artist of your financial legacy, succession planning becomes your final, yet enduring, signature. It signifies your commitment to ensuring that your creative vision doesn't merely fade away, but continues to flourish and inspire. In this way, your legacy becomes an eternal work of art, forever evolving and leaving an indelible mark on the canvas of time.

In the symphony of life, Chapter 11 conducts the creation of a lasting financial masterpiece. By building sustainable wealth, planning for retirement, crafting an effective estate plan, and leaving a profound legacy, you compose a harmonious opus that resonates across generations. Remember, every stroke of financial management is a note in your grand composition, and with careful consideration and collaboration, you create a legacy that will stand the test of time.

Chapter 12 Conclusion

12.1 Recap of Financial Control Blueprint

Our voyage through the Financial Control Blueprint has been nothing short of a symphonic expedition into the realm of effective financial management. This comprehensive guide has illuminated a pathway towards growth and triumph, equipping us with an array of instruments to navigate the intricate composition of our financial lives.

Our journey commenced with a recognition of the universal importance of financial control, an indispensable cornerstone for both individuals and businesses. From this initial note, we embarked on a captivating odyssey through the diverse movements of our financial opus, each orchestrated with precision and purpose.

The overture of our exploration involved the assessment of our financial standing, a process that laid the bedrock for the chapters that ensued. The artful crafting of budgets taught us to wield our financial instruments, creating a harmonious cash flow that resonated with fiscal equilibrium. In the subsequent movement, we mastered the symphony of debt control, composing a melody that harmonized with the liberating tones of financial independence.

As our expedition unfolded, we transitioned into the enchanting realm of investment, where strategic choices conducted the crescendo of growth. In this movement, we artfully orchestrated insurance as a protective ensemble, safeguarding our financial symphony against the discordant strains of unforeseen risks.

The emergence of tax planning served as a pivotal conductor, orchestrating the harmonious fusion of our fiscal arrangements with the intricate legal landscape. And finally, our journey culminated with a powerful crescendo in the long-term wealth creation chapter – a masterwork crafted over time, ensuring a legacy that resonates through the ages.

As we conclude this chapter, let us reflect on the harmonious ensemble we have composed. Each principle and practice serves as a note, each chapter a movement, and together they form a symphony of financial mastery. With the Financial Control Blueprint as our guide, we are now poised to conduct our financial futures with the finesse of a maestro, crafting a composition that resonates with growth, security, and enduring success.

12.2 Encouragement for Taking Action

In the symphony of financial management, knowledge serves as the sheet music, guiding our hands and minds to produce a harmonious arrangement. Yet, let us remember that knowledge alone is but an instrument waiting to be played. It is through the skillful plucking of the strings of action that our symphony truly comes to life. Armed with the insights woven into the tapestry of these pages, you now possess a virtuoso's array of tools – tools that have the power to transform your financial symphony into a magnificent and awe-inspiring performance.

Imagine this symphony as a grand orchestration of your life's journey, where each note, each decision, each movement contributes to the unfolding masterpiece. As you take your place as the conductor of this symphony, you hold the power to elicit melodies of prosperity, harmony, and fulfillment.

Undoubtedly, challenges will emerge along this melodic path. They may arrive as abrupt and dissonant chords, testing the mettle of your resolve. Yet, hold fast to the conductor's baton of persistence, wield the bow of discipline with unwavering precision, and let the melodious strains of your unwavering commitment resonate through every movement.

In this musical metaphor, your actions are the resonating vibrations that bring life to the notes on the page. Each financial decision plucks a string, setting in motion a sequence of events that reverberates through time. It is through these carefully orchestrated actions that your financial symphony evolves from mere notation to a living, breathing opus.

As you traverse this musical landscape, remember that each step you take, each note you play, contributes to the grandeur of your financial melody. Embrace both the triumphant crescendos that lift your spirits and the gentle, reflective interludes that allow for contemplation. For it is the interplay of these moments, skillfully woven together, that crafts a symphony of life defined by not just financial success, but by the richness of experiences, the harmony of dreams realized, and the legacy you leave for generations to come.

Your journey towards financial mastery is your opus, and every action you take breathes life into its vibrant composition. The quiet determination of saving, the bold crescendo of strategic investments, the harmonious blend of risk management – these are the notes that combine to create the magnificent symphony of your financial life.

The road ahead may be marked by twists and turns, moments of high energy and times of serene contemplation. Yet, in the tapestry of it all, the notes you play – the actions you take – will define the melody of your financial journey. Remember that this symphony is uniquely yours. It's not just about the final movement; it's about every note, every beat, every pause in between. Each action is an integral part of the composition, contributing to the overall resonance and beauty of your financial symphony.

So, let the score of your financial journey guide you, but let your actions infuse it with life. With each step, with each decision, you're adding depth, texture, and soul to your symphony. The crescendos and the softer moments, the high notes and the low – they all come together to create a tapestry of sound that is uniquely yours. And as you stand at the conductor's podium of your financial destiny, remember that your actions, when played in harmony, have the power to create a symphony that resounds through time.

12.3 Embracing a Path to Growth and Success

As you stand at the threshold of your financial journey, embracing the Financial Control Blueprint, you are poised on the precipice of a symphony of growth and success. But this is no mere performance – it's a lifelong symphony, meticulously composed with the elements of dedication, learning, and adaptability.

Consider this journey as the composition of a symphony. Just as a composer carefully selects each note to create a harmonious masterpiece, you too have the power to shape your financial destiny. The Financial Control Blueprint serves as your musical score, guiding you through the intricacies of financial management.

As you embark on this melodic path, remember that financial control is more than just the accumulation of wealth. It is the instrument of financial freedom, the soothing melody of peace of mind, and the ability to compose a legacy that reverberates through generations. Your financial decisions play the role of a conductor, orchestrating a harmonious arrangement that reflects your values and aspirations.

Much like a composer refines their composition, you must continuously monitor and fine-tune your financial strategies. Embrace the rhythm of change and remain adaptable in the face of evolving circumstances. Just as a symphony adapts to different tempos and key changes, your financial plan should flex and adjust to life's ever-shifting dynamics.

In this journey, you are not alone. Seek the guidance of experts when the composition becomes intricate. Just as a conductor relies on the expertise of skilled musicians, you can rely on financial advisors, accountants, and legal professionals to provide the knowledge and insight needed to navigate complex financial landscapes.

As you conclude this chapter, remember that your financial symphony is a masterpiece in the making. Every note, every challenge, and every triumph contributes to the harmonious arrangement of your financial journey. With the Financial Control Blueprint as your guiding score, you stand ready to orchestrate a life of abundance, security, and enduring impact.

Now is the time to seize control of your financial destiny. The stage is set, the instruments are in tune, and the audience awaits your performance. Begin implementing the Financial Control Blueprint, and let your financial symphony unfold. Through dedicated action, thoughtful decisions, and a commitment to your financial goals, you are not only composing a brighter future for yourself but also leaving a lasting legacy for those who will follow in your footsteps.

The baton is in your hand, and the melody of your financial symphony is waiting to be played. Start today, and let the music of growth and success resonate throughout your life's composition.

Don't miss out!

Visit the website below and you can sign up to receive emails whenever DG. Junior publishes a new book. There's no charge and no obligation.

https://books2read.com/r/B-A-NRUY-THBKC

BOOKS 2 READ

Connecting independent readers to independent writers.

Also by DG. Junior

Essential Coputer Skills

Basics of Programming: A Comprehensive Guide for Beginners

Get Your Finances In Order

Where Can I Invest? Unlocking a World of Opportunities

FROM IDEA TO PROFIT: A Guide for New Entrepreneurs on Building a Successful Business

Standalone

Financial Control Blueprint: Building a Path to Growth and Success

About the Author

DG Junior is a Computer Scientist, dynamic financial expert, author, and entrepreneur dedicated to helping individuals and businesses achieve financial control and unlock their path to growth and success. With a wealth of experience in the finance industry, DG has developed a keen understanding of strategic financial planning, investment management, and business growth strategies.

In "Financial Control Blueprint: Building a Path to Growth and Success," DG Junior shares practical guidance and actionable insights to demystify complex financial concepts. His ability to simplify intricate principles and communicate them clearly has made him a sought-after speaker, consultant, and educator.

DG Junior's passion for financial literacy stems from his own journey, rising from humble beginnings to achieve remarkable success. Through his book, he empowers readers to take charge of their financial future, whether as individuals seeking personal financial stability or business owners aiming to optimize their financial performance.

Beyond his work as an author, DG Junior runs a financial consulting firm, where he has helped numerous clients achieve their financial goals. Embrace the transformative power of financial control with DG Junior's "Financial Control Blueprint: Building a Path to Growth and Success," and embark on a journey toward prosperity, security, and lasting success.

www.ingramcontent.com/pod-product-compliance
Lightning Source LLC
LaVergne TN
LVHW090256210926
848480LV00001B/43
* 9 7 9 8 2 2 3 0 1 9 3 4 3 *